I0004155

The Cybersecurity Blueprint
Building and Operationalizing a
Complete Defensive Strategy

Bill Johns
Peninsula Network Security, LLC
2025

DEDICATIONS

To my peers — John, Casey, Cynthia, Mario, and Eric —

For the countless hours we've spent navigating complex technical and regulatory terrain together. Your expertise, creativity, and persistence turned even the most challenging moments into opportunities for growth and problem-solving. The long brainstorming sessions that stretched into weeks, and the unexpected detours — you were there for all of it, bringing not only your technical insight but also your humor and resilience.

More than just colleagues, you became trusted friends. Whether we were troubleshooting a stubborn issue or celebrating a hard-earned success, your support and camaraderie made all the difference. You reminded me that even in the face of complexity, solutions are possible — and that the journey matters just as much as the destination.

I couldn't have asked for a better team to share this adventure with. Thank you for standing beside me, challenging me, and pushing me to be better. Your guidance and friendship have shaped not just this work, but also the way I approach every problem and challenge. I am deeply grateful for each of you.

TABLE OF CONTENTS

THE CYBERSECURITY BLUEPRINT: BUILDING AND OPERATIONALIZING A COMPLETE DEFENSIVE STRATEGY

Foreword

In a world where cyber threats have become a constant and evolving danger, the need for a structured and strategic approach to cybersecurity has never been greater. Cyberattacks are no longer limited to isolated incidents of data theft or disruption—they have become instruments of economic warfare, political influence, and large-scale infrastructure sabotage. From nation-state actors targeting critical infrastructure to organized criminal groups executing sophisticated ransomware campaigns, the cyber threat landscape continues to grow in both complexity and scale.

Cybersecurity is no longer just a technical challenge; it is a business imperative. Organizations that fail to recognize the strategic nature of cyber threats put not only their data at risk but also their reputation, operational stability, and long-term viability. Effective cybersecurity is not just about installing the latest firewall or deploying endpoint protection—it requires building a comprehensive security program that integrates strategy, governance, risk management, and operational resilience.

This book serves as a definitive guide to building such a program. It does not catalog threats or defensive tactics in great technical detail. By the time you read this, the threats and tactics will likely have changed. Instead, it provides a structured approach to designing, implementing, and maintaining a complete and dynamic cybersecurity framework. From understanding the foundational principles of cybersecurity to addressing advanced threats like nation-state attacks and supply chain compromises, the book lays out a blueprint for success.

The strength of this work lies in its holistic approach. It addresses the organizational, operational, and human dimensions of cybersecurity, recognizing that true resilience comes from a balanced and adaptive strategy. By combining strategic foresight with operational execution, the book equips readers with the tools to not only defend against attacks but also to recover quickly and adapt to future challenges.

Cybersecurity is no longer the responsibility of IT departments alone—it is a business-wide mandate that requires executive alignment, employee engagement, and a culture of vigilance. The guidance in this book reflects the realities of the modern threat landscape and provides actionable insights for building an effective security program from the ground up.

For security professionals, business leaders, and anyone tasked with protecting an organization's digital assets, this book offers not just knowledge—but a framework for action. It is a valuable resource that bridges the gap between theory and practice, ensuring that organizations are not only prepared for today's threats but also resilient against those of tomorrow.

INTRODUCTION

Cybersecurity is now a strategic necessity. In today's hyper-connected world, the risk of cyberattacks is not just a technical concern; it is a business and operational threat that affects every aspect of an organization. From financial institutions and healthcare providers to government agencies and manufacturing firms, no sector is immune from the reach of cybercriminals and state-sponsored threat actors. The digital infrastructure that supports modern business has become a prime target for those seeking financial gain, political leverage, or operational disruption.

The growing frequency and sophistication of cyberattacks highlight how vulnerable even the most technologically advanced organizations can be. High-profile breaches at companies like Equifax, Target, and Sony Pictures have exposed the personal information of millions, while attacks like NotPetya and WannaCry have demonstrated how a single piece of malicious code can disrupt entire industries. The SolarWinds supply chain attack in 2020 revealed that even trusted software providers could be used as entry points for espionage and long-term network infiltration. The Colonial Pipeline attack in 2021 underscored how ransomware can cripple critical infrastructure and lead to economic and operational consequences on a national scale. The reality is that cyberattacks have become not only more frequent but also more damaging and far-reaching.

Yet despite the growing threat landscape, many organizations remain unprepared. Cybersecurity is often treated as a technical issue—left to IT teams to manage through firewalls, antivirus software, and network monitoring. This reactive approach is no longer sufficient. Cybersecurity must be approached as a strategic business function—embedded into the fabric of an organization's operations, governance structure, and risk management framework. A successful cybersecurity program is not one that simply blocks incoming threats; it is one that anticipates them, adapts to them, and recovers from them with minimal disruption. The reality is that no system is entirely immune to attack. Therefore, resilience—rather than absolute protection—has become the defining goal of modern cybersecurity.

The book describes a few core cybersecurity principles that provide the foundation for building and maintaining an effective security program. While the threat landscape constantly evolves, certain guiding principles remain constant. Understanding and applying these principles is essential for anyone involved in designing, implementing, or managing a cybersecurity framework. These principles provide a strategic and operational blueprint for protecting systems, data, and people.

This book provides a structured framework for building and maintaining such a program. It goes beyond technical solutions and provides a comprehensive guide to designing a cybersecurity strategy that aligns with business goals and operational priorities. The book covers the foundational elements of cybersecurity, including the CIA triad (confidentiality, integrity, and availability) and the importance of defense in depth. It explores the strategic dimensions of cybersecurity, including governance, risk management, and compliance, and provides detailed guidance on how to operationalize these principles through effective policies, procedures, and controls. A strong cybersecurity program is not built on technology alone—it requires leadership, coordination, and the right culture.

The book also addresses the evolving nature of cyber threats. Traditional cyberattacks, such as malware and denial-of-service (DoS) attacks, have been joined by more sophisticated tactics, including Advanced Persistent Threats (APTs), supply chain compromises, and nation-state cyber warfare. Attackers are no longer interested solely in quick financial gain—they seek strategic advantage, long-term espionage, and even the ability to disrupt critical infrastructure. Responding to these threats requires more than just defensive measures—it demands a proactive approach that combines threat intelligence, real-time monitoring, and adaptive response strategies. This book outlines how to establish and refine these capabilities, ensuring that security programs remain resilient in the face of changing tactics and technologies.

A key theme of this book is that cybersecurity is not static. Technology evolves rapidly, and so do the tactics of threat actors. A cybersecurity program that works today may be outdated tomorrow. This book emphasizes the importance of adaptability—continuously testing, refining, and improving security controls based on emerging threats and changing business needs. The principles of threat intelligence, behavioral analytics, and machine learning play an important role in this adaptability. By understanding how attackers operate and identifying patterns of malicious behavior, organizations can adjust their defenses in real-time and stay one step ahead of adversaries.

The concept of cyber resilience is central to this book. While traditional cybersecurity focuses on keeping attackers out, resilience focuses on how to respond when attackers inevitably get in. It is not enough to prevent an attack; organizations must be able to contain the damage, recover quickly, and continue operating even under adverse conditions. This requires a combination of incident response planning, backup and recovery systems, and strong business continuity measures. A resilient organization is not one that never experiences a breach —it is one that emerges stronger after the breach.

Developing a cybersecurity program is not just about technology —it's about people and processes. The human factor remains one of the most significant vulnerabilities in any security framework. Social engineering, phishing, and insider threats continue to account for a significant percentage of successful breaches. This book provides strategies for addressing the human element of cybersecurity through security awareness training, access controls, and cultural reinforcement. Employees are often the weakest link in a security program—but when properly trained and supported, they can also be one of the strongest defenses.

The role of governance and leadership in cybersecurity is another key focus of this book. Cybersecurity is no longer just an IT issue—it is a board-level responsibility. Executive leadership must align security strategies with business objectives, ensure adequate funding for security initiatives, and hold business units accountable for adhering to security policies. The rise of regulatory frameworks like GDPR (General Data Protection Regulation) and CCPA (California Consumer Privacy Act) has added a new layer of complexity to cybersecurity governance. Compliance is no longer optional—it is a legal requirement, and organizations face significant financial and reputational penalties for failing to protect customer data.

This book offers a blueprint for navigating these challenges. It provides practical guidance for building a security framework from the ground up, establishing security policies and procedures, implementing effective controls, and responding to incidents with speed and precision. It also emphasizes the importance of measuring the effectiveness of security controls through regular audits, penetration testing, and threat simulations. A cybersecurity program is not a one-time project —it is a continuous process of monitoring, improvement, and adaptation.

The audience for this book includes security professionals, business leaders, and anyone responsible for managing risk in an organization. For security professionals, this book provides a detailed guide to implementing technical defenses, managing threats, and responding to incidents. For business leaders, it explains how cybersecurity aligns with business strategy and how to build a culture of security awareness at all levels of the organization. For general readers, it provides insight into the evolving threat landscape and the practical steps that organizations can take to protect themselves.

Ultimately, this book is not just about defending against cyberattacks—it is about building resilience. It is about creating a security program that can withstand breaches, recover quickly, and adapt to future challenges. The goal is not just to survive the next attack, but to emerge stronger from it.

Whether you are a cybersecurity professional, a business executive, or someone tasked with managing risk in your organization, this book provides the tools and insights you need to succeed. Cybersecurity is not a one-time project; it is an ongoing process of adaptation and improvement. The strategies and frameworks presented here will help you build a security program that is not only effective today but prepared for the threats of tomorrow.

This is not a theoretical exercise—it is a practical guide to building cybersecurity success. The path to security is not passive—it requires strategic vision, operational discipline, and a commitment to continuous improvement. This book lays out that path—step by step—and provides the blueprint for creating a resilient and secure future.

CHAPTER 1: CYBERSECURITY IS NOT OPTIONAL

"Cybersecurity is a strategic imperative. In today's digital age, cyber threats are as real and dangerous as any physical threat. Our interconnected world demands a comprehensive approach that not only safeguards our information but also protects our critical infrastructure and way of life. It is a constant battle that requires vigilance, innovation, and cooperation across all sectors."
— General Keith Alexander

General Keith Alexander's quote highlights the essential and strategic nature of cybersecurity in the modern world. His comparison of cyber threats to physical threats underscores the severity and immediacy of the risks posed by cyberattacks. Traditionally, security concerns were centered around physical protection—guarding buildings, securing physical assets, and ensuring the safety of individuals. However, in the digital age, the battlefield has expanded to the virtual realm. Cyberattacks can now cause the same level of disruption, financial damage, and societal harm as traditional physical attacks, making cybersecurity an essential component of national and economic security.

Alexander's use of the term "strategic imperative" signals that cybersecurity is not just a technical issue to be handled by IT departments—it is a critical element of business strategy, governance, and national defense. In a world where financial systems, healthcare infrastructure, communications networks, and even military operations are interconnected and reliant on digital platforms, the consequences of cyberattacks can extend far beyond individual businesses or institutions. A successful attack on a power grid, transportation network, or financial system could cripple an entire economy or compromise national security. In recent years, emerging technologies and the rapid pace of digital transformation have only deepened these interdependencies, making every new digital initiative a potential target for exploitation.

The phrase "our interconnected world" reflects the complexity and scale of modern cybersecurity challenges. Globalization and technological advancement have created an environment where information flows freely across borders and networks. While this interconnectivity enhances efficiency and convenience, it also creates vulnerabilities. A single breach in one part of a supply chain can have cascading effects on businesses and governments worldwide. This interconnectedness demands a coordinated and comprehensive approach to cybersecurity— one that integrates technical defenses with strategic planning, regulatory compliance, and international cooperation. Moreover, as new technologies such as the Internet of Things, cloud computing, and artificial intelligence reshape the digital landscape, the attack surface continues to expand, requiring organizations to rethink and continuously update their security strategies.

Alexander's reference to "a comprehensive approach" points to the need for a layered defense strategy. Effective cybersecurity is not achieved through a single technology or process—it requires a combination of measures, including network segmentation, encryption, multi-factor authentication, employee training, real-time monitoring, and incident response protocols. A comprehensive approach also involves aligning cybersecurity efforts with business goals, legal requirements, and industry best practices to ensure that defenses are both effective and sustainable. This multi-layered strategy has become even more critical as adversaries employ increasingly sophisticated techniques that can bypass isolated defenses; it is through redundancy and diversity in security controls that organizations can build true resilience.

The statement that "cybersecurity is a constant battle" reflects the dynamic and evolving nature of cyber threats. Unlike physical threats, which may remain stable over time, cyber threats are constantly changing as attackers develop new methods and exploit new vulnerabilities. This creates an environment where static or outdated security measures are ineffective. Vigilance—the ability to continuously monitor for threats and respond swiftly—is crucial. Moreover, innovation is essential to staying ahead of adversaries. Just as attackers adapt, defenders must continually evolve their tools and strategies to counter new threats. Recent advances in threat intelligence and automated defense mechanisms illustrate the ongoing race between attackers and defenders, emphasizing that maintaining a secure posture requires perpetual learning and adaptation.

Finally, Alexander emphasizes the importance of "cooperation across all sectors." Cybersecurity is not the responsibility of a single entity or industry—it requires collaboration between governments, private businesses, technology providers, and regulatory bodies. Information sharing, coordinated incident response, and joint investment in security research and development are essential to creating a unified defense against sophisticated cyber threats. As cyber incidents increasingly cross national borders and affect diverse sectors, international partnerships and public-private collaborations have become critical components in the global fight against cybercrime.

In summary, General Keith Alexander's quote encapsulates the modern reality of cybersecurity: it is a strategic priority that affects not only individual organizations but also global stability and security. The quote frames cybersecurity as a continuous and collective responsibility, where success depends on strategic foresight, technological innovation, and broad-based cooperation. It sets the tone for the book by positioning cybersecurity not just as a technical challenge, but as a critical element of organizational resilience and national security in an interconnected and increasingly vulnerable digital world. Recent case studies from various industries further underline that no single solution exists; rather, it is the continuous evolution of strategies and technologies that enables organizations to withstand the ever-changing threat landscape.

Cybersecurity is not a luxury—it's an absolute necessity. Every online interaction—from checking email to managing bank accounts—leaves behind a trail of data that can be exploited by cybercriminals. In the early days of the internet, breaches were often isolated incidents. Today, cyberattacks are sophisticated, frequent, and far-reaching, impacting individuals, small businesses, and multinational corporations alike. As technology evolves, so do the methods attackers use, making it critical to adopt a proactive, informed approach to digital security. This text lays the groundwork for understanding these threats and explains why robust cybersecurity practices are essential for protecting not only your devices but also your privacy, financial health, and overall reputation. The rapid growth of digital services, coupled with the emergence of new cybercriminal tactics, means that staying ahead of the threat curve is more important now than ever before.

Cybersecurity is the art and science of protecting computers, networks, programs, and data from unauthorized access, damage, or attack. It encompasses a wide array of practices, technologies, and controls that work together to safeguard digital assets against threats such as malware, ransomware, phishing, and insider breaches. As industries continue to integrate digital solutions into their operations, the need for comprehensive, adaptive security measures becomes increasingly evident.

In IT environments, cybersecurity efforts primarily focus on protecting data, systems, and infrastructure from unauthorized access, malware, and data breaches. IT systems are generally characterized by dynamic networks, complex user access patterns, and the need for scalability. The focus in IT environments is on implementing strong access controls, network segmentation, real-time threat detection, and encryption protocols. Monitoring and logging solutions are used to analyze traffic patterns and detect anomalies, while automated tools help prevent misconfigurations and vulnerabilities. With the advent of cloud computing and remote work, these challenges have become even more pronounced, prompting organizations to invest in sophisticated monitoring and adaptive security solutions.

The consequences of a failure in an IT environment can be significant. A breach or outage can result in data loss, system downtime, and financial damage. Customer data, intellectual property, and trade secrets are prime targets for cybercriminals. A ransomware attack, for example, can lock down critical systems and prevent access to data, forcing businesses to pay costly ransoms or risk losing valuable information. Moreover, customer trust and reputation can suffer long-term damage if sensitive data is exposed or misused. Financial institutions and healthcare organizations are especially vulnerable because a single breach can lead to significant regulatory fines and legal penalties under data protection laws such as the GDPR and HIPAA. The increasing frequency of such incidents has driven both public and private sectors to re-evaluate their risk management strategies and invest in more resilient security infrastructures.

In contrast, OT (Operational Technology) and ICS (Industrial Control Systems) environments have fundamentally different requirements. OT/ICS systems control physical processes—such as energy generation, water treatment, manufacturing, and transportation. Security in OT/ICS environments emphasizes system integrity, availability, and physical safety over traditional data confidentiality. This distinct focus stems from the fact that disruptions in these systems can lead not only to financial losses but also to severe public safety issues and environmental hazards.

The consequences of a failure in an OT/ICS environment can be catastrophic. A successful attack could result in physical damage to equipment, environmental contamination, and even loss of human life. The 2015 cyberattack on Ukraine's power grid, which caused a widespread blackout affecting over 230,000 people, illustrates the real-world impact of a breach in critical infrastructure. Attacks on manufacturing plants could result in production halts, equipment damage, and dangerous chemical spills. A breach in a water treatment facility could lead to contaminated water supplies or disruption in water distribution, directly threatening public health. As these systems often rely on legacy technology that is not designed to handle modern cyber threats, the integration of updated security measures is not only challenging but also vital for ensuring public safety.

Many OT/ICS systems operate with legacy hardware and software that cannot be easily patched or updated without significant downtime. For this reason, alternate controls—such as network segmentation, strict access controls, and specialized monitoring—are often necessary. A successful attack on an OT/ICS environment could have catastrophic consequences, including physical damage, environmental harm, and threats to human safety. In recent years, there has been a growing emphasis on developing specialized security frameworks for OT/ICS environments that balance the need for robust protection with the operational realities of industrial systems.

Financial losses are often the most immediate and measurable consequence of a cyberattack. Direct costs may include ransom payments to attackers, expenses related to data recovery and system restoration, and fines for failing to meet regulatory requirements. However, the hidden financial toll can be even more damaging. Lost business opportunities, diminished customer trust, and declining stock value are common after a breach becomes public. The 2017 Equifax breach, for example, is estimated to have cost the company over $700 million in settlements and penalties alone—an amount that doesn't even account for the long-term reputational damage and loss of customer confidence. Increasingly, organizations are realizing that the true cost of a cyberattack extends far beyond immediate financial impacts, affecting long-term strategic positioning and market value.

Operational disruption is another serious consequence. When key systems are compromised, businesses may be forced to shut down essential functions, leading to significant downtime and supply chain disruptions. The 2021 Colonial Pipeline ransomware attack is a prime example of how an isolated cyberattack can escalate into a national crisis. The attack forced the company to shut down a major fuel supply network, which resulted in fuel shortages, panic buying, and price spikes across the U.S. East Coast. Similar disruptions have been observed in the healthcare sector, where ransomware attacks on hospital networks have forced staff to revert to manual processes, delaying patient care and increasing risks to patient safety. Manufacturing and transportation systems have also been targeted, with production lines grinding to a halt and logistical operations thrown into chaos. These incidents underscore the need for comprehensive business continuity planning and the integration of cybersecurity into overall risk management strategies.

The reputational damage caused by a cyberattack can linger for years, often far longer than the financial or operational impacts. Trust, once lost, is difficult to rebuild. The 2013 Target data breach, which exposed the personal information of over 40 million customers, severely damaged customer confidence and drove down sales in the following quarters. Even customers who weren't directly affected may hesitate to do business with a company that has been the victim of a high-profile breach. The erosion of trust can have a compounding effect, making it more difficult for the company to attract new customers and partners. In today's competitive market, maintaining a reputation for robust cybersecurity can be a significant strategic advantage.

Legal and regulatory penalties can further compound the damage. Data protection laws like the General Data Protection Regulation (GDPR) in the European Union and the California Consumer Privacy Act (CCPA) in the United States impose strict requirements on organizations to protect customer data. When these requirements are not met, regulators can impose steep fines and other penalties. The GDPR alone has issued fines exceeding $1 billion since its implementation in 2018. In addition to financial penalties, companies can face class-action lawsuits, government investigations, and reputational fallout from their perceived negligence in protecting customer data. This regulatory pressure has pushed organizations to adopt more rigorous cybersecurity measures and invest heavily in compliance and risk management programs.

Cyberattacks can also pose a direct threat to national security. Attacks on critical infrastructure such as power grids, water treatment facilities, and transportation networks can have far-reaching consequences for public safety and national defense. Stuxnet, the sophisticated worm deployed in 2010 to sabotage Iran's nuclear program, demonstrated how cyberattacks could be weaponized to disrupt and destroy physical infrastructure. More recently, ransomware attacks on government agencies and public sector networks have highlighted vulnerabilities in state and local infrastructure. When these systems are compromised, the consequences can include interruptions in essential services, exposure of sensitive government data, and increased vulnerability to further attacks. As geopolitical tensions rise in the digital realm, governments around the world are working to strengthen their cyber defenses and establish frameworks for international cybersecurity cooperation.

The consequences of a cyberattack are rarely contained to a single event or organization. The financial, operational, reputational, and geopolitical fallout can create a ripple effect across industries and nations. This underscores why cybersecurity is not just an IT problem—it is a strategic imperative that requires attention and investment at the highest levels of leadership. An organization's ability to anticipate, prevent, and respond to cyber threats is now directly tied to its long-term viability and success in an increasingly interconnected and volatile digital landscape. The evolving nature of cyber threats demands that leaders at all levels remain engaged with cybersecurity as a core element of organizational strategy.

In the face of such severe and far-reaching consequences, a robust cybersecurity program is not just a technical necessity —it is a strategic imperative for the survival and success of any organization. The financial, operational, reputational, and national security risks posed by cyberattacks underscore the critical need for a well-defined and continuously evolving cybersecurity program. Without a structured approach to identifying vulnerabilities, implementing protective measures, and responding swiftly to incidents, organizations are left vulnerable to increasingly sophisticated and targeted threats. Recent trends in cyber insurance and risk quantification are pushing companies to adopt more proactive measures, further emphasizing the strategic nature of cybersecurity investments.

A mature cybersecurity program establishes clear frameworks, controls, and response protocols that enable organizations to minimize damage, recover quickly, and maintain business continuity even in the event of a breach. Furthermore, a strong cybersecurity posture helps build trust with customers, partners, and stakeholders by demonstrating a proactive commitment to protecting sensitive data and critical infrastructure. In an environment where cyber threats are constantly evolving, a comprehensive and adaptable cybersecurity program is essential to safeguarding not only organizational assets but also long-term stability and reputation. As technological innovations such as quantum computing and artificial intelligence continue to emerge, the importance of an agile, forward-looking cybersecurity strategy will only grow.

Cybersecurity programs are influenced by, and can differ significantly, depending on the size and resources of an organization, even though the core principles remain consistent. Small businesses, mid-sized organizations, and large enterprises each face distinct challenges and require different approaches to building and maintaining an effective cybersecurity program. The diversity of organizational needs has led to a broad spectrum of solutions in the market, ranging from affordable, easy-to-deploy tools for small companies to sophisticated, enterprise-grade systems for large organizations.

For small organizations, resource constraints often dictate a focus on cost-effective solutions that still provide robust security. Small entities must carefully balance affordability with effectiveness. The focus is usually on fundamental protections such as using strong passwords, implementing two-factor authentication, deploying firewalls and antivirus software, and training employees to recognize phishing attempts. Small businesses may rely on integrated security solutions that combine multiple functions (e.g., endpoint protection and email filtering) to simplify management and reduce costs. Despite limited resources, establishing basic data backup protocols and incident response procedures is critical for recovering quickly from attacks. A single breach could cripple a small business, especially if sensitive customer data is exposed or core systems are rendered inoperable by ransomware. In recent years, the availability of cloud-based security services has helped small organizations access advanced protection without the need for significant upfront investment.

For a small organization, the next step might involve moving beyond basic protections and investing in more structured policies and procedures. A small business that has implemented endpoint protection and employee training may look to improve by deploying network segmentation, configuring a secure VPN for remote workers, or formalizing an incident response plan. Developing a cybersecurity plan that outlines key assets, threats, and protective measures can help small businesses prioritize their limited resources more effectively. Strengthening employee training to address emerging threats like deepfake phishing or business email compromise (BEC) scams could also represent a key area of improvement. A small business might also create more detailed policies for data handling, password management, and third-party access to establish greater consistency and accountability. Even at a small scale, having a written cybersecurity plan and clear operational procedures helps ensure that security efforts remain focused and consistent as the business grows.

Mid-sized organizations face more complex security needs due to their growing networks and expanding digital footprint. Unlike small businesses, they are more likely to have formal security teams and dedicated resources for managing cybersecurity. Mid-sized companies typically establish more detailed security policies and deploy centralized monitoring tools such as Security Information and Event Management (SIEM) systems. Employee training becomes more formalized, and threat detection systems are integrated to enable real-time monitoring and response. The challenge for mid-sized organizations lies in scaling security controls effectively without introducing complexity that slows down business processes. A successful attack on a mid-sized company could disrupt operations, expose proprietary data, and lead to significant reputational harm. As these organizations grow, they often find that incremental investments in security infrastructure yield substantial returns in risk reduction and operational resilience.

A mid-sized organization that has established fundamental controls may focus on expanding its threat detection and incident response capabilities. The next step might involve deploying a Security Information and Event Management

(SIEM) system to centralize and analyze security alerts in real time or adopting a Zero Trust framework to tighten access controls. Mid-sized companies might also strengthen their vendor risk management programs or develop more comprehensive disaster recovery and business continuity plans to minimize the impact of an attack. Enhancing the maturity of the cybersecurity program at this stage often involves improving the cybersecurity plan itself—expanding its scope to include more detailed risk assessments, establishing defined response protocols for different threat scenarios, and aligning security strategy with broader business goals. Updating policies and procedures to reflect new business operations, compliance requirements, and technological changes ensures that security practices remain effective and consistent. Mid-sized companies might also begin conducting regular internal audits and tabletop exercises to validate the effectiveness of their security plan and response processes.

For large organizations, cybersecurity programs must address a broad spectrum of threats and protect a wide range of assets. Large enterprises maintain complex networks with multiple data centers, global operations, and diverse endpoints. Their security programs are typically managed by a Chief Information Security Officer (CISO) and supported by dedicated teams specializing in risk management, incident response, and compliance. Large organizations deploy advanced threat detection systems, real-time monitoring platforms, and artificial intelligence (AI)-based tools to identify and respond to emerging threats. Security measures are multi-layered, with segmented networks, Zero Trust models, and strict access controls to prevent lateral movement within the network. Large organizations also face greater regulatory scrutiny and must align their security programs with industry standards such as the NIST Cybersecurity Framework, ISO/IEC 27001, and PCI DSS. A major breach could lead to operational paralysis, shareholder lawsuits, and regulatory fines. With the increasing complexity of global operations, many large enterprises are now integrating risk management into their corporate governance structures, ensuring that cybersecurity is a board-level priority.

For a large enterprise, increasing maturity might involve automating more aspects of threat detection and response through artificial intelligence and machine learning. Integrating threat intelligence feeds, enhancing endpoint detection and response (EDR) capabilities, and expanding red team/blue team exercises to simulate sophisticated attacks could represent logical next steps. Large organizations may also focus on improving governance, aligning security strategy with broader business objectives, and conducting more detailed risk assessments across global operations. Expanding cross-departmental collaboration and improving employee accountability for security protocols are also critical steps for increasing program maturity. The scale and diversity of threats faced by large organizations necessitate a proactive and dynamic approach to cybersecurity that is continuously refined through regular testing, training, and strategic investment.

The cybersecurity plan in a large enterprise becomes more complex, encompassing not only IT infrastructure but also third-party risk, supply chain security, and operational resilience. Updating policies and procedures to reflect these expanding responsibilities is essential to maintaining alignment across business units and ensuring that all stakeholders understand their role in securing the organization's infrastructure and data. A large enterprise may also focus on improving the agility of its incident response processes, developing specialized playbooks for different types of attacks, and ensuring that incident response teams are well-trained and prepared for evolving threats.

While the maturity of a cybersecurity program may reflect the influences of organizational size and the availability of resources, the underlying goal remains the same: to protect data, systems, and business continuity from an increasingly complex threat landscape. A well-designed cybersecurity program scales with the organization, adapting to changes in business operations, technology infrastructure, and emerging threats. The ultimate goal is always to advance the maturity of its cybersecurity program. This pursuit of maturity is a continuous journey that involves both technological upgrades and cultural shifts within an organization, fostering an environment where security is an integral part of every decision.

Cybersecurity is not a static achievement—it is an ongoing process that requires constant evaluation, adaptation, and improvement. The threat landscape evolves rapidly, with attackers developing new methods to bypass defenses and exploit vulnerabilities. A mature cybersecurity program is one that recognizes this reality and continually seeks to strengthen its defenses, close gaps, and improve response capabilities. At the core of this ongoing evolution is the development or enhancement of a cybersecurity plan, supported by well-defined policies and procedures that operationalize the strategic goals of the program. New research and emerging technologies continually reshape best practices, urging organizations to remain agile and forward-thinking.

What defines a mature cybersecurity program is not the specific tools or frameworks deployed, but rather the organization's ability to adapt, anticipate, and respond effectively to emerging threats. Every improvement in maturity creates new opportunities to strengthen defenses and identify vulnerabilities before they are exploited. Cybersecurity maturity is a moving target—there is no finish line. The goal is to build a program that is resilient, responsive, and capable of evolving alongside both the threat landscape and the organization's changing business environment. The next step is always about refining and improving—no matter how advanced the current state of the program may be. A well-developed and continuously updated cybersecurity plan, supported by clear and actionable policies and procedures, serves as the foundation for sustaining and advancing cybersecurity maturity over time.

Understanding the maturity of your cybersecurity program is essential. Are you just starting out? Are you working to establish foundational protections? Or are you operating a mature program that requires continuous improvement? Regardless of the stage, effective cybersecurity programs require ongoing training, strong leadership, and a commitment to adapting to the evolving threat landscape. The integration of emerging trends, such as behavioral analytics and threat intelligence sharing, can further empower organizations to anticipate and neutralize risks before they materialize.

This book is designed to benefit a wide range of readers by addressing the complexities and challenges of building and maintaining a secure cybersecurity program. Security professionals and IT staff will gain practical insights into how to strengthen security controls, improve threat detection and response, and align security initiatives with broader business goals. For professionals already working in cybersecurity, this book provides a roadmap for enhancing existing programs and identifying areas for improvement.

Executive leadership and business managers will better understand the strategic importance of cybersecurity and how to allocate resources effectively to mitigate risk. Cybersecurity is not just a technical concern—it is a critical business issue that impacts customer trust, operational continuity, and long-term financial health. By understanding the business impact of cyber threats, leaders can make more informed decisions and prioritize security investments accordingly.

For compliance officers and legal teams, the book offers valuable guidance on aligning security practices with regulatory requirements. Data protection laws such as the General Data Protection Regulation (GDPR) and the California Consumer Privacy Act (CCPA) impose strict requirements on how organizations handle sensitive data and respond to breaches.

Understanding how to implement security controls that meet these requirements is essential for avoiding fines and legal exposure.

Small business owners will benefit from foundational advice on setting up basic protections, such as firewalls, endpoint security, and employee training. Small organizations often lack the resources to build comprehensive security programs, but even simple steps—like enabling multi-factor authentication and training employees to recognize phishing attempts—can significantly reduce risk. This book provides practical recommendations that small businesses can implement immediately, helping them establish a security foundation that can scale as the business grows.

Finally, non-technical employees and stakeholders will benefit from a broader understanding of cybersecurity's role in protecting business operations and personal data. Cybersecurity is not just the responsibility of IT teams—it's a shared responsibility that requires awareness and participation at all levels of the organization. When employees understand the potential consequences of a breach and know how to spot suspicious activity, they become an essential part of the organization's defense strategy.

By helping readers at all levels understand the complexities and challenges of cybersecurity, this book aims to foster a culture of shared responsibility and collective defense. Everyone—from front-line employees to executive leadership—plays a role in maintaining a secure operating environment. Cybersecurity is no longer just an IT issue; it is a business issue, a legal issue, and a reputational issue. The more stakeholders understand their role in supporting cybersecurity, the more effective the overall program becomes.

This is not a theoretical exercise—it is a practical guide to building cybersecurity success. The path to security is not passive—it requires strategic vision, operational discipline, and a commitment to continuous improvement. This book lays out that path—step by step—and provides the blueprint for creating a resilient and secure future. As new challenges emerge and technologies evolve, the principles outlined here will continue to serve as a foundation for innovative and adaptive security strategies.

CHAPTER 2: THE EVOLUTION AND SCOPE OF CYBERSECURITY

"Cybersecurity is not just about protecting data—it's about protecting our way of life."
— *Kevin Mitnick*

Kevin Mitnick's famous statement underscores that cybersecurity transcends the mere safeguarding of information. In today's digital age, where technology is woven into every facet of life—from healthcare and transportation to finance and personal communication—the risks extend far beyond simple data breaches. Understanding the evolution of cybersecurity is crucial to grasp the challenges and solutions we face today. Over the decades, as incidents exposed new vulnerabilities, cybersecurity practices adapted in response. This evolution is a story of continuous learning and adaptation, with each era marked by innovations spurred by real-world events.

In the early days, computers were rare, expensive machines confined to research laboratories, government institutions, and select academic environments. These early systems were housed in secure facilities and protected primarily by physical measures and rudimentary user authentication. For instance, in the 1960s, when institutions like MIT implemented the Compatible Time-Sharing System (CTSS), security was largely about controlling physical access to mainframes. However, even these pioneering systems planted the seeds of modern cybersecurity practices. When early users began sharing resources over time-sharing systems, administrators quickly recognized the need for more sophisticated methods of access control—leading to early forms of logging user activities and enforcing stricter terminal access policies. These measures, though primitive by today's standards, set the groundwork for later innovations.

During the 1960s and 1970s, computing remained an experimental field. Hardware was enormous and costly, and systems were so isolated that physical security was the primary means of defense. Yet even then, a few incidents hinted at future challenges. As organizations began experimenting with remote access and time-sharing, the inherent risks of multiple users accessing a single system became apparent. Administrators started to introduce rudimentary auditing practices to monitor who logged in and when—a practice that would later evolve into sophisticated Security Information and Event Management (SIEM) systems. The concept of accountability was born out of necessity; early computer centers implemented strict sign-in logs and physical key controls, which over time evolved into digital access control mechanisms using passwords and eventually two-factor authentication.

As the 1970s progressed, the emergence of ARPANET marked a significant turning point. ARPANET, the precursor to the modern Internet, connected disparate computer systems across vast distances. This interconnection, while revolutionary, also introduced new vulnerabilities. One of the earliest examples was the Creeper program, developed in 1971. The Creeper was a self-replicating piece of code that moved from one computer to another, demonstrating that even in a controlled network environment, malicious code could propagate. Although its intent was not malicious by today's standards—it merely displayed a message on infected machines—the Creeper program highlighted the potential for digital contagion and spurred early discussions on the need for countermeasures.

The expansion of ARPANET during the 1980s and 1990s heralded an era of rapid technological innovation and widespread connectivity. As computers began to appear in homes, businesses, and government offices around the globe, the interconnectivity that once seemed like a scientific curiosity became a foundational aspect of modern life. With the democratization of access to computing resources came a proliferation of new threats. The Morris Worm of 1988, one of the first widely publicized Internet-based attacks, exploited vulnerabilities in Unix systems and spread uncontrollably across the network, affecting thousands of machines. This incident underscored the risks of self-replicating code and served as a wake-up call to the nascent cybersecurity community. It was no longer sufficient to rely on physical security or simple password mechanisms; new approaches and technologies were needed to address the increasingly complex landscape of networked systems.

The evolution of cybersecurity is a story of reactive innovation. In the early days, many threats were theoretical constructs —vulnerabilities discussed in academic circles or highlighted as potential risks in isolated systems. However, as digital networks expanded and interconnections multiplied, these once-perceived threats began manifesting as real, damaging attacks. Early warnings turned into full-blown crises, and vulnerabilities that were once considered remote or unlikely were suddenly exploited by malicious actors, forcing the security community to rethink and redesign protective measures.

Throughout the 1990s, the evolution of malware continued with viruses such as the CIH (Chernobyl) virus and the Melissa virus. The CIH virus became notorious for its ability to corrupt data and even overwrite the system BIOS, demonstrating that malicious code could inflict physical damage on hardware— a concept that blurred the lines between digital and physical realms. In contrast, the Melissa virus spread via email and exploited the trust inherent in electronic communication, reminding everyone that human behavior was an integral part of the security equation. These early viruses revealed that cyber threats were not limited to isolated incidents; they could spread rapidly, cause widespread disruption, and inflict significant economic damage, setting the stage for the sophisticated attacks that would follow.

The early 1990s also witnessed the rise of individuals who would become synonymous with the term "hacker." Figures like Kevin Mitnick exploited not only technical vulnerabilities but also the weaknesses inherent in human psychology. Mitnick's exploits relied heavily on social engineering tactics— manipulating individuals into divulging sensitive information and bypassing even the most sophisticated technical safeguards. His activities underscored the need for comprehensive security measures that extended beyond technology, highlighting the importance of rigorous training and awareness programs for all users. This era marked a turning point in cybersecurity—a recognition that the human element was both the weakest link and a critical point of defense.

The evolution of cybersecurity has been largely in response to the ever-expanding and evolving threat landscape. In the early days, many vulnerabilities were theoretical concerns discussed in academic forums; however, as networks expanded and interconnected, these perceived threats quickly materialized into real-life attacks. What once seemed like an unlikely scenario—such as a worm spreading uncontrollably across a network—became a dramatic reality that forced organizations to implement proactive defense measures. Every new breach revealed weaknesses that had not been foreseen, compelling the security community to constantly revise its strategies and tools.

Real-life cyberattacks repeatedly exposed vulnerabilities that defied conventional expectations. Seemingly minor oversights —a misconfigured server, outdated software, or weak user passwords—often became the entry points for sophisticated intrusions. Incidents such as the Morris Worm or later, the Stuxnet attack, demonstrated that the consequences of a single overlooked flaw could escalate into catastrophic events. In response, cybersecurity practices evolved from relying solely on reactive measures to embracing proactive strategies, such as continuous vulnerability assessments, rigorous patch management, and comprehensive incident response planning.

As the threat landscape grew increasingly complex, so too did the tactics of the adversaries. Cybercriminals quickly learned to exploit any overlooked weakness, evolving their methods to bypass traditional security measures. The transition from theoretical risk to actual attack led to a fundamental shift: cybersecurity was no longer about defending against static, isolated threats but about countering a dynamic, relentless adversary. Each major incident—whether it was the rapid dissemination of a worm or the targeted disruption of industrial systems—served as a catalyst for the development of new technologies and strategies designed to anticipate and neutralize future threats.

This relentless cycle of attack and response has driven the entire field of cybersecurity into a state of perpetual evolution. Defensive measures that were once considered sufficient quickly became obsolete as new, unforeseen methods of attack emerged. The process of learning from each incident, incorporating those lessons into enhanced defenses, and then facing yet another wave of innovative threats has become the norm. Today's cybersecurity frameworks, built on the principles of layered defense and continuous monitoring, are direct responses to the real-world lessons learned from past breaches.

With the advent of the World Wide Web in the mid-1990s, the digital landscape transformed almost overnight. The Web's explosive growth opened up an array of services—from online shopping and banking to social media—that became potential targets for cyberattacks. This period saw the emergence of e-commerce giants, whose security challenges spurred the development of technologies like Secure Sockets Layer (SSL) encryption, which evolved into the modern Transport Layer Security (TLS) protocols. The push for secure online transactions forced financial institutions and retailers to invest heavily in encryption technologies and secure coding practices, establishing the foundation for modern web security.

The turn of the millennium further complicated the cybersecurity landscape. As organizations increasingly relied on digital platforms for everything from financial transactions to email communications, the attack surface expanded dramatically. Broadband internet, mobile devices, and cloud computing transformed traditional networks into complex ecosystems where data flowed freely across multiple environments. Malware evolved into complex, multi-faceted threats that employed polymorphic techniques to evade detection. In response, cybersecurity practices advanced from reactive antivirus programs to heuristic and behavior-based detection systems. Organizations began to implement advanced endpoint security solutions, intrusion detection systems, and real-time monitoring platforms—all measures designed to address a threat landscape that was becoming both larger and more unpredictable.

One of the most transformative developments of the past decade has been the rise of Advanced Persistent Threats (APTs). Unlike the relatively unsophisticated attacks of earlier eras, APTs are characterized by their stealth, persistence, and the significant resources that state-sponsored groups or organized criminal syndicates devote to them. The discovery of the Stuxnet worm in 2010 is one of the most illustrative examples of this evolution. Stuxnet was designed specifically to target industrial control systems by exploiting multiple zero-day vulnerabilities. It successfully breached an air-gapped network —long considered a nearly impenetrable defense—by using infected USB drives and exploiting side-channel vulnerabilities. The fallout from Stuxnet forced the cybersecurity industry to reconsider the security of isolated systems. In response, new practices evolved: organizations began to implement stricter controls on removable media, enhanced physical security around critical infrastructure, and developed comprehensive monitoring even for systems that were traditionally considered isolated. The Stuxnet attack fundamentally changed the approach to industrial cybersecurity, emphasizing the need for a multi-layered defense that integrated both physical and digital safeguards.

In the years following Stuxnet, additional high-profile incidents continued to shape cybersecurity practices. The 2016 Mirai Botnet attack, for instance, exploited default credentials on Internet of Things (IoT) devices—such as security cameras and routers—to create a massive botnet capable of launching coordinated Distributed Denial of Service (DDoS) attacks. This event underscored the critical importance of securing every device connected to a network and led to widespread changes in IoT security practices, including the mandate to change default passwords and the development of IoT-specific security protocols. Similarly, regulatory measures such as the GDPR and CCPA have pushed organizations worldwide to adopt robust encryption methods, improved access controls, and regular security audits, ensuring that evolving threats are met with equally dynamic defensive strategies.

The rapid evolution of technology in recent years has brought both new challenges and opportunities. Mobile devices and cloud computing have revolutionized the way people work and interact, but they have also introduced complexities in securing data as it moves between on-premise systems and the cloud. In response, cybersecurity practices have evolved to include advanced cloud security protocols and mobile device management solutions. Enterprises now deploy unified threat management systems that consolidate multiple security functions into a single platform. Moreover, artificial intelligence and machine learning technologies are beginning to play a pivotal role in detecting anomalous behavior and automating responses, further illustrating how cybersecurity practices continue to evolve in direct response to an ever-changing threat landscape.

At the same time, the human dimension of cybersecurity

remains a critical focus. Despite technological advances, many successful attacks still hinge on human error. Cybercriminals exploit trust through social engineering techniques such as phishing, pretexting, and baiting. In response, organizations have ramped up user education and training programs, implementing regular simulated phishing exercises and interactive workshops to reinforce the importance of vigilance. This evolution in training practices—moving from simple awareness programs to comprehensive, behavior-focused initiatives—has been driven by real-world incidents that demonstrated how easily human error can compromise even the most advanced technical defenses.

International cooperation has also grown in response to the increasingly global nature of cyber threats. Cyberattacks rarely respect national borders, and their attribution often involves complex geopolitical factors. In response, governments, industry groups, and international organizations have established platforms for sharing threat intelligence, coordinating responses, and developing common standards for cybersecurity. Initiatives such as the NATO Cooperative Cyber Defence Centre of Excellence and various public-private partnerships have become vital components of a unified global defense strategy. These collaborative efforts have led to standardized protocols and best practices that organizations worldwide now rely on, reinforcing the understanding that cybersecurity is a collective responsibility.

Another significant evolution has occurred in the realm of supply chain security. As organizations increasingly depend on third-party vendors, cloud services, and interconnected systems, the risk that a compromise in one link of the supply chain could cascade into broader network disruptions has grown dramatically. High-profile breaches involving trusted software vendors have forced companies to adopt rigorous third-party risk management practices, including continuous monitoring of vendor security, comprehensive due diligence, and contractual obligations to adhere to strict cybersecurity standards. These measures ensure that security is not limited to an organization's internal network but extends throughout its entire supply chain.

Looking forward, emerging technologies such as quantum computing present both opportunities and challenges. Quantum computing promises to solve complex problems that are intractable for classical computers, yet its immense processing power also threatens to render current encryption methods obsolete. Researchers and industry experts are actively developing quantum-resistant cryptographic algorithms—a proactive effort to secure data against future quantum-based attacks. This area of research highlights the forward-looking nature of cybersecurity: as new technologies emerge, so too must the defensive strategies evolve to mitigate risks that may only become apparent in the future.

Throughout its evolution, cybersecurity has been defined by its continuous adaptation to an ever-changing threat landscape. Each era—whether marked by the theoretical vulnerabilities of early computing, the explosive connectivity of the Internet age, or the sophisticated, multi-layered attacks of the modern era— has driven the development of innovative defensive practices. Real-life attacks repeatedly exposed vulnerabilities that defied conventional expectations, transforming theoretical risks into tangible challenges and forcing the security community to continuously reinvent itself. This relentless cycle of attack and response serves as the engine of innovation in cybersecurity, ensuring that every new vulnerability uncovered leads to the development of more robust, comprehensive defenses.

Ultimately, the evolution of cybersecurity is not a static achievement but a continuous process of learning from the past, adapting to the present, and preparing for the future. Each unanticipated breach reinforces the need for perpetual vigilance, ensuring that the systems we depend on remain resilient in the face of an ever-expanding threat landscape. As emerging challenges such as quantum computing, advanced AI-driven attacks, and increasingly interconnected supply chains come to the forefront, the commitment to cybersecurity must also evolve, embracing new technologies and strategies while never losing sight of the human element that is often the first line of defense.

In this ever-changing landscape, every incident—from the earliest network worms to the sophisticated state-sponsored intrusions of today—has served as a catalyst for change. The evolution and scope of cybersecurity are a testament to the resilience and ingenuity of a global community committed to protecting our way of life in an increasingly digital world. As emerging threats continue to test our defenses, the journey of cybersecurity remains a dynamic, ongoing process marked by continuous adaptation, collaboration, and innovation—a process that is as essential as it is never complete.

Ultimately, the evolution of cybersecurity is a story of reactive innovation—a journey from theoretical vulnerabilities to real-life attacks that have forced the industry to confront weaknesses that were once unimaginable. Each phase of this evolution, driven by incidents that exposed critical flaws, has led to the development of defensive practices that are more robust, adaptive, and integrated than ever before. The dynamic interplay between emerging threats and innovative countermeasures underscores that cybersecurity is not a destination, but a continuous commitment to protecting the digital fabric of our society.

CHAPTER 3: THE CIA TRIAD

"Selecting the most important principle in the CIA Triad is like trying to select your favorite child. You love your children equally, but they each have one uniqueness that separates them from the others. Same with the CIA triad. They are all important but for different reasons."
— Antonio Sanchez

This statement, offered by Antonio Sanchez, encapsulates a perspective that resonates deeply with both the seasoned security professional and the inquisitive newcomer. It is a reminder that while the elements of confidentiality, integrity, and availability might be dissected and analyzed separately, in practice they interweave into a singular, robust fabric that underpins every security strategy. No single component can be isolated as more important than the others because each one contributes a vital function, much like the distinctive qualities of a beloved child that, when brought together, form the essence of a family's strength.

In an era defined by digital transformation, the importance of protecting data has surged to the forefront of every organization's strategic priorities. The digital landscape has grown from a simple network of isolated computers to an intricate, interconnected ecosystem where every device, application, and user plays a role in a vast exchange of information. As the Internet, cloud computing, and the Internet of Things have expanded the boundaries of our digital universe, they have simultaneously multiplied the avenues through which data can be exposed, intercepted, or even altered. The CIA triad—comprising confidentiality, integrity, and availability—serves as the cornerstone of any robust security framework, providing the guiding principles that inform the design and implementation of security measures across myriad environments. It is a framework that has evolved over decades, continuously refined in response to new challenges and emerging threats, always maintaining its relevance in a world where the only constant is change.

The journey toward understanding and implementing the CIA triad begins with the notion of confidentiality, which can be likened to a high-security vault in a bustling metropolis. In the early days of computing, confidentiality was often a secondary consideration. Basic file permissions and rudimentary password protection were considered sufficient defenses. However, as networks grew larger and the stakes became higher, it became apparent that the mechanisms protecting sensitive information needed to evolve dramatically. The introduction of data encryption, which transforms readable information into a ciphered format accessible only through the correct decryption key, revolutionized the way organizations viewed and enforced confidentiality. The development of advanced encryption standards, such as AES, and the widespread adoption of protocols like SSL/TLS have created layers of defense that protect data both in transit and at rest. In modern systems, confidentiality is not simply a matter of keeping information hidden—it is about ensuring that every piece of data is accessible only to those with explicit authorization, a goal achieved through sophisticated authentication protocols that range from passwords to biometrics and multi-factor authentication. These mechanisms not only verify the identity of users but also ensure that unauthorized entities, even if they manage to breach the outer layers of security, are met with insurmountable barriers that prevent them from accessing valuable information.

The evolution of confidentiality is further highlighted by practices such as data masking and tokenization, which allow organizations to protect sensitive data during processes that do not require full visibility of the original information. This is particularly important in environments where data must be analyzed or processed without exposing the raw, unprotected data itself. The evolution of these techniques was driven by early experiences with unencrypted communications and unauthorized data access, where even brief lapses in security led to significant breaches. Over time, as attackers refined their techniques, organizations learned that a multi-layered approach to confidentiality was essential. Employee training and the establishment of comprehensive security policies became as important as technical safeguards, reinforcing a culture in which data protection was not merely a technical challenge but a core organizational value. The story of confidentiality is one of continual adaptation, where each advancement in technology has been met with an equally innovative response from the security community, creating an ongoing arms race that defines much of modern cybersecurity.

While confidentiality focuses on protecting data from unauthorized access, the principle of integrity is equally crucial in maintaining trust in our digital systems. Integrity is the assurance that data remains accurate, unaltered, and reliable from the moment it is created until it is no longer needed. In a world where information flows ceaselessly across networks and is subject to constant updates and modifications, ensuring that data has not been tampered with is paramount. Early systems that relied on manual audits or periodic checks were quickly outpaced by the rapid pace of digital transformation. The advent of techniques such as hashing, which produces a unique digital fingerprint for data, enabled the development of systems that could detect even the smallest changes. Digital signatures further cemented this capability by providing a means to verify not only the integrity of the data but also its origin. This technological progression was driven in part by incidents where minor alterations in financial records or medical data went unnoticed until the consequences of those changes became apparent. The need for automated, continuous monitoring became evident, and organizations soon implemented systems that could track every alteration in real time, ensuring that any deviation from the expected data pattern was quickly identified and addressed.

Ensuring the integrity of data is not solely a technical challenge; it is also an organizational one. The introduction of rigorous version control systems and the practice of periodic audits have become standard in industries where accuracy is not just preferred but required. In financial sectors, for example, even the slightest discrepancy in transaction records can lead to significant monetary losses and erode the trust of stakeholders. In healthcare, the integrity of patient records can mean the difference between a correct diagnosis and a life-threatening error. These experiences underscored that integrity is about more than just maintaining data—it is about preserving the trust that is essential for any digital interaction. The constant vigilance required to maintain data integrity has driven the development of advanced monitoring systems that can detect unauthorized modifications almost instantaneously, reducing the window of opportunity for potential attackers. In this way, the principle of integrity is both a technical safeguard and a fundamental component of an organization's reputation and operational reliability.

Availability, the final pillar of the CIA triad, is perhaps the most immediately perceptible in everyday operations. It represents the assurance that data and systems remain accessible to those who need them at the right time. In the early days of computing, availability was taken for granted; systems were designed around the assumption that they would operate continuously and without interruption. However, as digital dependence grew, so too did the recognition that any downtime —whether due to technical failure, cyberattack, or natural disaster—could have catastrophic consequences. In sectors such as finance, healthcare, and critical infrastructure, the inability to access data in a timely manner can lead to severe operational disruptions and even pose risks to human safety. The response to early system outages was the development of redundant architectures, designed to eliminate single points of failure. Techniques such as load balancing, which distributes workloads evenly across multiple servers, and the establishment of geographically dispersed data centers have become standard practices in ensuring that systems remain resilient in the face of unforeseen disruptions.

The history of availability is marked by both tragedy and triumph. Early incidents involving system outages led to the realization that continuity planning was not just an IT concern but a critical business imperative. Organizations that once relied on single, centralized systems had to rethink their strategies and invest in robust disaster recovery and business continuity plans. These plans, which outline detailed procedures for restoring systems and data after an incident, have evolved into sophisticated protocols that incorporate automated failover mechanisms and real-time monitoring of system health. The emphasis on availability has spurred technological innovations that allow systems to operate seamlessly even when individual components fail. Modern infrastructures are designed with resilience in mind, ensuring that critical services remain uninterrupted regardless of the challenges that may arise.

Balancing the three principles of the CIA triad in an integrated IT environment requires a nuanced and context-driven approach. Mission-critical systems, those that support financial transactions, customer data management, or strategic decision-making, often demand a tailored blend of security measures. In some scenarios, ensuring the confidentiality of sensitive data may require significant investments in advanced encryption and strict access controls. In other situations, particularly where the immediate availability of data is critical, systems must be designed to prioritize uptime, even if that means accepting a certain level of risk regarding confidentiality or integrity. Over time, the interplay among these three principles has driven the evolution of security strategies. For instance, the rise of ransomware—a type of cyberattack that can simultaneously compromise confidentiality, integrity, and availability—has forced organizations to adopt holistic, integrated security measures. These measures encompass the entire data lifecycle, from creation and storage to transmission and eventual disposal, ensuring that a breach in one area does not precipitate a cascade of failures across the system.

In the specialized world of Operational Technology (OT) and Industrial Control Systems (ICS), the application of the CIA triad takes on additional layers of complexity. These systems, which govern everything from power generation to manufacturing and water treatment, operate in environments where even minor disruptions can have far-reaching consequences. In these settings, the continuous availability of data is not just a convenience—it is a necessity that can affect the safety of entire communities. The design of OT and ICS systems often requires a delicate balance: while confidentiality is important to protect against espionage and sabotage, the methods used in traditional IT environments, such as heavy encryption, may introduce unacceptable delays in time-sensitive operations. Consequently, the security measures implemented in these systems are often carefully calibrated to preserve the performance and responsiveness that industrial processes demand. Historical incidents, such as cyberattacks on power grids or water treatment facilities, have underscored the need for specialized strategies that address the unique challenges of these environments. Techniques such as network segmentation, dedicated security gateways, and the use of air-gapped systems are common in OT/ICS, where the cost of a security breach can be measured not just in lost data but in physical damage and human risk.

The evolution of cybersecurity has also brought about a convergence of IT and OT security practices, prompting a reassessment of traditional paradigms. While the vulnerabilities inherent in IT systems—often characterized by open networks and standardized protocols—differ in some respects from those found in OT environments, there is growing recognition that the two worlds are inextricably linked. The potential for an attacker to leverage weaknesses in an IT network to gain access to an OT system has driven organizations to adopt integrated security approaches. This convergence has led to the development of secure communication protocols, unified threat management systems, and continuous risk assessments that span both domains. The lessons learned from high-profile breaches in IT environments have informed the strategies employed in OT settings, fostering a culture of continuous improvement and cross-disciplinary collaboration. In many organizations, the successful integration of IT and OT security measures has become a cornerstone of modern cybersecurity strategies, ensuring that the benefits of digital innovation are not undermined by vulnerabilities at the intersection of these two critical domains.

Beyond the technical dimensions of confidentiality, integrity, and availability, the broader context of cybersecurity encompasses a range of regulatory, legal, and organizational factors. Over the years, government regulations and industry standards have played a significant role in shaping the practices that govern data protection. Frameworks such as the Health Insurance Portability and Accountability Act, the Payment Card Industry Data Security Standard, and various international privacy regulations have imposed strict requirements on how organizations must handle sensitive information. These regulatory imperatives have driven the adoption of best practices that align closely with the principles of the CIA triad. For example, the need to secure patient data in the healthcare industry has led to the widespread implementation of encryption, access controls, and rigorous auditing practices, all of which are designed to uphold the confidentiality, integrity, and availability of critical information. The influence of regulatory bodies has ensured that security is not merely a matter of technical capability but also a matter of compliance and accountability, fostering an environment in which organizations are continuously pushed to refine and improve their security postures.

The dynamic interplay among the three components of the CIA triad is further illustrated by the evolving nature of cyber threats. In the past, security breaches were often the result of isolated incidents—errors made by individuals or the exploitation of a single vulnerability. Today, however, cyberattacks are sophisticated, multifaceted operations that often involve coordinated efforts by highly skilled adversaries. A single incident, such as a ransomware attack, can simultaneously compromise the confidentiality of data, alter its integrity, and render systems unavailable to legitimate users. This confluence of threats has reinforced the need for security measures that are not only robust in isolation but also capable of operating cohesively as part of an integrated defense strategy. The continuous evolution of attack techniques has necessitated a corresponding evolution in defensive strategies, leading to the development of security solutions that combine traditional measures with advanced analytics, machine learning, and real-time monitoring. These innovations are designed to detect and respond to threats as they emerge, ensuring that any disruption is contained before it can spread and cause extensive damage.

It is not lost on those who work in cybersecurity that the battle for secure information is ongoing and ever-changing. Every breakthrough in technology is met by a new challenge, every innovative tool is eventually countered by an equally inventive exploit. This cycle of adaptation has instilled a sense of urgency and resilience in organizations across every sector. The CIA triad, in its enduring simplicity, serves as both a reminder of fundamental principles and a beacon guiding the future of cybersecurity. The principles of confidentiality, integrity, and availability are as relevant today as they were in the early days of digital communication, and their continued evolution is a testament to the collective effort of the global security community.

Stories from the front lines of cybersecurity offer powerful insights into the real-world impact of these principles. Consider the case of a major financial institution that suffered a significant data breach several years ago. The attackers exploited a vulnerability in the institution's network, compromising customer data and undermining the trust that the institution had painstakingly built over decades. In the aftermath of the breach, the organization embarked on a comprehensive overhaul of its security architecture. Investments were made in state-of-the-art encryption systems, and access controls were tightened to ensure that only authorized personnel could access sensitive information. Simultaneously, automated integrity checks were introduced to monitor data for unauthorized changes, and redundant systems were deployed to guarantee that critical services would remain operational even in the event of an attack. The incident served as a stark reminder that neglecting even one aspect of the CIA triad could have catastrophic consequences, and it spurred a transformation that not only restored confidence but also set new benchmarks for security across the industry.

A similar narrative unfolds in the realm of healthcare, where the protection of patient records is a matter of life and death. Hospitals and clinics, once content with basic security measures, have now embraced a more holistic approach that addresses all three elements of the CIA triad. Advanced encryption techniques protect patient data from unauthorized access, while automated systems continuously verify the integrity of electronic health records. At the same time, investments in redundant network infrastructures ensure that medical personnel can access critical information at a moment's notice, even in the face of cyberattacks or system failures. In these environments, the principles of confidentiality, integrity, and availability are not abstract concepts but practical necessities that directly affect patient outcomes. The evolution of these practices in healthcare is a powerful testament to the impact that a balanced approach to cybersecurity can have on human lives.

The journey toward achieving a secure, resilient digital environment is an ongoing process that demands continuous learning and adaptation. Every incident, whether it be a minor data anomaly or a full-blown cyberattack, provides valuable lessons that drive further innovation in security practices. The evolution of the CIA triad is marked by a constant interplay between defensive measures and the ever-creative methods employed by attackers. In this dynamic landscape, organizations are not only tasked with implementing cutting-edge technologies but also with fostering a culture of security that permeates every level of the enterprise. Regular training, rigorous audits, and an unwavering commitment to continuous improvement have become indispensable components of a modern security strategy. The lessons learned from past breaches and the innovations spurred by those experiences form the bedrock upon which future advancements are built, ensuring that as the threats evolve, so too does the defensive framework that protects against them.

Reflecting on the historical evolution of cybersecurity, one cannot help but marvel at the resilience and ingenuity that have characterized the field. From the early days of simple password protection to today's sophisticated, multi-layered security architectures, the journey has been one of relentless progress. Each new challenge has spurred the development of innovative solutions that not only address immediate vulnerabilities but also anticipate future threats. The story of the CIA triad is a narrative of evolution and adaptation, a chronicle of how the fundamental principles of confidentiality, integrity, and availability have been reimagined to meet the demands of an increasingly interconnected world.

It is a story that underscores the importance of remaining vigilant, of continuously questioning and refining our security practices, and of recognizing that in the realm of cybersecurity, complacency is the enemy of progress.

The dynamic interplay between emerging technologies and evolving threats continues to shape the future of cybersecurity. As organizations increasingly rely on cloud services, mobile platforms, and artificial intelligence, the traditional boundaries between IT and OT are blurring. New challenges emerge from every corner, and the principles of the CIA triad remain as relevant as ever. The expansion of digital ecosystems means that data now flows across diverse platforms and geographies, each with its own set of risks and vulnerabilities. In this complex environment, the ability to protect data through robust confidentiality measures, ensure its unaltered state through rigorous integrity checks, and guarantee its availability even in adverse conditions is more critical than ever. The evolving nature of cyber threats compels us to remain agile, to constantly adapt our defenses in anticipation of the next breakthrough from adversaries, and to recognize that the strength of our digital infrastructure ultimately rests on the balanced application of these timeless principles.

The evolution of the CIA triad is not merely a tale of technological advancement but also a reflection of the human element in cybersecurity. Behind every encryption algorithm, every integrity check, and every redundant system, there are teams of dedicated professionals who labor tirelessly to protect the digital fabric of our society. Their efforts, often unseen by the end users who benefit from seamless connectivity and uninterrupted services, are a testament to the importance of diligence, innovation, and collaboration. These professionals understand that cybersecurity is as much about people and processes as it is about technology. They work to instill a mindset of security awareness that transcends individual tasks and becomes a fundamental part of an organization's culture.

The evolution of the CIA triad thus mirrors the evolution of our collective approach to security—a gradual, ongoing process of learning, adapting, and ultimately fortifying the digital defenses that underpin every aspect of modern life.

Looking to the future, the continued relevance of the CIA triad will depend on our ability to anticipate and counter new threats. The rapid pace of technological innovation brings with it both promise and peril. As emerging technologies such as quantum computing, the Internet of Things, and next-generation artificial intelligence reshape our world, they will also introduce novel vulnerabilities that challenge our current security paradigms. The lessons of the past, encapsulated in the principles of confidentiality, integrity, and availability, provide a robust framework for addressing these challenges. However, the future will undoubtedly require us to push the boundaries of innovation even further, to develop new methods of protecting data and systems in ways that we can scarcely imagine today. The spirit of continuous improvement that has driven the evolution of the CIA triad for decades will remain the guiding light as we navigate the uncertain terrain of tomorrow's cybersecurity landscape.

In many ways, the journey of understanding and implementing the CIA triad is emblematic of the broader challenges faced by society in the digital age. It is a journey marked by a delicate balance between progress and protection, between innovation and security. Every advancement in technology brings with it a host of new opportunities, as well as new risks that must be managed with equal vigor. The principles of confidentiality, integrity, and availability are not relics of a bygone era but living, dynamic guidelines that continue to shape the way we interact with and protect our digital world. They remind us that in an environment where the stakes are continually rising, a holistic, integrated approach to security is not just desirable—it is essential.

As we reflect on the evolution of cybersecurity practices,

it becomes clear that every innovation, every procedural improvement, and every new technological breakthrough is part of a larger tapestry of resilience. The lessons learned from early experiments in digital security, from the humble beginnings of password protection to the complex, multi-layered strategies of today, are interwoven with the experiences of countless professionals who have dedicated their careers to this ever-evolving field. Their stories, though often unsung, form the backbone of our modern understanding of security. The CIA triad, in its elegant simplicity, captures the essence of their endeavors—a constant reminder that the pursuit of secure, reliable, and accessible information is a journey without end, one that demands perpetual vigilance and unwavering commitment.

In the final analysis, the principles of confidentiality, integrity, and availability are more than mere technical constructs; they are the embodiment of a philosophy that recognizes the intrinsic value of information in our modern world. They serve as a constant reminder that no matter how advanced our technologies become, the core tenets of security remain unchanged. They are the guardians of trust, the sentinels of data, and the architects of a digital future that is as resilient as it is innovative. As cyber threats continue to evolve and the boundaries of technology are pushed ever further, the enduring wisdom of the CIA triad offers both a roadmap and a reassurance: that with careful, balanced, and continuous effort, it is possible to build a digital world where information remains secure, trustworthy, and ever available to those who need it.

In the quiet determination of every security professional lies an understanding that the journey is far from over. With every breakthrough in technology comes a new frontier of vulnerabilities to explore and fortify. Yet, even as new challenges emerge, the foundational principles of confidentiality, integrity, and availability stand as beacons of stability in a tumultuous digital landscape. The evolution of these principles is a story of learning from adversity, of adapting to the ever-changing dynamics of technology, and of a shared commitment to protecting the very essence of what makes our digital lives possible.

Ultimately, the narrative of the CIA triad is a testament to the unyielding human spirit—a spirit that, in the face of relentless challenges and ceaseless innovation, remains steadfast in its resolve to build a safer, more secure digital future. It is a story of continuous improvement, of resilience in the face of adversity, and of a future that is defined not by the inevitability of cyber threats, but by the promise of human ingenuity and the enduring commitment to secure the flow of information that shapes our world.

CHAPTER 4: DEFENSIVE ARCHITECTURE

"Iraq has no depth."
- General Norman Schwarzkopf

When General Norman Schwarzkopf uttered those words, he encapsulated a truth that transcends the battlefield and speaks to the very core of modern cybersecurity. That single statement serves as a stark reminder that no solitary barrier, however formidable it might seem, can ever provide absolute protection for our most vital assets. In an era defined by rapid technological advances and increasingly sophisticated adversaries, relying on one line of defense is like trusting a delicate dam to hold back an unyielding torrent—a dam that may offer temporary respite but is ultimately destined to succumb to persistent, evolving pressure.

In the annals of military history, great fortifications were never built with just one line of defense. Consider the medieval castle: a marvel of engineering designed not as a single wall but as an intricate series of obstacles. Moats encircled the structure, high walls and drawbridges deterred direct assault, and inner keeps served as the final sanctuary for those who survived the initial onslaught. Every component was crafted to slow, frustrate, and ultimately deter invaders, forcing them to navigate a gauntlet of defenses before they could reach the heart of the stronghold. Today, this same layered principle forms the basis of what we call defense in depth. If one barrier is breached, another stands ready to delay the threat, granting defenders invaluable time to detect, analyze, and neutralize the incursion.

In the early days of computer security, the idea of isolation was almost revered. Critical systems were often separated from the sprawling digital network by employing what was known as an air gap—a deliberate physical disconnection designed to render these systems immune to remote attacks. The logic was compelling: without a network connection, malicious actors would have no avenue to infiltrate. However, as our digital landscape expanded and interconnectedness became the norm, so did the ingenuity of those intent on breaching these defenses. The myth of an impregnable air gap began to crumble as attackers discovered that even isolated systems could be compromised through contaminated USB drives, side-channel attacks that exploited subtle electromagnetic emissions, or the inadvertent introduction of vulnerabilities by insiders. These incidents underscored a harsh reality: no measure of isolation, however rigorously maintained, is entirely impervious.

Yet, to dismiss the air gap as a relic of the past would be a grave misjudgment. Its role has evolved rather than diminished. Today, we understand the air gap in a dual sense —encompassing both a physical barrier that isolates critical systems from less secure networks and a logical partition within digital architectures that safeguards the very core of an organization's data. Consider the stringent security measures in US nuclear power plants. In these facilities, where even the smallest misstep could have catastrophic consequences, defense is built on multiple, interlocking layers. At the outermost level, physical air gaps are maintained through the construction of secure, fortified buildings equipped with robust access controls, armed guards, biometric scanners, and continuous surveillance. Within these walls, these controls are replicated, and even strengthened, moving inward into the defensive architecture. Logical air gaps are achieved via multiple layers of meticulous network segmentation and micro segmentation, advanced firewalls, diodes, and strict authentication protocols. Each defensive layer is managed through a comprehensive cybersecurity plan complimented by extensive policies and implementing procedures. Even if an adversary were to breach the outer defenses, they would encounter a digital fortress designed to protect the systems that regulate critical nuclear processes.

Another particularly instructive example of layered security is found in the Purdue model—a framework originally developed for securing industrial control systems. The Purdue model divides a network into distinct hierarchical levels, each engineered with its own set of security controls to protect the industrial process at its core. At Level 0 lie the physical processes: sensors, actuators, and machinery that directly interact with the environment. Level 1 contains the basic control functions managed by programmable logic controllers. Level 2 introduces supervisory control, where systems monitor and coordinate the activities of Level 1 devices. Higher levels, such as Levels 3 and 4, extend into the realm of enterprise networks, handling production management and corporate decision-making. The genius of the Purdue model lies in its insistence on isolating each layer from the next. Should an adversary breach one level, they must contend with additional, independently secured layers before reaching the heart of the industrial process. This not only reinforces the evolved concept of the air gap—both physical and logical—but also vividly illustrates the effectiveness of defense in depth.

Beyond these structured models, the evolution of defense in depth is also a narrative of convergence—where the physical and digital realms intertwine to create a resilient and adaptive security posture. Our modern adversaries are not lone wolves working from the shadows; they are organized entities, sometimes state-sponsored, equipped with resources and methodologies that enable them to exploit even the smallest vulnerabilities. In this landscape, a breach in one layer can cascade into a full-scale compromise unless overlapping safeguards are in place. The necessity for layered security is thus not merely an option—it is an imperative dictated by the very nature of contemporary threats.

Imagine for a moment that your most prized assets are positioned at the center of a series of concentric rings. The outer ring is comprised of tangible, physical security measures —a fortified building with impenetrable walls, secure entry points manned by vigilant guards, and an array of surveillance systems monitoring every movement. As one moves inward, the defenses transition from the physical to include the technical realm – increasing the defensive architecture at each of the inner rings. Advanced firewalls scrutinize every data packet attempting to cross into the network; intrusion detection systems monitor for even the faintest hint of anomalous activity; and robust encryption protocols ensure that even if data is intercepted, it remains indecipherable. The innermost layer may even be protected by deterministic devices such as data diodes – and the networks within this layer may each be protected from lateral movement through the use of firewalls or diodes. Each successive layer acts as an independent barrier, forcing any attacker to expend considerable time and resources just to reach the next level. This redundancy—the seamless integration of physical and logical defenses—transforms isolated measures into an unyielding fortress.

The historical reliance on singular security measures, such as the early air gap, offered a veneer of protection—a temporary illusion of safety that eventually proved insufficient. The notorious Stuxnet worm, which infiltrated industrial control systems presumed secure due to their isolation, serves as a stark reminder of this vulnerability. Such incidents drive home an essential lesson: no defense can ever be complete when it stands alone. Instead, each measure must be woven into a broader, integrated strategy—a tapestry of defenses in which every thread reinforces the others, and the collective strength far exceeds that of any single component.

Modern cybersecurity challenges are as multifaceted as they are relentless. Attackers exploit vulnerabilities on multiple fronts —human error, software flaws, and even lapses in physical security. A well-orchestrated phishing campaign might trick an unsuspecting employee into divulging login credentials, creating a gateway for further exploitation. Yet even in such cases, layered defenses can significantly mitigate the damage. Multi-factor authentication can prevent an attacker from gaining full access even if a password is compromised, while robust endpoint protection can halt malware in its tracks before it spreads throughout the network. In essence, each additional layer acts as a safety net, catching threats that manage to slip past earlier defenses and ensuring that the overall security posture remains intact.

The interplay between these layers is not static; it is a dynamic, ever-changing dance—a continuous adaptation to emerging threats. Modern security architectures are designed to not only withstand attacks but to evolve in response to them. Every new vulnerability discovered and every novel attack vector exploited compels a reassessment of existing defenses, leading to refinements that enhance overall resilience. This perpetual cycle of threat and response is the essence of defense in depth— a strategy built on the understanding that while no system can be made completely impervious, it is possible to create a defense that forces adversaries to expend disproportionate effort for minimal gain.

Integral to this evolutionary process is the adoption of cutting-edge technologies such as artificial intelligence and machine learning. These tools have revolutionized our ability to monitor vast networks in real time, sifting through enormous volumes of data to identify subtle patterns and anomalies that may signal an ongoing attack. In many instances, these AI-driven systems are capable of initiating automated responses that neutralize threats before they can inflict significant damage. The integration of such advanced technologies into the broader defense in depth strategy not only enhances the effectiveness of individual layers but also contributes to the overall synergy and robustness of the security framework.

Yet, amid all these technological advancements, the human element remains an irreplaceable cornerstone of effective defense. It is often said that the greatest vulnerability in any security system is not the technology itself but the people who operate it. Even the most sophisticated defenses can be undermined by a single moment of human error—a misdirected email, a poorly chosen password, or an inadvertent click on a malicious link. This reality underscores the critical importance of continuous training, fostering a culture of vigilance, and instilling a deep sense of shared responsibility across all levels of an organization. In high-stakes environments such as nuclear power plants, where the margin for error is negligible, the commitment to security must be ingrained in every individual's daily routine. Rigorous training programs, regular simulated attack exercises, and an unwavering emphasis on accountability help transform every employee into a vital component of the collective defense—a human firewall that works in concert with technological safeguards.

As we reflect on the evolution of defense in depth, we cannot help but draw parallels with the age-old strategies of historical fortifications. The ancient castle, with its multiple layers of walls, moats, and inner keeps, remains a powerful metaphor for our modern approach to cybersecurity. Just as those stone fortresses were designed to sap the strength and resolve of invaders through successive, exhausting challenges, our digital defenses are constructed to delay, expose, and ultimately thwart any malicious effort. The transformation of the air gap—from a simple physical disconnection to a sophisticated blend of physical and logical isolation—is emblematic of this enduring principle. In critical infrastructures such as US nuclear power plants, where the consequences of a breach can be catastrophic, the layered approach is not merely an academic concept but a rigorously implemented strategy that protects both lives and national security.

The Purdue model, with its clear delineation of operational

levels, offers a vivid example of how such layered defenses are applied in industrial settings. By segmenting a network into distinct layers—each with tailored security controls—the Purdue model ensures that even if an adversary breaches an outer layer, they must confront additional, independently secured barriers before reaching the core processes. At Level 0, raw physical processes are closely monitored and controlled by sensors and actuators; Level 1 oversees these devices with programmable controllers; Level 2 provides a supervisory layer to coordinate and manage operations; and higher levels integrate these functions into comprehensive enterprise systems. This hierarchical segmentation creates a series of virtual air gaps, each one isolating and protecting the inner sanctum from external threats. It is a brilliant demonstration of defense in depth—a testament to the power of combining multiple layers of protection into a cohesive, adaptive system.

Beyond the realm of industrial control systems, the principles of defense in depth have far-reaching applications in nearly every sector. Financial institutions safeguard sensitive customer data by isolating external-facing applications from internal processing systems. Healthcare organizations protect patient information through the integration of advanced encryption, continuous monitoring, and strict access controls. Even small businesses, despite their limited resources, are increasingly recognizing the imperative of a layered approach —deploying everything from firewalls and antivirus software to comprehensive staff training and rigorous data backup protocols. The underlying message is clear: no single security measure, regardless of its sophistication, can offer complete protection. Instead, it is the interplay of multiple, overlapping defenses that creates a resilient system capable of withstanding the relentless pressures of an ever-evolving threat landscape.

As our digital and physical worlds continue to converge, the challenges we face become ever more complex. The interconnected nature of modern technology means that every device, every network, and every process is part of a larger, interdependent ecosystem. With this interdependence comes new risks—vulnerabilities that can emerge from the most unexpected quarters. Supply chain attacks, for instance, exploit the very connectivity that drives global commerce, compromising a single vendor to gain access to an entire network. Insider threats, driven by human error or malice, exploit the privileges that are essential for operational efficiency. In this context, defense in depth is not merely a reactive strategy but a proactive philosophy—one that anticipates every potential point of failure and seeks to mitigate it through redundancy and resilience.

The rapid pace of technological change further complicates the security landscape. Each day, new tools and techniques emerge —both for those who protect and those who attack. While this dynamism fuels innovation, it also means that the security measures of yesterday can quickly become obsolete. Continuous reassessment, adaptation, and improvement are therefore not optional but essential. Every vulnerability uncovered, every breach attempted, contributes to a growing body of knowledge that informs and refines our defenses. It is a relentless cycle of threat and response—a modern arms race in which the only constant is change. In such an environment, the layered approach of defense in depth stands as the most effective strategy, acknowledging that while perfection is unattainable, resilience is very much within our reach.

Zero Trust is a security framework built on the principle that no user, device, or network component should be inherently trusted—regardless of whether it resides inside or outside the traditional network perimeter. This approach mandates that every access request is continuously verified, authenticated, and authorized before granting any level of access. It operates under the concept of least privilege, ensuring that users and devices have only the minimum necessary permissions to perform their functions. By treating every interaction as potentially hostile,

Zero Trust effectively minimizes the risk of lateral movement by attackers, fortifying an organization's defenses against evolving cyber threats.

Zero Trust and Defense in Depth are two intertwined security paradigms that, while distinct in their origins and implementations, ultimately work towards the same goal: reducing the risk of a security breach. Defense in Depth, rooted in the concept of layered security, builds multiple independent barriers to protect critical assets. In contrast, Zero Trust starts from the premise that no entity—whether inside or outside the network—should be inherently trusted.

The relationship between these models is both complementary and synergistic. Defense in Depth creates a robust infrastructure by stacking various security controls—physical, network, application, and data—so that even if one layer fails, the others continue to safeguard sensitive information. Zero Trust, on the other hand, refines this approach by applying strict identity verification and access policies across all layers. It reinforces the concept of least privilege and continuous validation, ensuring that even if an attacker bypasses one of the layered defenses, they still face rigorous scrutiny at every subsequent step.

In practical terms, integrating Zero Trust principles into a Defense in Depth strategy means that each layer is not merely a passive barrier but an active checkpoint. For example, in a traditional layered model, network segmentation and firewalls might block unauthorized access at the perimeter. Zero Trust takes this further by requiring that every device and user undergo continuous authentication, regardless of their location within the network. This dynamic approach ensures that even internal traffic is subject to rigorous checks, significantly reducing the risk posed by insider threats or lateral movement after a breach.

Ultimately, the fusion of Zero Trust with Defense in Depth creates a more resilient security framework. While Defense in

Depth offers a broad, multi-layered safety net, Zero Trust injects a granular, risk-aware mindset into each layer. Together, they form a comprehensive strategy that not only delays and deters attackers but also minimizes the impact of any breach that does occur, ensuring that every access point is continuously scrutinized and every vulnerability is promptly addressed.

Looking ahead, emerging technologies hold the promise of further enhancing our layered defenses. Blockchain technology, for instance, offers revolutionary methods for ensuring data integrity and creating immutable audit trails that can detect tampering and ensure accountability. Cloud-native security solutions are redefining traditional network boundaries, enabling dynamic, scalable defenses that adapt in real time to shifting conditions. The integration of artificial intelligence and machine learning into security systems is already transforming the way we detect and neutralize threats—allowing us to identify, analyze, and respond to attacks with unprecedented speed and precision. Even as these innovations push the envelope of what is possible, the fundamental tenets of defense in depth remain unchanged. They serve as a timeless reminder that true security is not achieved through any single breakthrough but through the thoughtful integration of multiple, interlocking defenses.

In the final analysis, the narrative of defense in depth is one of resilience, adaptation, and unwavering commitment—a story that spans centuries, from the fortified walls of ancient castles to the cutting-edge cybersecurity systems that safeguard our digital and physical worlds today. It teaches us that while no single measure can guarantee absolute security, the careful orchestration of multiple, overlapping defenses can create a fortress capable of withstanding even the most determined adversaries. As we continue our journey into an increasingly interconnected future, we do so with the understanding that our defenses must evolve in tandem with the threats we face.

This evolution is not just a matter of technology, but also one of organizational culture and human commitment. Building a resilient defense in depth strategy requires that every member of an organization—from the boardroom to the break room —embrace security as a core value. It means fostering an environment where continuous learning, rigorous training, and proactive vigilance are the norm. It means investing not only in cutting-edge technologies but also in the people who operate them, recognizing that the human element is both our greatest asset and our most significant vulnerability.

In this relentless pursuit of security, the dual nature of the modern air gap—encompassing both physical and logical isolation—stands as a potent symbol of our adaptive ingenuity. Whether manifested in the layered defenses of the Purdue model or the stringent protocols safeguarding nuclear power plants, the principle is consistent: every additional barrier fortifies the whole, transforming potential vulnerabilities into formidable strengths. As new challenges emerge and the threat landscape evolves, our commitment to defense in depth remains our most powerful weapon—a testament to our ability to innovate, adapt, and ultimately protect what matters most.

In the end, the story of defense in depth is not one of despair, but of hope and resilience—a narrative of continuous improvement, where every challenge is met with a renewed commitment to excellence. It is a story that reminds us that while no single barrier can withstand the full force of a determined adversary, a well-constructed, multi-layered fortress can indeed hold the line. And it is a story that will continue to unfold, as long as we remain dedicated to the principles of layered, adaptive, and resilient security.

CHAPTER 5: CYBERSECURITY LIFECYCLE

"Security is a process, not a product. It is not a state to be achieved but a continuous effort that must adapt to the ever-changing threat landscape. The challenge of cybersecurity is not in implementing a single solution, but in weaving security into the fabric of every system, every interaction, and every decision."
— Bruce Schneier

Security is a process, not a product. These words by Bruce Schneier capture the essence of a challenge that has evolved alongside the digital age—a challenge that demands perpetual attention rather than a one-time fix. In today's environment, where every new technological innovation brings with it potential vulnerabilities and every threat adapts to overcome static defenses, cybersecurity must be viewed as an unceasing journey. It is not a destination reached with a final patch or a single piece of hardware, but rather a continuous cycle of vigilance, adaptation, and improvement. This understanding forms the backbone of the Cybersecurity Lifecycle, a structured framework that guides organizations in protecting their digital assets against an ever-shifting array of cyber threats.

At its core, the Cybersecurity Lifecycle is an endless loop composed of five interconnected phases: Identify, Protect, Detect, Respond, and Recover. Each phase is integral to building and maintaining a resilient security posture. The framework is not merely a sequential checklist; it is an iterative process in which the insights gained in one stage feed back into the others, ensuring that organizations not only address current threats but also prepare for those yet to emerge. This chapter endeavors to expand on the original narrative by delving deeper into each phase, enriching the language and detail while retaining the foundational content that defines our understanding of cybersecurity.

The journey begins with the Identify phase, a foundational step that lays the groundwork for every subsequent effort. In this stage, an organization embarks on a comprehensive examination of its entire digital ecosystem. It is here that one must inventory every asset, from servers and networks to endpoints and cloud services, and catalog not only their existence but also their vulnerabilities and potential exposure. This phase is akin to taking a detailed map of an expansive territory, where every device, application, and data repository is scrutinized to reveal both its value and its risk. Small businesses may rely on simple spreadsheets or basic asset management platforms, while larger enterprises invest in sophisticated risk management systems that deliver real-time dashboards and predictive analytics. The process demands that organizations confront their own digital landscape with brutal honesty, acknowledging weaknesses that could serve as entry points for malicious actors. It is an exercise in self-awareness— a deliberate, systematic effort to understand not just what one owns, but how each component interacts within the broader context of the organization's operations.

As organizations map their environments, they also conduct thorough risk assessments. These assessments combine qualitative insights with quantitative data to form a complete picture of potential threats. In this stage, every identified asset is measured against the likelihood and impact of its compromise, creating a risk profile that informs every decision moving forward. The Identify phase is not static; it is a continuous process. As new systems are deployed or as the threat landscape evolves, this phase must be revisited and updated. The narrative here is one of constant vigilance, a relentless pursuit of knowledge about one's own operations. In a way, it is the act of "knowing thyself" in the digital realm, a critical first step that informs every other security measure. The integrity of this phase determines the quality of all that follows; without a clear understanding of the environment, subsequent efforts to protect, detect, respond, and recover may be misdirected or incomplete.

Building upon this foundational knowledge, the Protect phase transforms insight into tangible defense measures. It is here that the raw data of the Identify phase is put to practical use in fortifying the organization against potential attacks. This phase is characterized by the deployment of an array of technical controls designed to secure networks, safeguard data, and restrict access to sensitive systems. The narrative of protection is one of layered defenses—an approach where multiple security measures are interwoven to create a robust barrier against intrusion. Basic firewalls, antivirus software, and encryption protocols represent the first line of defense, ensuring that data remains secure both in transit and at rest. More advanced measures such as intrusion prevention systems, biometric authentication, and privileged access management add additional layers of security, forming a complex web that deters and deflects would-be attackers.

For a small business, the Protect phase might begin with simple, cost-effective solutions: configuring a secure Wi-Fi network, enabling automatic updates to patch vulnerabilities, and educating employees about the dangers of weak passwords and phishing scams. These measures, while seemingly modest, lay the groundwork for a secure environment by closing off common avenues of attack. In contrast, a medium-sized organization may adopt a more comprehensive strategy, integrating centralized security systems that monitor and manage endpoints, segmenting networks to contain breaches, and establishing detailed access controls that define and restrict user privileges. Large enterprises, with their sprawling infrastructures and critical data assets, often deploy an arsenal of advanced technologies. They combine state-of-the-art endpoint detection and response systems with sophisticated security information and event management (SIEM) platforms, and they regularly conduct penetration tests and security audits to verify that every layer of defense remains impenetrable.

The act of protection is not solely a technical challenge— it is also deeply human. Effective security depends on the people who manage it, from IT professionals to every employee who accesses the network. As such, comprehensive protection strategies incorporate robust training and awareness programs, ensuring that everyone understands their role in the collective defense. The language of protection, while technical in nature, is ultimately about creating a culture of security—where each individual becomes a vital link in the chain of defense. This phase, in its extended narrative, is as much about building a resilient organizational mindset as it is about installing firewalls and encryption protocols. It is the synthesis of technology and human behavior, where every secure configuration, every updated policy, and every informed employee contributes to the overall safety of the organization.

Once defenses are in place, the Detect phase assumes the role of a vigilant sentinel, ever watchful for signs of intrusion. Detection is not a one-off event; it is a continuous, dynamic process that monitors network traffic, system logs, and user behaviors for any anomalies that might indicate a security incident. In small organizations, detection might rely on basic intrusion detection systems (IDS) that alert administrators to suspicious activities, while larger entities leverage centralized SIEM systems and even artificial intelligence to scrutinize vast amounts of data in real time. The essence of the Detect phase is early warning —a sophisticated interplay between automated systems and the critical thinking of cybersecurity professionals. Every alert generated, every anomaly flagged, is a potential clue in the puzzle of an emerging threat.

The narrative of detection is fraught with challenges. Amid the sea of benign activities, subtle indicators of malicious behavior can be easily overlooked. It is a stage where the margin for error is razor-thin, and the cost of oversight can be enormous. For medium-sized organizations, this might mean implementing behavioral-based anomaly detection systems that learn the normal patterns of network activity and then highlight deviations. In large enterprises, the stakes are higher, and the tools more advanced: AI-driven threat detection platforms work in tandem with Security Operations Centers (SOCs) staffed by analysts who monitor real-time dashboards, ready to respond at a moment's notice. Detection is the phase where the art of cybersecurity converges with the science of data analysis—a relentless pursuit of the smallest detail that might portend a larger attack. It is a narrative of continuous alertness, where every piece of data is a potential harbinger of danger, and every detection capability is a testament to the organization's commitment to staying one step ahead of adversaries.

When a security incident is finally identified, the narrative shifts dramatically into the Respond phase—a moment when theory is put into immediate practice. Response is the phase where swift, decisive action is required to contain the threat, mitigate damage, and set the stage for recovery. It is a high-pressure, high-stakes juncture, often compared to a well-drilled emergency response in the physical world. For small organizations, responding to an incident may involve straightforward steps: isolating affected systems, resetting compromised passwords, and calling in external experts if necessary. Even in these smaller setups, the response must be prompt and coordinated to prevent further damage. Medium-sized organizations typically develop more elaborate incident response plans, complete with predefined playbooks for various types of cyberattacks, from ransomware intrusions to data breaches. They engage in forensic analysis to understand the root cause of the incident and coordinate communication with stakeholders to manage the fallout. In large enterprises, response strategies are even more sophisticated. Automated containment tools can instantly quarantine affected segments of a network, and dedicated incident response teams work around the clock to neutralize threats. These teams follow meticulously crafted protocols, engaging in forensic investigations, legal communications, and even liaising with law enforcement or regulatory agencies. The narrative of response is one of urgency and precision—a time when every second counts, and every action must be executed with the utmost clarity and coordination. It is during this phase that an organization's resilience is truly tested, and the lessons learned become invaluable for fortifying future defenses.

After the immediate crisis has been managed, the focus naturally turns to the Recover phase—a stage dedicated to restoring normal operations and learning from the incident. Recovery is not merely about returning to a pre-incident state; it is a process of introspection, reflection, and transformation. In a small business, recovery might involve painstakingly reinstalling software, verifying the integrity of data, and revisiting security policies to close any gaps that the incident revealed. Medium-sized organizations approach recovery as a collaborative effort, assembling cross-functional teams to conduct comprehensive post-incident reviews. These reviews are essential for understanding the timeline of the breach, assessing the effectiveness of the response, and identifying improvements to both technical systems and organizational processes. Large enterprises, with their complex infrastructures and extensive resources, treat recovery as an enterprise-wide initiative. Detailed audits and strategic planning sessions become the norm, ensuring that every lesson learned is incorporated into updated security policies, incident response plans, and training programs.

The narrative of recovery is as much about human resilience as it is about technical remediation. It is the phase where the scars of an attack are not hidden but examined closely, each one serving as a reminder of vulnerabilities that must be addressed.

Recovery is a process of transformation—an opportunity to rebuild stronger and wiser than before. The process feeds directly back into the Identify phase, as lessons learned prompt a reassessment of risks and the introduction of new measures to preempt future incidents. Recovery is not a finite end, but rather a necessary, continuous loop that reinforces the cyclical nature of the Cybersecurity Lifecycle. It is a narrative of renewal, where every setback becomes a stepping stone towards a more resilient future.

Throughout this lifecycle, the phases of Identify, Protect, Detect, Respond, and Recover are not isolated silos but parts of an interconnected whole. The insights gained during the Identify phase shape the defensive measures deployed during Protect, while the capabilities built in Detect ensure that any breach is swiftly recognized. In turn, the efficiency and effectiveness of the response during the Respond phase set the stage for a meaningful recovery, which then feeds back into the cycle through renewed identification and analysis of vulnerabilities. The integration of these phases creates a dynamic and evolving security posture, one that is capable of adapting to the relentless pace of technological change and the myriad threats that accompany it.

The extended narrative of the Cybersecurity Lifecycle is particularly compelling when viewed through the lens of different organizational contexts. In smaller organizations, the cycle may be implemented with limited resources, yet the fundamental principles remain intact. The journey often begins with a modest but earnest effort to map out digital assets and identify vulnerabilities. Each step, though simple, carries a weight of urgency and importance—every device, every connection, every policy is scrutinized with the understanding that even the smallest oversight could open the door to an attacker. The narrative here is one of ingenuity and perseverance, where creative solutions and cost-effective measures combine to form a surprisingly robust defense. Even with limited budgets and personnel, small organizations can achieve significant resilience by focusing on the fundamentals of the lifecycle and continuously improving through experience and incremental innovation.

Medium-sized enterprises, caught between the agility of small businesses and the vast resources of large organizations, often face a delicate balancing act. Their cybersecurity narratives are enriched by the need to scale solutions without sacrificing the personalized touch that can be lost in larger bureaucracies. In these environments, the Identify phase might involve more advanced tools and processes—integrated risk management platforms that continuously monitor assets and flag potential issues. Protection strategies become more layered and complex, incorporating both technical solutions and rigorous employee training programs. Detection systems, too, evolve from basic alert mechanisms into more sophisticated platforms that employ behavioral analytics and machine learning to distinguish between normal operations and potential threats. The response plans in these organizations are detailed and rehearsed, reflecting the need for swift, coordinated action in the face of growing cyber threats. Recovery, then, becomes a collaborative effort that draws on the collective experience of cross-functional teams, ensuring that every incident contributes to the maturation of the organization's security posture.

Large enterprises, with their expansive digital landscapes and critical data assets, tell a narrative of cybersecurity on an almost epic scale. In these organizations, the Identify phase is a continuous, never-ending process. Advanced risk management platforms, powered by real-time data and predictive analytics, constantly scan sprawling networks for vulnerabilities. Every asset, regardless of size or function, is catalogued and monitored, creating a dynamic, ever-updating map of the digital terrain. The Protect phase in these settings is characterized by a multi-layered defense strategy that leaves little to chance.

Enterprise-grade firewalls, intrusion detection and prevention systems, endpoint detection and response platforms, and advanced encryption protocols work in concert to create an almost impenetrable barrier. Yet even the most sophisticated defenses require human oversight, and large enterprises invest heavily in training programs, simulation exercises, and automated systems that assist in managing the complexity of their networks.

Detection in large organizations is an exercise in precision and scale. With vast amounts of data flowing through multiple channels, the challenge is to sift through the noise to find the true signals of malicious activity. Here, artificial intelligence and machine learning play critical roles, analyzing patterns and identifying anomalies that might elude human observers. Security Operations Centers, staffed by highly trained analysts working around the clock, serve as the nerve centers of this phase. Every alert is meticulously investigated, and the lessons learned from each incident feed into the continuous improvement of detection algorithms. The Respond phase, when activated, is a full-scale operation. Automated systems quickly isolate compromised segments, while dedicated incident response teams launch coordinated efforts to neutralize threats. For large enterprises, response is not merely a technical exercise but a matter of strategic importance, with clear protocols for communication, legal considerations, and even coordination with law enforcement. The subsequent Recover phase involves comprehensive audits, deep forensic investigations, and strategic overhauls designed to ensure that every weakness is addressed and that the organization emerges stronger from the crisis.

What unifies these diverse narratives is the understanding that the Cybersecurity Lifecycle is not a linear progression but a continuous, iterative process. Each phase is intimately connected to the others, creating a loop of perpetual improvement. As organizations identify new vulnerabilities, they must adapt their protective measures; as they detect new threats, they refine their response strategies; and as they recover from incidents, they gather insights that enhance every future phase. This interdependence is the lifeblood of a resilient cybersecurity program, one that acknowledges the reality that no system is ever truly secure. Instead, security is a dynamic state—constantly in flux, continuously evolving, and always demanding the full attention of every stakeholder.

The enduring truth of Bruce Schneier's observation resonates throughout this lifecycle: security is not a product to be purchased or a state to be achieved, but a continuous effort —a journey marked by discovery, innovation, and relentless adaptation. As organizations navigate the complexities of the digital age, they must embrace the reality that cybersecurity is a perpetual challenge. It requires a holistic approach that integrates cutting-edge technology with human insight, detailed planning with agile execution, and a culture of continuous improvement that permeates every level of the organization. Each phase of the lifecycle is a chapter in an ongoing story of resilience—a story that is written in real time, with every decision and every action contributing to a broader narrative of defense against an ever-evolving enemy.

In the end, the Cybersecurity Lifecycle is more than just a framework; it is a philosophy. It is a recognition that the only constant in the world of cybersecurity is change, and that the only effective defense is one that is as dynamic and adaptable as the threats it faces. It is a call to action for organizations of all sizes to take a proactive, integrated approach to security— one that acknowledges the complexity of the digital landscape while remaining committed to the fundamental principles of risk management, protection, detection, response, and recovery. Through this continuous cycle of improvement, organizations not only safeguard their assets but also build a culture of resilience that can withstand the trials of tomorrow.

This chapter, with its extended narratives and detailed

exploration of each phase, seeks to capture the essence of that ongoing journey. It retains the original insights that have long defined our understanding of cybersecurity, while enriching the narrative with additional detail and depth. By weaving together the technical, the strategic, and the human elements of cybersecurity, we hope to provide a comprehensive portrait of what it means to defend in a digital world. The story of cybersecurity is one of constant evolution—a narrative where every vulnerability identified, every defense implemented, every threat detected, every incident responded to, and every system recovered contributes to a legacy of continuous improvement. It is a story that reminds us that the battle for security is never won once and for all, but is fought every day, in every system, and by every individual dedicated to the cause.

In embracing this journey, organizations commit themselves to a state of perpetual readiness, understanding that every phase of the lifecycle is critical to building and maintaining a secure future. They learn that identifying risks is not a one-time exercise but an ongoing dialogue with the digital environment, that protecting assets is a layered effort combining technology with human diligence, that detecting intrusions requires both sophisticated tools and a keen eye for anomalies, that responding to incidents demands both speed and strategic coordination, and that recovering from breaches is an opportunity for reflection, learning, and renewal. The Cybersecurity Lifecycle is a testament to the power of continuous adaptation—a narrative that evolves with every technological advancement and every emerging threat.

As we move forward in an era defined by rapid innovation and persistent cyber risks, the principles outlined in this lifecycle remain our most reliable guideposts. They are reminders that the strength of our defenses lies not in any single measure, but in the continuous, integrated effort to identify, protect, detect, respond, and recover. This is the enduring truth of cybersecurity —a truth that demands not complacency but constant vigilance, not temporary fixes but sustained commitment, and not isolated actions but a cohesive, dynamic strategy. It is a journey that each organization must undertake with determination and with the full understanding that security is, above all, a continuous process—a process that, like the digital world itself, is ever-changing, ever-challenging, and ever-inspiring.

In the final analysis, the narrative of the Cybersecurity Lifecycle is one of transformation and hope. It is a story in which every setback is transformed into an opportunity to learn, every breach into a lesson in resilience, and every recovery into a stepping stone towards a safer digital future. It is a story that we, as stewards of cybersecurity, are privileged to write—one chapter at a time, one phase after another, in a continuous cycle of discovery, protection, vigilance, and renewal. As we stand on the front lines of this ongoing battle, we are reminded that true security is not a destination but a journey—one that we must travel with unwavering commitment, relentless curiosity, and the profound understanding that every effort, no matter how small, contributes to the larger story of defense in an ever-evolving digital age.

CHAPTER 6: ATTACK VECTORS AND PATHWAYS

"It's impossible to be completely protected from every vulnerability. That's because the good guys must protect against every possible vulnerability, while the bad guys only need one small crack in a company's armor to get in."
— *Keri Pearlson*

In the ever-evolving landscape of cybersecurity, understanding how attackers breach systems and navigate complex networks is akin to studying the intricate blueprints of an ancient fortress. Every digital asset—whether it is a small corporate network, a sprawling enterprise infrastructure, or an interwoven collection of cloud-based applications—is constructed with multiple layers of defense. Each layer is designed with a specific purpose, yet each also presents its own potential vulnerabilities. Attack vectors are the distinct methods by which adversaries exploit these vulnerabilities, while attack pathways are the subsequent routes they use to expand their access once the initial breach has occurred. This chapter embarks on an extensive exploration of these ideas, drawing on historical context, technical analysis, and lessons gleaned from real-world incidents. In addition, it highlights the crucial role of analytical tools such as the MITRE ATT&CK framework and the strategic insights provided by control frameworks like those from NIST—frameworks that conceptualize every control as the answer to a specific security question.

From ancient times to the modern digital era, the art of exploiting vulnerabilities has been central to the conduct of warfare. In days of yore, generals would study castle walls and defensive perimeters, looking for a crumbling stone or an unguarded gate that could be exploited. Modern cyber attackers perform a similar function—scanning lines of code, scrutinizing network architectures, and even observing human behavior—to pinpoint that one overlooked flaw that will allow them access. Early cyber conflicts were marked by crude methods, such as unsophisticated spam emails and basic viruses. Today's adversaries, however, are far more adept at identifying the minutest misconfigurations or software bugs, exploiting them with techniques that are as psychological as they are technical. This historical evolution underscores an enduring truth: while defenders must patch every potential entry point, attackers need only find one weakness to succeed.

One of the most pervasive and effective attack vectors in today's environment is phishing. In a phishing attack, a malicious actor crafts a communication—typically an email or a text message —that appears to originate from a trusted source. The attacker invests significant effort into mimicking the visual style, language, and even the urgency of legitimate correspondence. When the recipient is convinced by the facade, they click on a malicious link or download an infected attachment, unwittingly opening a door into the network. Because many organizations design their internal communications to be highly trusted, once a user takes that action, the attacker gains an initial foothold. Numerous real-world incidents have demonstrated how a single phishing email can trigger a cascade of breaches, enabling adversaries to harvest sensitive credentials and install malware that silently permeates the network. Detailed studies of these incidents have revealed subtle behavioral indicators that often precede such attacks, prompting improvements in email filtering, targeted user training, and the deployment of multi-factor authentication measures.

Yet, the breach achieved by a phishing attack is only the opening act. Once the initial entry is secured, attackers typically move laterally through the network—a process known as lateral movement or pivoting. With a foothold established, adversaries launch reconnaissance operations to map the internal network. They harvest additional credentials, escalate privileges, and install persistent backdoors that ensure long-term access. The internal network is rarely a simple, linear configuration; it is more like a labyrinth where each segment offers a potential route to critical assets. For example, after compromising a single workstation, an attacker may search for servers hosting financial data, human resources files, or proprietary intellectual property. Every step of this process is informed by lessons from past breaches, underscoring the importance of rapid detection and segmentation. Real-world case studies consistently show that the faster defenders can isolate a compromised segment, the less damage an attacker can inflict.

Malware represents another critical attack vector that has grown ever more sophisticated. Viruses, worms, trojans, ransomware—each of these forms of malicious software is designed to either disrupt operations or covertly exfiltrate data once it infiltrates a system. The delivery methods for malware are varied: some are introduced via compromised email attachments or malicious downloads, while others are delivered through compromised websites or even through physical media like USB drives. Modern malware is particularly elusive. Many strains now employ polymorphic techniques, constantly altering their code to evade detection by signature-based antivirus systems. In some instances, attackers exploit zero-day vulnerabilities—flaws unknown to the vendor and unpatched at the time of exploitation—to deliver their payloads before defenses can be updated. High-profile ransomware attacks, where critical data is encrypted and held hostage until a ransom is paid, serve as stark reminders of the potentially devastating impact of malware. These incidents have driven the development of layered defense strategies that combine signature-based detection with behavioral analytics, endpoint detection and response (EDR) systems, and real-time threat intelligence feeds.

While technical exploits such as phishing and malware are critical to understanding modern cyber threats, the human element remains a frequently exploited vulnerability. Social engineering attacks target the human psyche rather than technical systems. In these scenarios, the attacker leverages natural human tendencies—trust, curiosity, and even fear—to manipulate individuals into divulging sensitive information or bypassing security protocols. A classic example is when an attacker impersonates a senior executive or trusted vendor, convincing an employee to provide confidential data or to disable security measures temporarily. Such attacks demonstrate that even the most advanced technical defenses can be rendered ineffective if the people behind them are not adequately prepared. The study of numerous social engineering incidents reinforces the importance of comprehensive training programs, regular simulated phishing exercises, and fostering a culture of healthy skepticism. In many cases, technical defenses have been bolstered only after an organization has learned from a breach that exploited human error, underscoring the interplay between technology and human behavior.

The vulnerabilities of physical systems also add to the complexity of the threat landscape. Although much of modern cybersecurity focuses on digital defenses, the physical security of devices and facilities remains paramount. Attackers who gain physical access can bypass digital safeguards with relative ease. For instance, an intruder who manages to tailgate into a restricted area may plug a malicious USB drive into an unattended computer, installing software that opens a covert backdoor into the network. Real-world examples of physical breaches have resulted in significant data losses and long-term security compromises, leading many organizations to invest in robust physical security measures such as biometric access controls, surveillance systems, and strict visitor protocols. These measures work in tandem with digital defenses, ensuring that every potential attack vector—whether digital or physical—

is addressed.

Wireless networks, which offer the flexibility of mobility and convenience, come with their own unique set of vulnerabilities. Unlike wired networks, which benefit from the physical constraints of cables and controlled access points, wireless networks broadcast data through the air, making them inherently more susceptible to interception and unauthorized access. Adversaries can easily set up rogue access points that mimic legitimate networks, luring unsuspecting users into connecting and exposing their data. Several high-profile breaches have demonstrated that poorly secured or misconfigured wireless networks can serve as gateways for significant intrusions. To mitigate these risks, organizations have adopted robust encryption standards such as WPA3, coupled with continuous monitoring systems that detect unauthorized signals and rogue devices. Viewed through the lens of frameworks like NIST, each technical control for wireless security is designed as a precise answer to the threat posed by these vulnerabilities.

Another modern challenge arises from the intricacies of supply chains. In today's interconnected global economy, organizations are seldom isolated; they depend on a network of vendors, suppliers, and partners for critical components, software, and services. Supply chain attacks exploit this interdependence by targeting the weakest link in the chain rather than the primary organization itself. An attacker might compromise a third-party vendor by tampering with software updates or injecting malicious code into hardware components, thereby gaining indirect access to the target organization. The fallout from such breaches can be extensive, affecting not only the compromised vendor but also every organization that relies on their products or services. High-profile supply chain attacks have prompted companies to rethink their vendor management practices, leading to more rigorous assessments, continuous monitoring, and the implementation of stringent access controls that extend to external collaborators. When viewed in the context of NIST control frameworks, every measure designed to secure the supply chain is a targeted response to the question: How can we protect our organization from vulnerabilities introduced by external partners?

In the quest to counter these multifaceted threats, one indispensable resource stands out: the MITRE ATT&CK framework. This comprehensive knowledge base meticulously documents the tactics, techniques, and procedures (TTPs) that adversaries have used in real-world cyber incidents. With over 300 distinct techniques organized across a wide array of tactical categories, the MITRE ATT&CK framework serves as both a reference and a practical guide for defenders. By studying this framework, cybersecurity professionals can discern patterns in adversary behavior, anticipate potential future threats, and tailor their defense strategies to address specific attack methods. The framework is dynamic—continuously updated to reflect new insights and emerging trends—and its detailed mappings enable defenders to translate abstract threat concepts into actionable intelligence. As a result, the MITRE framework not only informs immediate defensive measures but also contributes to long-term strategic planning, ensuring that every layer of security is designed with an understanding of how attackers might attempt to bypass it.

The real value of frameworks such as MITRE ATT&CK becomes even more apparent when they are integrated with the guidance provided by standards like NIST. When cybersecurity professionals study NIST control frameworks, it is useful to view each control not as a bureaucratic mandate but as a carefully crafted answer to a specific question: What potential attack vector or method does this control address? For example, a control mandating regular patch management is a direct countermeasure against vulnerabilities exploited by malware or zero-day attacks. Similarly, the requirement for multi-factor authentication is a purposeful response to the threat of credential theft—a common tactic in phishing and social engineering. By conceptualizing every control as a targeted solution, organizations can implement a coherent and comprehensive defense strategy where every measure has a clear purpose, and no potential attack vector is left unaddressed.

Beyond these technical and procedural considerations, the human and organizational dimensions of cybersecurity are equally critical. Modern cybersecurity is not solely about deploying advanced software or hardware solutions; it is also about cultivating a culture of continuous learning and vigilance. Real-world examples of cyber attacks often reveal that the most sophisticated defenses can be undermined by human error or organizational complacency. Therefore, organizations must invest not only in technological solutions but also in training programs, simulation exercises, and collaborative initiatives that promote a deep, shared understanding of the threat landscape. When employees are well-informed about the tactics used by adversaries—whether through simulated phishing exercises or detailed analyses of past incidents—they become active participants in the defense strategy. This human element, when combined with the technical capabilities of modern cybersecurity systems, creates a resilient posture that is much harder for attackers to breach.

In today's interconnected world, the threat landscape is further complicated by emerging technologies and the rapid pace of innovation. The Internet of Things (IoT), for example, has brought a proliferation of connected devices into nearly every facet of our lives—from smart home systems to industrial control networks. While these technologies offer immense benefits, they also expand the potential attack surface, introducing new vectors that adversaries can exploit. Vulnerabilities in IoT devices, which often have less robust security measures than traditional IT systems, can provide attackers with entry points into larger networks. Real-world incidents involving compromised IoT devices have demonstrated that attackers can leverage these weaknesses not only to gain unauthorized access but also to disrupt critical infrastructure. As a result, securing IoT ecosystems has become a major focus for cybersecurity professionals, requiring specialized strategies that address both the technical and operational challenges posed by these devices.

Another emerging frontier in the battle against cyber threats is the use of machine learning and artificial intelligence (AI) in both offensive and defensive capacities. On the offensive side, attackers are beginning to harness AI to automate the reconnaissance process, analyze large datasets for vulnerabilities, and even craft more convincing social engineering attacks. Conversely, defenders are leveraging machine learning to enhance threat detection, automate incident response, and predict potential breaches before they occur. These advanced technologies represent a double-edged sword; while they can significantly bolster an organization's security posture, they also raise the stakes in the ongoing arms race between attackers and defenders. As machine learning tools become more sophisticated, the insights gleaned from real-world attacks and analytical frameworks like MITRE will be essential in calibrating these systems to distinguish between benign anomalies and genuine threats.

Collaboration and information sharing have emerged as indispensable components of modern cybersecurity. In a landscape where threats are both global and dynamic, no single organization can afford to operate in isolation. Governments, private enterprises, and international bodies increasingly recognize the value of sharing threat intelligence and best practices. Initiatives such as information sharing and analysis centers (ISACs) provide platforms where organizations can exchange insights about emerging attack vectors, share detailed case studies of breaches, and collectively refine defensive strategies. This collaborative approach not only accelerates the identification of new threats but also enhances the overall resilience of the digital ecosystem. When combined with the detailed mappings provided by frameworks like MITRE ATT&CK and the structured guidance of NIST controls, information sharing creates a feedback loop that continuously informs and improves cybersecurity practices on a global scale.

The role of simulation and red-teaming exercises in this environment cannot be overstated. These practices, which involve simulating real-world cyber attacks under controlled conditions, offer organizations a practical way to test their defenses, identify gaps, and refine their incident response strategies. Through red-teaming exercises, organizations can observe firsthand how an attacker might exploit specific vulnerabilities and traverse attack pathways. The insights gained from such exercises are invaluable; they provide concrete evidence of the strengths and weaknesses of existing security measures and offer clear guidance on how to fortify defenses. Many organizations now integrate regular simulation exercises into their cybersecurity programs, ensuring that both technical systems and human operators are well-prepared to face emerging threats.

Moreover, the evolving regulatory landscape is shaping how organizations approach cybersecurity. Governments around the world are increasingly imposing stringent cybersecurity requirements, driven by high-profile breaches and the growing recognition of the risks posed by cyber threats. Regulations such as the General Data Protection Regulation (GDPR) in Europe and various cybersecurity directives in other regions mandate rigorous standards for protecting personal and sensitive data. These regulatory frameworks often echo the principles found in NIST and other industry standards, reinforcing the idea that every control must be understood as a response to a specific threat. Compliance with these regulations not only enhances security but also builds trust with customers and partners, who recognize that robust cybersecurity practices are fundamental to protecting their interests in an interconnected digital world.

Ethical and legal considerations also play a significant role in shaping modern cybersecurity strategies. As organizations deploy increasingly sophisticated surveillance and monitoring tools to detect and counter cyber attacks, they must balance these measures against the need to protect individual privacy and civil liberties. The debate over encryption, data retention, and governmental oversight continues to influence how security controls are designed and implemented. Ethical cybersecurity practices require transparency, accountability, and a commitment to upholding the rights of all stakeholders, even as defenders work to close every potential attack vector. These ethical challenges further complicate the task of securing digital infrastructures, demanding that security professionals not only address technical vulnerabilities but also navigate complex legal and societal expectations.

The continuous interplay between attackers and defenders is a dynamic process marked by perpetual evolution. Each new attack vector or pathway that is discovered fuels the development of innovative countermeasures. In this relentless cycle, every successful breach, every narrowly thwarted attempt, contributes to the collective knowledge that drives the field of cybersecurity forward. Defenders learn from the ingenuity of their adversaries, incorporating those lessons into enhanced monitoring systems, more effective training programs, and tighter network architectures. In turn, attackers refine their tactics, seeking ever-more subtle and sophisticated ways to bypass defenses. This ongoing contest is at the heart of modern cybersecurity—a battle in which the only constant is change, and where the goal is not absolute invulnerability but a resilient, adaptive defense that can withstand the inevitable onslaught of new threats.

Ultimately, the study of attack vectors and pathways is more than a technical analysis; it is a narrative that encapsulates the entire ethos of cybersecurity. It is the story of how human creativity, technological innovation, and strategic foresight converge to build defenses capable of protecting our most critical digital assets. By learning from real-world incidents, employing comprehensive frameworks like MITRE ATT&CK, and interpreting each NIST control as a deliberate answer to a specific threat, organizations can transform vulnerabilities into strengths. Every piece of intelligence, every simulation exercise, and every regulatory guideline contributes to a mosaic of defenses that is as dynamic and multifaceted as the threats it is designed to counter.

As we look to the future, it becomes increasingly clear that the challenges of cybersecurity will continue to expand. New technologies, such as artificial intelligence, the Internet of Things, and quantum computing, will introduce both unprecedented opportunities and novel vulnerabilities. The digital ecosystem will only grow more complex, and the potential pathways for attack will multiply. In this uncertain and rapidly evolving environment, the importance of continuous learning, robust collaboration, and proactive adaptation cannot be overstated. Each real-world attack is a lesson, each defense a building block in the ongoing effort to secure our interconnected world.

This chapter, therefore, stands as a comprehensive narrative of the current state of cyber threats—a detailed chronicle of attack vectors and pathways that weaves together historical insights, technical analyses, and the critical lessons of real-world experience. It is a call to arms for every cybersecurity professional: to study diligently, to adapt relentlessly, and to innovate continuously. The tools we use—the MITRE ATT&CK framework, the rigorous standards of NIST, and the collaborative spirit of information sharing—are not merely checklists but living components of a defense strategy that evolves with every threat encountered.

In the final analysis, our journey through the complex terrain of attack vectors and pathways reaffirms that cybersecurity is not a destination but a continuous voyage. It is a voyage marked by relentless adaptation, constant vigilance, and an unwavering commitment to transforming every vulnerability into an opportunity for improvement. Every breach is a lesson, every control a targeted answer to a critical security question, and every real-world incident a reminder that the battle for digital security is fought daily on countless fronts. As we continue to document and learn from these experiences, we build a future where every small crack in our armor is mended by collective strength, innovation, and an enduring resolve to protect the digital realm.

This narrative, enriched by additional insights into emerging technologies, ethical challenges, regulatory pressures, and the evolving nature of threat intelligence, serves not only as an academic treatise but also as a practical guide. It is the story of our times—a chronicle of the ever-changing digital battlefield where every defensive measure is carefully calibrated to counter a specific threat, and where the wisdom gained from real-world examples shapes the strategies of tomorrow. As we stand on the front lines of this continuous struggle, let us embrace the lessons of the past, remain agile in the present, and be ever-prepared for the future—a future in which our collective resilience transforms every attack vector into a stepping stone toward a safer, more secure digital world.

The opening quote by Keri Pearlson—"It's impossible to be completely protected from every vulnerability. That's because the good guys must protect against every possible vulnerability, while the bad guys only need one small crack in a company's armor to get in."—perfectly encapsulates the challenges we face today. In the context of the MITRE ATT&CK framework, which catalogs over 300 techniques across 14 tactical categories, the quote highlights the immense scope of the threat landscape. While defenders must strive to secure every potential vector, attackers can focus on exploiting even a single overlooked vulnerability. As adversary tactics continue to evolve, this framework serves as a powerful tool for anticipating emerging threats and reinforcing defenses accordingly.

CHAPTER 7 - THE ATTACK SURFACE

"Cyber attacks rain down on us from many places. You have to make your systems secure and safe and teach your people cyber hygiene."
— Kersti Kaljulaid

In today's hyper-connected world, the notion of an attack surface has emerged as one of the most critical concepts in cybersecurity. Every organization, from a small startup to a multinational conglomerate, must contend with an array of potential vulnerabilities that span both the physical and digital realms. The attack surface is, in essence, the total sum of all the points—both tangible and intangible—where an unauthorized actor might attempt to gain access to or extract data from a system. It encompasses everything from hardware and software to networks and even the human elements that interact with these systems. A comprehensive understanding of the attack surface is paramount because it not only highlights the immediate areas of exposure but also reveals deeper, interconnected vulnerabilities that can be exploited in a cascading fashion.

Imagine, if you will, an ancient fortress designed with multiple layers of defense: thick stone walls, a moat, towers, and guarded gates. In that medieval structure, every wall, door, and even the surrounding landscape represents a potential point of weakness—an entry point that an attacker might target. Modern organizations, though built in the digital realm, are no different. Their "fortresses" are composed of interconnected servers, cloud services, user devices, communication protocols, and even the people who use them. Each component is a potential entry point that can be exploited if not properly secured. This holistic perspective is essential because even the most advanced technical safeguards can be rendered ineffective by a single overlooked vulnerability or an unexpected human error.

The attack surface is composed of two primary types of components: tangible and intangible. Tangible components refer to the physical assets that can be seen, touched, and directly managed. These include computers, servers, mobile devices, Internet of Things (IoT) gadgets, and other hardware that forms the backbone of an organization's technological infrastructure. The physical security of these devices is as important as their digital security. For instance, a server left in an unsecured room or an IoT device installed in a remote location without proper access controls can serve as an easy target for physical tampering or theft. History has shown that physical breaches—such as an intruder gaining access to a data center or even a simple act of plugging in an unauthorized device—can lead to catastrophic data breaches long before any digital exploitation occurs.

In contrast, intangible components encompass the digital elements that facilitate the flow of information and operations across networks. These include software applications, APIs, open ports, databases, and communication protocols. Unlike tangible assets, intangible elements exist in a virtual space that spans on-premises systems, cloud environments, and hybrid infrastructures. Their distributed and dynamic nature makes them more elusive and challenging to secure consistently. For example, a misconfigured application programming interface (API) or an unpatched vulnerability in a widely used software application can expose sensitive data to remote attackers without any need for physical proximity. The fluidity and ubiquity of digital interactions demand that organizations continuously monitor and update their security measures to keep pace with emerging threats.

The importance of understanding the attack surface becomes even more evident when one considers the varied nature of modern IT environments. In traditional Information Technology (IT) settings, the primary focus is on protecting data, applications, and network infrastructure. These environments are typically dynamic—systems are updated, patched, and monitored in real time to address vulnerabilities as they arise. The objective in IT is to maintain the confidentiality, integrity, and availability of data while ensuring that operations continue smoothly in a rapidly changing digital landscape. To achieve this, cybersecurity teams deploy an arsenal of tools including vulnerability scanners, intrusion detection systems, and automated patch management solutions. These tools help identify and remediate weaknesses in the digital fabric of an organization, thereby reducing the overall attack surface.

However, many organizations also operate within Operational Technology (OT) or Industrial Control Systems (ICS) environments, which are designed to control physical processes. OT/ICS systems are found in industries such as energy, manufacturing, transportation, and critical infrastructure, where the primary concern is not just data but the continuous operation of physical processes. The attack surface in these environments is fundamentally different. Legacy systems that were never designed with modern cybersecurity in mind, combined with the need for uninterrupted operation, create a unique set of challenges. In these settings, a successful cyber attack can have immediate physical consequences— ranging from the disruption of production lines to potentially catastrophic failures in critical infrastructure. As a result, organizations in OT/ICS sectors must carefully balance the imperative of security with the equally critical need for operational continuity. They adopt specialized measures, such as network segmentation, strict change management, and rigorous testing protocols, to minimize risks while ensuring that their systems remain robust and reliable.

Beyond the traditional IT and OT domains, the modern digital ecosystem is further complicated by the rise of cloud computing, remote work, and mobile connectivity. Each of these trends expands the attack surface exponentially. Cloud environments, while offering tremendous flexibility and scalability, present new challenges in securing data that is stored off-premises and accessed over the internet. The shared responsibility model of cloud security means that while cloud providers secure the infrastructure, organizations are still responsible for configuring and managing their data within the cloud. Misconfigurations, such as improperly set permissions or unencrypted data storage, can create glaring vulnerabilities that attackers can exploit. Similarly, the surge in remote work, accelerated by global events and evolving business practices, has led to a proliferation of endpoints outside the traditional corporate firewall. Employees accessing corporate systems from home networks, using personal devices, or connecting through unsecured Wi-Fi networks all contribute to a vastly expanded attack surface. Each of these endpoints is a potential gateway for cyber attacks, necessitating comprehensive endpoint security strategies and constant vigilance.

Managing and reducing the attack surface is a continuous, iterative process that begins with thorough asset discovery. Organizations must develop a detailed inventory of every asset —both tangible and intangible—that is part of their operational ecosystem. This involves not only cataloging hardware and software but also understanding how different systems interact and how people engage with these systems on a daily basis. Without a clear and up-to-date inventory, even the most sophisticated security measures can fail because there is simply no way to protect what is not known to exist. Asset discovery is the foundation upon which effective vulnerability management is built. Once all assets are identified, organizations can employ vulnerability assessments and penetration testing to uncover weaknesses. These proactive measures simulate the actions of a determined attacker, revealing potential vulnerabilities before they can be exploited in a real-world scenario.

Once vulnerabilities have been identified, the next step is to map the entire attack surface and prioritize remediation efforts. This mapping process involves a strategic review of all entry points, allowing security teams to visually assess which areas are most exposed to potential threats. Vulnerabilities are evaluated based on their severity, the likelihood of exploitation, and the potential impact on the organization. In IT environments, high-risk vulnerabilities might result in massive data breaches or extended service outages, while in OT/ICS environments, the same vulnerabilities could lead to dangerous operational disruptions or even loss of life. With a prioritized list in hand, organizations can allocate resources more effectively, focusing on closing the most critical gaps first. The process of mapping and prioritization is dynamic—it must be revisited continuously as new assets are added, software is updated, and the threat landscape evolves.

Reducing the attack surface involves a multifaceted approach that combines technical controls, policy enforcement, and human-focused strategies. One of the most effective methods is minimization—eliminating unnecessary services, applications, or network ports that do not serve a vital business function. By streamlining the number of potential entry points, organizations naturally reduce the number of vulnerabilities that need to be managed. For instance, decommissioning outdated systems and disabling unused network services can dramatically lower the risk profile. Network segmentation is another critical strategy. By dividing a network into smaller, isolated zones with strict access controls, organizations can contain breaches and prevent attackers from moving laterally. This segmentation is particularly important in IT environments, where the isolation of sensitive data can limit the impact of a breach, and in OT/ICS settings, where preventing the spread of an intrusion can mean the difference between a minor incident and a catastrophic failure.

Regular updates and patch management are essential to keeping the attack surface as small as possible. In the fast-paced world of IT, vulnerabilities are discovered daily, and timely patches are crucial in closing security gaps. Automated patch management systems have become indispensable, allowing organizations to quickly apply updates across their infrastructure. In OT/ICS environments, however, patching is often more complicated due to the need for continuous operation and the use of legacy systems that may not support modern update protocols. Here, organizations must balance the urgency of security with the operational imperatives of maintaining stability. Rigorous testing, controlled rollouts, and contingency planning are all part of an effective patch management strategy in these settings.

Educating employees about cybersecurity best practices is another cornerstone of reducing the attack surface. Human error is often the weakest link in any security system, and even the most advanced technical safeguards can be undermined by a single lapse in judgment. Comprehensive training programs help employees recognize the signs of phishing, understand the importance of password hygiene, and follow secure protocols when handling sensitive information. Organizations that prioritize employee education often see a significant reduction in the incidence of social engineering attacks and other human-centric vulnerabilities. Regular training sessions, combined with simulated phishing exercises and clear communication about emerging threats, empower employees to become active defenders rather than inadvertent liabilities.

The rise of Zero Trust architecture represents a modern evolution in reducing the attack surface. At its core, Zero Trust is predicated on the idea that no user or device, whether inside or outside the network, should be automatically trusted. Every access request is continuously verified, and even internal communications are subject to stringent authentication protocols. By eliminating the assumption of inherent trust, Zero Trust dramatically reduces the risk of lateral movement following an initial breach. In IT environments, this model confines any potential intruder to a very limited portion of the network, while in OT/ICS settings, Zero Trust principles must be carefully adapted to ensure that operational processes remain uninterrupted while still providing robust security. The implementation of Zero Trust is a testament to the idea that reducing the attack surface is not solely about adding layers of protection but about fundamentally rethinking the way trust is established and maintained within a network.

As organizations expand their digital footprints, the role of emerging technologies further complicates the attack surface. The Internet of Things has ushered in an era where everyday devices—from smart thermostats to industrial sensors—are connected to the internet. While these devices offer tremendous benefits in terms of automation and efficiency, they often lack robust security measures, making them attractive targets for attackers. A compromised IoT device can serve as a gateway into a larger network, providing access to sensitive data or critical systems. Cloud computing has similarly revolutionized the way organizations store and manage data, but it also introduces new challenges. The shared responsibility model in the cloud means that while providers secure the underlying infrastructure, organizations are still responsible for configuring and managing their data securely. Misconfigurations in cloud storage or databases can expose vast troves of information to malicious actors. The surge in remote work further expands the attack surface, as employees access corporate resources from diverse, often unsecured environments. Each of these trends—IoT, cloud computing, remote work—adds layers of complexity, demanding that security strategies evolve continuously to address these new vulnerabilities.

Beyond the technical realm, the physical security of assets remains a crucial part of managing the attack surface. Even in a digital age, the physical security of hardware, facilities, and network infrastructure cannot be overlooked. An attacker who gains physical access to an organization's premises may bypass digital security measures entirely. Incidents of unauthorized entry, theft of devices, or tampering with hardware have underscored the necessity of integrating physical security protocols into the overall cybersecurity strategy. Measures such as biometric access controls, video surveillance, alarm systems, and strict visitor policies serve as vital complements to digital defenses, ensuring that every potential entry point—physical or digital—is guarded against intrusion.

The complexity of the modern attack surface necessitates the use of advanced analytical tools and comprehensive frameworks. One such invaluable tool is the MITRE ATT&CK framework, which meticulously documents the tactics, techniques, and procedures (TTPs) employed by adversaries in real-world cyber incidents. This framework, with its extensive catalog of over 300 techniques, enables cybersecurity professionals to map out the likely paths that attackers might take through a network. By understanding these patterns, defenders can anticipate where vulnerabilities may be exploited and tailor their defensive measures accordingly. The MITRE framework is a living repository that is continuously updated with insights from the latest cyber incidents, making it an essential resource for anyone tasked with managing a complex attack surface.

Complementing the MITRE framework are the structured guidelines provided by control frameworks such as those from NIST. When examining NIST's recommendations, it is helpful to view every control as the answer to a precise question: what potential attack vector or method does this control mitigate? For example, a control that mandates regular patch management is directly aimed at closing vulnerabilities that could be exploited by malware or zero-day attacks. Multi-factor authentication is not simply an extra step in the login process; it is a targeted response to the threat of credential theft and social engineering. This perspective transforms a seemingly long list of controls into a coherent, purpose-driven strategy, where each measure has a clear rationale grounded in real-world experience. By integrating these controls into a unified framework, organizations can develop a robust security posture that systematically reduces the attack surface.

The process of managing the attack surface is inherently dynamic. Cyber threats are not static; they evolve constantly as attackers develop new methods and as technology advances. Continuous monitoring, regular vulnerability assessments, and proactive penetration testing are therefore indispensable components of an effective defense strategy. Organizations must remain vigilant, regularly reassessing their attack surfaces and updating their security measures to address new vulnerabilities as they emerge. This iterative process—where every breach, every near-miss, and every successful defensive action contributes to a growing body of knowledge—is what ultimately drives the evolution of cybersecurity.

Collaboration and information sharing have become critical in this ongoing battle. In today's interconnected world, no organization operates in isolation. Cyber attacks can have far-reaching impacts that transcend individual companies or even industries. Recognizing this, many organizations have joined forces through initiatives such as information sharing and analysis centers (ISACs) where threat intelligence, case studies, and best practices are exchanged openly. Such collaborative efforts not only enhance the collective ability to detect and respond to threats but also contribute to a more comprehensive understanding of the attack surface across diverse environments. This shared knowledge helps to refine frameworks like MITRE ATT&CK and ensures that guidelines from NIST remain relevant in the face of emerging trends.

An additional layer of complexity in managing the attack surface arises from the need to balance security with operational efficiency. Organizations must protect their assets without hindering productivity or innovation. This balancing act is particularly challenging in environments where rapid digital transformation is essential for maintaining a competitive edge. For example, in industries where agile development is key, new software features and updates are deployed frequently. Each new release can introduce unanticipated vulnerabilities, expanding the attack surface if not managed carefully. To address this, organizations are increasingly integrating security into every stage of the development lifecycle—a practice known as DevSecOps. By embedding security considerations into the development process from the outset, teams can identify and remediate vulnerabilities early, ensuring that new features do not inadvertently widen the attack surface.

The concept of cyber hygiene is also central to managing the attack surface. Just as personal hygiene involves routine practices to maintain health and prevent disease, cyber hygiene encompasses the regular, systematic measures taken to secure digital systems. This includes tasks such as updating software, reviewing access controls, conducting regular backups, and educating users about safe practices. A strong culture of cyber hygiene reduces the number of vulnerabilities that can be exploited and ensures that even if an attack does occur, its impact is minimized. Organizations that prioritize cyber hygiene tend to be more resilient, as they continuously reinforce their defenses against the ever-changing landscape of cyber threats.

Furthermore, the growing use of artificial intelligence and machine learning in cybersecurity is transforming how organizations manage their attack surfaces. On one hand, attackers are beginning to leverage these technologies to automate the reconnaissance process, analyze vulnerabilities at scale, and craft more convincing social engineering attacks. On the other hand, defenders are employing machine learning algorithms to sift through vast amounts of network data, detect anomalies in real time, and predict potential breaches before they occur. These advanced technologies offer the promise of enhanced precision and speed in identifying vulnerabilities, but they also add new layers of complexity to the attack surface. As AI tools become more sophisticated, the interplay between human judgment and machine intelligence will be critical in ensuring that security measures remain both effective and adaptive.

At its core, managing the attack surface is about understanding that every component—every piece of hardware, every line of code, and every human interaction—is part of a larger ecosystem that must be protected. It is a holistic approach that requires constant vigilance, continuous improvement, and an unwavering commitment to learning from every incident. Every breach that occurs, every vulnerability that is discovered, serves as a lesson that can be used to strengthen defenses. Over time, these incremental improvements build a resilient security posture that is capable of withstanding even the most sophisticated attacks.

The narrative of the attack surface is, ultimately, a story of balance and resilience. It is the story of how organizations can transform a sprawling, seemingly unmanageable array of vulnerabilities into a well-defined and continuously refined system of defense. It is a journey that involves not only the deployment of advanced technologies and the adherence to rigorous standards but also the cultivation of a security-minded culture that permeates every level of an organization. Through diligent asset discovery, continuous monitoring, proactive vulnerability management, and comprehensive user education, organizations can reduce their attack surfaces to a manageable scope, even in the face of rapidly evolving cyber threats.

As we look to the future, the challenges of managing the attack surface will only grow more complex. New technologies, evolving threat landscapes, and shifting business practices will continually redefine what constitutes an attack surface. However, by embracing a philosophy of continuous improvement, organizations can remain agile and resilient. Every new piece of technology, every process innovation, must be viewed through the lens of security from the outset. The integration of frameworks like MITRE ATT&CK and NIST controls into everyday operations is not merely a best practice —it is a necessity in an age where every digital interaction can potentially serve as an entry point for an adversary.

In conclusion, the concept of the attack surface encapsulates the entirety of an organization's vulnerabilities—both digital and physical, both technical and human. It is a dynamic, ever-changing landscape that must be continuously monitored, assessed, and managed. By adopting a comprehensive approach that combines robust technical controls with proactive human-focused strategies, organizations can significantly reduce their exposure to cyber threats. The insights provided by real-world examples, the analytical power of the MITRE ATT&CK framework, and the targeted guidance of NIST controls all serve as essential tools in this ongoing endeavor. Every control is not an isolated requirement but a carefully considered answer to a specific threat—a testament to the collective wisdom gained from years of experience in the field.

This narrative is a call to arms for all cybersecurity professionals and organizations alike: to understand, manage, and ultimately secure every facet of the attack surface. It is a continuous journey—one marked by perpetual vigilance, relentless adaptation, and an unwavering commitment to transforming every vulnerability into an opportunity for improvement. The future of cybersecurity depends on our ability to learn from the past, innovate in the present, and prepare for the challenges of tomorrow. As we strive to secure our digital and physical assets in an ever-connected world, let us remember that every small crack in our armor is not a sign of defeat, but rather an invitation to build stronger, more resilient defenses for the future.

CHAPTER 8: INVENTORY, ASSESSMENT, AND BASELINES

"You can't protect what you don't know you have."
— Dave DeWalt

This quote by Dave DeWalt, a leading cybersecurity expert, captures the core principle of effective security: understanding what you are protecting is the first and most important step in building a secure environment. Without a complete and accurate inventory of assets, it is impossible to develop an effective defense strategy. Security measures—no matter how sophisticated—can only protect what is known and accounted for. Undocumented or unidentified assets represent blind spots that attackers can exploit, creating hidden vulnerabilities within an organization's infrastructure.

Understanding and documenting your inventory and assessment is critical to defining and securing your attack surface. A complete inventory provides visibility into where the Confidentiality, Integrity, and Availability (CIA) emphasis lies for each system, allowing security teams to align defensive measures accordingly. It also defines the position of each asset within the organization's defensive architecture—both logically and physically—and clarifies which systems are vital to the business mission and must be protected at the highest level in the defensive architecture. Furthermore, a comprehensive inventory informs you of the full extent of your attack surface by identifying all potential entry points, communication pathways, and system dependencies that could be exploited by attackers. This awareness helps security teams to implement targeted defensive measures, close security gaps, and strengthen overall resilience.

Effective security begins with a clear understanding of what exists. In a world where digital and physical assets are in constant flux, the very first step in building a secure environment is to develop a complete and accurate inventory. This fundamental principle forms the backbone of any robust cybersecurity program. When organizations are unaware of the assets they own—be it hardware, software, network devices, or even undocumented systems—there remain gaps in their defenses that attackers can readily exploit. The ability to document and assess every asset provides critical visibility into where the emphasis of confidentiality, integrity, and availability must lie. This insight is essential not only for establishing protective measures but also for determining the hierarchy of critical systems that need to be safeguarded with the utmost care.

The process of creating an inventory is far more than compiling a list of devices and applications; it is about understanding the role each asset plays within the organization. Every component has a function, and by clearly documenting these functions, security teams can pinpoint which systems are vital to the business mission and which interconnections create potential vulnerabilities. An asset inventory must detail the lifecycle stage of each item, whether it is in development, production, maintenance, or nearing decommissioning. This information is not static—it evolves over time as new systems are deployed, existing ones are upgraded, and older systems are retired. Without this ongoing process of inventory management, organizations operate with blind spots that undermine even the most sophisticated security measures.

To fully grasp the scope of an organization's assets, one must consider both tangible and intangible components. Tangible assets are those physical items that can be seen and handled, such as servers, desktop computers, mobile devices, routers, and Internet of Things devices. These form the visible, physical backbone of any IT or operational technology environment. Yet, their physical nature means they are also subject to risks like theft, physical tampering, or environmental damage. For instance, a server left in an unsecured facility is as vulnerable to an intruder as it is to a natural disaster. In contrast, intangible assets exist in the digital realm. They include software applications, cloud-based services, APIs, communication protocols, and even the data itself. These digital components may be distributed across on-premises systems, private data centers, or public clouds, and they are often interconnected in complex ways that are difficult to visualize. A misconfigured API or an unpatched software vulnerability can provide a remote attacker with the very access needed to compromise sensitive information.

When organizations attempt to document their entire asset base, they must contend with the vast and ever-changing nature of modern IT and OT environments. Large enterprises may have thousands of interconnected devices spread over multiple geographic locations, with assets managed by different teams and even outsourced vendors. Smaller organizations, though less complex, can still suffer from the pitfalls of shadow IT —systems and applications installed without formal oversight. These undocumented assets are particularly dangerous because they fall outside the purview of established security controls. Whether the organization is large or small, it becomes clear that the inventory is finite, even if it appears overwhelming. By breaking down the task into manageable segments—such as grouping assets by function, department, or location—security teams can methodically work through the entire environment. This systematic approach is crucial, as each completed group brings the organization closer to a comprehensive understanding of its attack surface.

The importance of a complete asset inventory cannot be overstated because it directly informs risk management. Once every asset is cataloged, organizations can begin to assess vulnerabilities and determine the potential impact of a breach. This is where the concept of the Confidentiality, Integrity, and Availability (CIA) triad comes into play. By knowing what assets exist and understanding their criticality, security teams can align defensive measures to ensure that the most important systems receive the highest level of protection. For instance, a database that contains sensitive customer information must be secured with strict access controls and robust encryption, while a less critical system might warrant a more moderate level of protection. Without a full inventory, however, it is impossible to prioritize effectively, leaving some systems underprotected and others overprotected—both of which are inefficient and dangerous.

In addition to identifying assets, it is equally important to map out how these assets interact. The relationships between systems—the interconnections that allow data to flow and operations to occur—can reveal hidden vulnerabilities. Whether the interconnections are physical, such as network cables and wireless links, or virtual, such as shared cloud resources and API integrations, they can serve as conduits for lateral movement during an attack. A business application might rely on a shared database server, meaning that a breach in one system could have cascading effects across multiple applications. In operational technology environments, the stakes are even higher. Industrial control systems often depend on proprietary communication protocols and specialized hardware that were not designed with modern cybersecurity threats in mind. An attacker who compromises one controller could potentially disrupt entire manufacturing processes, leading to significant financial and operational damage.

The notion of establishing baselines is a critical next step after completing an inventory. A baseline represents the normal, expected state of a system, including its hardware configuration, software versions, network settings, and even typical user activity patterns. Establishing such baselines allows security teams to detect deviations that could indicate a breach or unauthorized change. For example, if a normally quiet server suddenly begins transmitting large volumes of data, this anomaly can trigger an investigation to determine whether malicious activity is underway. Baselines serve as a reference point for what is considered normal, and any deviation can be a potential red flag. In environments where continuous monitoring is impractical to achieve manually, automated systems play an essential role in comparing current asset behavior against the established baseline. These systems can quickly identify discrepancies, generate alerts, and allow for rapid response to potential security incidents.

Configuration baselines are equally important in maintaining a secure environment. They provide detailed records of how each asset is supposed to be configured—from operating system versions and installed patches to network settings and access controls. These baselines become critical during incident response and forensic investigations, as they allow security teams to determine whether changes to a system were legitimate or the result of a malicious attack. Over time, however, systems may drift from their original configuration due to unauthorized changes, misconfigurations, or ad-hoc updates—a phenomenon known as configuration drift. Drift complicates the security landscape because it creates inconsistencies that can be exploited by attackers. Regular audits and automated reconciliation processes are necessary to ensure that systems remain aligned with their intended configurations. In industrial settings, even minor configuration changes can have significant repercussions, potentially leading to process failures or unsafe operating conditions.

Managing an extensive inventory and establishing robust baselines are challenging tasks that vary significantly depending on the size and complexity of an organization. In small organizations, the number of assets may be relatively limited, and the infrastructure less complex, but resource constraints often present a challenge. Limited staffing and budget can mean that there is insufficient time to dedicate to comprehensive asset discovery and continuous monitoring. In such cases, prioritizing the most critical assets becomes essential. By focusing on business-critical systems —such as financial servers, key communication devices, or essential operational systems—small organizations can create a manageable, yet effective, inventory. Automated tools, cloud-based asset management solutions, and even external managed service providers can help bridge the resource gap, ensuring that the inventory is as complete as possible.

Medium-sized organizations face a different set of challenges. Their infrastructures are more complex, with multiple departments and a greater variety of interconnected systems. In these organizations, it is often necessary to adopt a phased approach to inventory and assessment. This might involve initially cataloging assets within specific business units or network segments before integrating them into a centralized database. A centralized configuration management database (CMDB) can consolidate information from various sources, enabling security teams to maintain an up-to-date, unified view of the asset landscape. Combining automated discovery tools with periodic manual reviews helps ensure both efficiency and accuracy. Medium-sized organizations often benefit from cross-departmental collaboration, where each unit takes responsibility for maintaining its portion of the inventory, while a central security team oversees the overall process.

Large organizations, with their vast and often geographically dispersed infrastructures, present the most complex challenges. With thousands of assets spread across multiple networks, data centers, and cloud environments, the task of inventory and baseline management becomes monumental. Large enterprises often adopt a tiered approach, starting with critical assets and gradually expanding the inventory to include peripheral systems. In these environments, continuous monitoring and automated tools become indispensable. Advanced endpoint detection and response (EDR) platforms, network monitoring solutions, and automated vulnerability scanners are integrated with the CMDB to provide a real-time view of the entire ecosystem. Additionally, role-based access controls and rigorous change management protocols ensure that any alterations to the configuration are documented and reviewed. In such dynamic environments, regular red-team exercises and physical walkdowns complement automated systems, verifying that the inventory reflects the true state of the organization.

The complexity of modern infrastructures means that some assets might escape automated discovery entirely. Stand-alone systems, legacy devices, and equipment on isolated network segments are all examples of assets that may not be detected by automated scans. In these cases, manual audits and physical walkdowns become essential. A walkdown provides an opportunity for security teams to visually confirm the presence, condition, and connectivity of assets that might otherwise remain hidden. These inspections also allow teams to assess environmental factors such as physical security controls and even verify the effectiveness of existing documentation. By combining automated tools with manual validation, organizations can achieve a level of accuracy that is critical for comprehensive risk management.

Once the inventory is complete and baselines have been established, the next phase in a robust cybersecurity program is continuous monitoring and periodic reassessment. In today's rapidly evolving threat landscape, an asset inventory is not a one-time project but an ongoing process. New devices are constantly being added, configurations change, and the threat environment evolves. As a result, organizations must treat their inventory and baselines as living documents that require regular updates. Automated systems can facilitate this by continuously scanning the network and comparing current configurations against the established baselines. When discrepancies are detected, these systems generate alerts for further investigation, allowing security teams to react swiftly to potential anomalies before they can be exploited.

The value of maintaining an accurate inventory extends beyond simply knowing what assets exist. It serves as the foundation for every other aspect of a comprehensive security strategy. A complete inventory allows organizations to identify the full scope of their attack surface, ensuring that every potential point of entry is considered when designing defensive measures. By mapping out interconnections between assets, security teams can identify critical dependencies and potential avenues for lateral movement. This knowledge is essential when prioritizing remediation efforts, as it enables teams to focus on closing the most significant gaps first. Without a clear understanding of the asset landscape, security policies and controls may be misaligned, leaving the organization vulnerable to unexpected breaches.

Furthermore, a detailed asset inventory supports a risk-based approach to security. Not all assets are created equal; some are mission-critical and require a higher level of protection than others. By assessing the criticality of each asset and its role within the organization, security teams can tailor their defensive measures accordingly. For example, an asset that processes sensitive customer data may be subject to more rigorous controls—such as enhanced encryption, tighter access controls, and more frequent audits—than a system that supports less critical functions. This stratified approach not only optimizes resource allocation but also ensures that the most valuable or vulnerable systems receive the attention they require.

Another significant benefit of a robust inventory and assessment process is its ability to support effective change management. In any dynamic organization, systems and configurations are subject to change—whether through routine updates, emergency patches, or complete overhauls. A well-documented baseline provides a reference point for evaluating the impact of these changes. Security teams can use the baseline to determine whether a change introduces new risks or deviates from the intended configuration. In this way, the inventory serves as both a proactive and reactive tool: it helps prevent security breaches by highlighting potential vulnerabilities before they can be exploited, and it aids in incident response by providing a clear record of the asset's original state.

In many ways, the process of inventory, assessment, and establishing baselines is an exercise in continuous improvement. Every asset that is documented, every interconnection that is mapped, and every baseline that is established represents a step toward a more secure environment. This process is not static; it evolves alongside the organization and the threat landscape. Lessons learned from past incidents—whether they involve configuration drift, unauthorized changes, or unforeseen vulnerabilities—inform future updates to the inventory and baseline. Over time, these incremental improvements build a resilient security posture that is better equipped to handle emerging threats.

For organizations operating in environments with both IT and OT/ICS systems, the challenges of inventory and baseline management are even more pronounced. IT systems are generally more dynamic, with frequent updates and constant changes. In contrast, OT/ICS environments tend to be more static, with long hardware lifecycles and legacy systems that may not support modern security protocols. The divergence between these two environments means that a one-size-fits-all approach is rarely effective. Instead, organizations must adopt tailored strategies for each environment. In IT, automated asset discovery and continuous monitoring may be highly effective, while in OT/ICS environments, manual inspections, physical walkdowns, and specialized tools that understand proprietary protocols may be necessary. The challenge is to integrate these disparate approaches into a unified security framework that provides comprehensive visibility and control across the entire enterprise.

The role of technology in facilitating a complete inventory cannot be understated. Automated discovery tools, network scanners, and endpoint detection and response (EDR) platforms can dramatically reduce the manual workload involved in asset identification. These tools can quickly identify devices connected to the network, gather information about installed software and configurations, and flag potential vulnerabilities. However, technology is not a panacea. Automated tools can miss assets that are offline, misidentify devices, or fail to capture critical configuration details that require a human touch. This is why manual validation, periodic audits, and physical walkdowns remain essential components of the process. The combination of automation and manual review ensures that the inventory is both comprehensive and accurate, capturing nuances that purely digital methods might overlook.

Another aspect of inventory and assessment that warrants attention is the challenge of managing "shadow IT." In many organizations, systems and applications are deployed by individual departments or employees without formal approval or oversight. While these systems may serve legitimate business needs, their existence outside of the official inventory creates blind spots in security coverage. Shadow IT can lead to inconsistent configurations, unpatched vulnerabilities, and gaps in monitoring, all of which increase the overall risk. Recognizing and incorporating these assets into the formal inventory is a critical step in achieving full visibility and control over the attack surface.

Once an inventory is established and baselines are in place, organizations can move on to the ongoing task of monitoring and maintenance. This continuous process is essential, as the digital environment is in a state of perpetual flux. New vulnerabilities emerge, configurations change, and assets are added or removed at a rapid pace. Continuous monitoring solutions can track these changes in real time, comparing current configurations against established baselines to detect deviations that might indicate a security incident. When anomalies are detected—such as unexpected changes in system performance, unauthorized modifications, or unusual network traffic—automated alerts enable security teams to respond quickly before the situation escalates. This proactive stance is vital in reducing the window of opportunity for attackers, ensuring that any breach is contained as soon as possible.

The benefits of a robust inventory, coupled with rigorous assessment and baseline management, extend well beyond immediate risk reduction. Such practices form the foundation for strategic decision-making in cybersecurity. With a clear understanding of the asset landscape, organizations can make informed decisions about resource allocation, risk mitigation, and long-term security investments. They can identify areas where additional controls are needed, prioritize systems that require the highest levels of protection, and develop incident response plans that are grounded in the reality of their operational environment. In this way, inventory and assessment become not only tools for day-to-day management but also strategic assets that drive overall security posture.

Moreover, a well-maintained inventory and set of baselines are indispensable when it comes to regulatory compliance. Many industry standards and government regulations require organizations to maintain accurate records of their assets and to demonstrate that they are taking appropriate steps to secure their environment. By maintaining comprehensive documentation and continuously monitoring for compliance with established baselines, organizations can not only reduce the risk of a security breach but also streamline audit processes and reduce the burden of regulatory oversight.

The process of inventory, assessment, and baseline management is, at its core, a commitment to understanding and protecting every facet of an organization's digital and physical ecosystem. It is an ongoing journey that requires diligence, persistence, and a willingness to adapt to new challenges. As technology evolves and the threat landscape continues to change, organizations that invest in comprehensive asset management will be better positioned to anticipate and counter emerging risks. This continuous process of learning, monitoring, and adapting ultimately builds a more resilient security posture, one that can withstand the myriad challenges of the modern digital world.

In reflecting on the wisdom of Dave DeWalt's words, one is reminded that true security is built on knowledge. Without knowing what exists within the organization's environment, no amount of sophisticated technology or security policy can provide adequate protection. The act of documenting every asset, every interconnection, and every configuration is the first step in the journey toward robust cybersecurity. It is an exercise in both diligence and humility—acknowledging that without complete visibility, even the best defenses are doomed to have blind spots.

The challenges of this process are many, but so too are the rewards. A comprehensive inventory and assessment not only reduce the attack surface but also empower organizations to implement targeted, effective security controls. By understanding the criticality of each asset, security teams can apply measures that are proportional to the risk, ensuring that high-value systems are fortified while lower-risk areas are managed appropriately. The result is a defense strategy that is both efficient and effective, one that evolves in tandem with the organization's needs and the ever-changing landscape of cyber threats.

Ultimately, the pursuit of a complete asset inventory and the establishment of rigorous baselines is a foundational element of a mature cybersecurity program. It is a process that underpins every other security measure, informing everything from access control policies to incident response plans. As organizations continue to face an increasingly complex array of threats, the ability to monitor, assess, and manage every asset becomes not just a best practice but a critical necessity. In this way, the journey of inventory and baseline management is not a one-time project but a continuous commitment—a commitment to knowing every part of the organization's digital and physical landscape, and to using that knowledge as the first line of defense against the ever-present tide of cyber threats.

In embracing this philosophy, organizations transform their security posture from one of reactive measures to proactive resilience. Every asset cataloged, every baseline established, and every interconnection mapped contributes to a comprehensive understanding of the environment—a mosaic of data that empowers security teams to respond rapidly to anomalies and to preempt potential breaches. It is this holistic approach, rooted in the fundamental truth that you cannot protect what you do not know, that ultimately forms the bedrock of effective cybersecurity.

The future of cybersecurity will undoubtedly present new challenges and evolving technologies. Yet, the principles of thorough inventory, diligent assessment, and continuous baseline management will remain constant. They serve as the indispensable starting point for any security initiative, a reminder that even in a world of rapid digital transformation, the most basic truth still holds: knowledge is power, and the only way to protect what you have is to first know what you have. This commitment to understanding every asset and every interconnection ensures that organizations remain agile, resilient, and ever-prepared to defend against the next wave of cyber threats.

As we look forward, the integration of advanced technologies such as artificial intelligence, machine learning, and automated analytics will further enhance the ability to manage the attack surface. These tools will offer deeper insights into asset behavior, enabling real-time detection of deviations from established baselines and more rapid identification of potential security incidents. However, no technology can replace the need for a meticulous, well-documented inventory. It is the synergy between human insight and technological innovation that will drive the next generation of cybersecurity practices.

In the end, the journey of inventory, assessment, and baseline management is one of continuous improvement and relentless vigilance. It is a commitment to transforming every potential vulnerability into a strength, every gap in knowledge into an opportunity for deeper understanding, and every asset into a fortified element of a secure environment. Through dedication, collaboration, and a proactive approach to managing the attack surface, organizations can build a future where security is not merely a series of reactive measures, but a robust, dynamic, and comprehensive strategy for protecting the digital and physical realms.

CHAPTER 9: THE CYBERSECURITY PLAN

"Cybersecurity is not a set of products – it's a set of practices."
– Ed Amoroso

This quote, widely attributed to Ed Amoroso and others, encapsulates a fundamental truth that has shaped modern security strategies: robust cybersecurity is not achieved by simply purchasing the latest technologies, but through the disciplined and systematic application of well-designed plans, policies, and procedures. A cybersecurity plan is not just a static document listing tools and configurations; it is the strategic blueprint that directs an organization's every effort to protect its critical assets, safeguard sensitive data, and ensure the resilience of its infrastructure in the face of ever-evolving threats. It is the foundation upon which all other security measures are built—a living guide that is continually refined as the organization grows and as new risks emerge.

At the core of any comprehensive cybersecurity plan is the understanding that risk is inherent in every digital and physical asset. Before any measures can be taken to protect an organization, it is imperative to identify and assess the risks it faces. This begins with a thorough risk assessment that considers the unique threat landscape in which the organization operates. Detailed analyses reveal which assets are most critical, what potential vulnerabilities exist, and how those vulnerabilities might be exploited by adversaries. Whether it is through external threats like hackers, malware, and sophisticated nation-state actors or internal vulnerabilities such as human error and insider threats, every risk must be cataloged. This process lays the groundwork for prioritizing security efforts; with a clear picture of where the most significant exposures lie, an organization can allocate resources effectively, ensuring that its most valuable assets receive the strongest protection.

Risk assessment is not a one-time event but an ongoing process. The digital environment is in a state of constant flux as new technologies are deployed, systems are updated, and attackers continually devise new tactics. Continuous monitoring, vulnerability scanning, and periodic audits ensure that any changes in risk levels are promptly detected and addressed. These assessments not only inform the development of technical controls such as firewalls, intrusion detection systems, and encryption protocols, but they also shape the policies and procedures that govern day-to-day operations. By integrating risk management into the very fabric of the cybersecurity plan, organizations are better prepared to adapt to emerging threats and to close gaps in their defenses before they can be exploited.

Once risks have been identified, the cybersecurity plan must outline the strategies and measures that will be employed to mitigate them. This includes a combination of technical, administrative, and physical controls that work together to create a multi-layered defense. Technical measures such as advanced threat detection systems, secure access controls, and endpoint protection solutions are critical; however, they are only as effective as the policies that dictate their use and the people who implement them. Administrative controls encompass the rules, guidelines, and procedures that govern security practices, ensuring that every employee understands their role in protecting the organization. Physical controls, including secure facilities, access badges, and surveillance systems, provide an essential line of defense for hardware and other tangible assets. In unison, these layers create a defense-in-depth strategy that ensures if one barrier is breached, others remain to protect the organization's critical assets.

A key pillar of the cybersecurity plan is its focus on incident response and recovery. Despite all preventive measures, no system is completely immune to breaches. The true measure of an organization's cybersecurity maturity is revealed in its ability to respond to incidents swiftly and effectively. The plan must define clear protocols for every stage of the incident response lifecycle: detection, analysis, containment, eradication, and recovery. Clear delineation of roles and responsibilities ensures that every team member—from the front-line technicians to the executive leadership—knows exactly what to do when an incident occurs. Detailed communication procedures must be established so that internal stakeholders, customers, regulators, and law enforcement are informed promptly and accurately. Regular training, drills, and simulated scenarios are essential for testing these procedures and ensuring that they function as intended under pressure. By preparing for incidents as if they were inevitable, organizations can reduce both the impact and the recovery time, thereby maintaining business continuity and protecting their reputations.

The scope of a cybersecurity plan must be tailored to the specific needs, size, and operational context of the organization. For individuals and small entities, the plan might focus primarily on personal security practices—such as managing passwords, using antivirus software, and backing up critical data—while also addressing basic measures for protecting business-critical systems. Small organizations, in particular, face the challenge of limited resources; however, even with constrained budgets and staffing, it is crucial to identify and secure the most vital assets. This often involves using off-the-shelf security solutions and leveraging external managed service providers to supplement internal capabilities. Training staff to recognize threats like phishing and social engineering becomes even more critical, as does ensuring that data is encrypted both in transit and at rest. The plan must be practical and achievable, offering a clear roadmap that can be scaled as the organization grows.

In larger organizations, the complexity and scale of operations demand a far more comprehensive approach. Cybersecurity plans for large enterprises must address an extensive range of threats, incorporate sophisticated risk management processes, and deploy advanced technical controls. These plans are often developed by dedicated security teams led by a Chief Information Security Officer (CISO) and overseen by a Cybersecurity Steering Committee. They encompass detailed security policies that align with industry standards and regulatory requirements, such as those outlined in NIST SP 800-53, ISO/IEC 27001, and the CIS Controls. For these organizations, the cybersecurity plan must also integrate a multi-tiered approach that distinguishes between different levels of asset criticality. High-value assets such as sensitive customer data, proprietary intellectual property, and core operational systems are typically housed in secure zones with stringent access controls, while less critical systems might reside in moderated zones that still offer significant protection. Such stratification not only optimizes resource allocation but also limits the potential impact of a breach by containing it within a specific segment of the network.

A central theme of the cybersecurity plan is the concept of defense in depth. This approach relies on implementing multiple, overlapping security controls so that if one layer is compromised, subsequent layers continue to provide protection. For instance, even if an attacker bypasses perimeter defenses such as firewalls or intrusion detection systems, they will still encounter internal safeguards like network segmentation and strict access controls. In many environments, especially those involving Operational Technology (OT) and Industrial Control Systems (ICS), the importance of defense in depth is magnified. In these contexts, the stakes are not just data loss or service disruption; a successful breach can have direct physical consequences, endangering processes, equipment, and even lives. Consequently, the cybersecurity plan must address both the technical and operational challenges unique to OT/ICS environments, incorporating specialized measures such as data diodes to enforce unidirectional data flows, as well as rigorous monitoring systems that detect anomalies in real time.

A robust cybersecurity plan is built upon clear, well-documented policies and procedures. These documents serve as both a reference and a guide, outlining the specific measures that must be taken to protect the organization's assets. Policies define the overarching rules and standards for security, while procedures detail the day-to-day actions required to implement these rules. For example, a policy might mandate that all sensitive data be encrypted using industry-standard protocols, and the accompanying procedures would specify how this encryption is to be applied, managed, and audited. This dual structure ensures that there is no disconnect between the strategic vision of the cybersecurity plan and its practical execution. The integration of policies and procedures into the cybersecurity plan not only clarifies roles and responsibilities but also creates a framework for accountability, ensuring that every employee is aware of their duties and that deviations from the plan are promptly addressed.

Human factors play a critical role in the overall security posture of an organization, and no cybersecurity plan can be complete without addressing them. People are often cited as the weakest link in cybersecurity, and the reality is that even the most advanced technical controls can be undermined by human error or deliberate insider actions. As such, fostering a culture of security is essential. This involves regular training and awareness programs that educate employees about the latest threats, such as phishing scams, social engineering tactics, and other common attack vectors. By instilling a sense of personal responsibility and emphasizing the importance of security in every role, organizations can significantly reduce the likelihood of human error leading to a breach. Furthermore, clear communication of security policies and continuous reinforcement of best practices ensure that the entire organization operates with a security-first mindset.

Modern cybersecurity plans must also account for the rapidly evolving technological landscape. The proliferation of cloud computing, mobile devices, and remote work has dramatically expanded the traditional network perimeter. Data and applications are no longer confined to a single location; instead, they are dispersed across various platforms and accessed from multiple endpoints. This decentralization requires that the cybersecurity plan be flexible and comprehensive enough to protect assets regardless of their physical location. Cloud-based services, for example, must be secured through robust access controls, data encryption, and continuous monitoring. Similarly, mobile devices and remote endpoints must be managed through advanced endpoint security solutions and secure connectivity protocols. The integration of these diverse technologies into a unified security strategy is essential for maintaining comprehensive protection in an increasingly dispersed digital environment.

An often underappreciated aspect of a cybersecurity plan is its alignment with established frameworks and regulatory requirements. Industry standards such as NIST SP 800-53, ISO/IEC 27001, and the CIS Controls provide a structured approach to building a security program that is both comprehensive and adaptable. These frameworks offer a common language and a set of best practices that help ensure the organization's security measures are robust and effective. Furthermore, regulatory mandates—such as HIPAA for healthcare, PCI DSS for payment card security, and NERC CIP for critical infrastructure —impose additional requirements that the cybersecurity plan must address. Aligning the plan with these standards not only enhances its effectiveness but also facilitates compliance, thereby reducing the risk of legal penalties and protecting the organization's reputation.

Another critical component of the cybersecurity plan is its emphasis on continuous improvement. The dynamic nature of the digital environment means that threats are constantly evolving, and what was considered secure yesterday may not be secure tomorrow. As such, the cybersecurity plan is not a static document but a living blueprint that must be regularly reviewed, updated, and refined. Continuous monitoring and periodic vulnerability assessments are essential for identifying new risks and ensuring that existing controls remain effective. Lessons learned from past incidents—whether minor breaches or major cyber attacks—must be systematically incorporated into the plan, driving a cycle of ongoing improvement. This commitment to continuous improvement not only enhances the organization's resilience but also ensures that the cybersecurity plan remains aligned with both current technologies and emerging threats.

The role of technology in supporting a robust cybersecurity plan cannot be overstated. Automated tools for asset discovery, vulnerability scanning, and continuous monitoring provide the data that drives informed decision-making. These tools enable security teams to maintain real-time visibility into the organization's environment, quickly identify anomalies, and respond to potential threats before they escalate. However, technology is only one piece of the puzzle; the insights gleaned from these tools must be integrated with the strategic vision of the cybersecurity plan and the practical expertise of security professionals. This synergy between technological innovation and human judgment is what transforms a collection of products into a cohesive set of practices—a set of practices that embodies the true spirit of cybersecurity.

Physical security measures are equally critical in a comprehensive cybersecurity plan. While much attention is given to digital defenses, the protection of physical assets—such as servers, network equipment, and even the facilities in which these assets reside—remains a vital aspect of overall security. Unauthorized physical access can compromise the integrity of even the most sophisticated digital controls. Measures such as secure access controls, surveillance systems, and environmental monitoring not only prevent unauthorized entry but also serve to complement and reinforce digital security measures. In environments where physical and digital assets intersect, such as data centers or industrial control systems, the integration of physical security into the cybersecurity plan is indispensable.

The cybersecurity plan must also clearly define roles and responsibilities across the organization. Leadership, spearheaded by the Chief Information Security Officer, must set the strategic vision and ensure that the cybersecurity plan aligns with the organization's overall objectives. A Cybersecurity Steering Committee or Policy Review Board is often established to oversee the plan's development and ongoing revision. In addition to executive oversight, every department and employee must understand their role in the collective effort to safeguard the organization. Clear communication channels, predefined escalation paths, and regular training sessions ensure that when an incident occurs, the response is coordinated and effective. This culture of accountability and preparedness is a critical enabler of rapid, decisive action in the face of a cyber threat.

For organizations that operate in environments with both IT and Operational Technology (OT) systems, the cybersecurity plan must address the unique challenges posed by each domain. IT environments are typically dynamic, with frequent changes and updates that require continuous monitoring and agile responses. In contrast, OT environments—such as those found in industrial control systems—are often characterized by legacy systems, proprietary protocols, and a critical need for operational continuity. In these cases, the cybersecurity plan must strike a balance between maintaining stringent security controls and ensuring that essential processes remain uninterrupted. This may involve implementing specialized monitoring solutions, strict network segmentation, and compensatory controls where traditional patching is not feasible. The ability to integrate these diverse approaches into a unified, coherent cybersecurity plan is essential for protecting the organization as a whole.

Furthermore, a comprehensive cybersecurity plan takes into account the broader external environment in which the organization operates. The rise of cloud computing, the proliferation of mobile devices, and the increasing prevalence of remote work have fundamentally altered the nature of the network perimeter. Data is no longer confined to a single physical location; it flows between on-premises systems, cloud platforms, and personal devices. This diffusion of assets necessitates a flexible, adaptive approach to security—one that ensures that robust controls are in place regardless of where the data resides. Strategies such as secure virtual private networks, strong encryption, and rigorous identity and access management become even more critical in this context. The cybersecurity plan must therefore articulate how these modern challenges will be addressed, ensuring that the organization's security measures remain effective in an increasingly decentralized digital landscape.

The integration of advanced technologies such as artificial intelligence and machine learning is also reshaping the way organizations approach cybersecurity. These technologies offer the potential to analyze vast amounts of data in real time, identify patterns indicative of emerging threats, and automate responses to contain breaches swiftly. While the deployment of AI-driven tools enhances the efficiency of threat detection and incident response, it also adds new layers of complexity to the cybersecurity plan. The plan must outline how these technologies will be integrated with existing systems, the criteria for triggering automated responses, and the protocols for human oversight to ensure that decisions made by automated systems are both accurate and appropriate. This balanced approach leverages the speed and scalability of machine intelligence while retaining the nuanced judgment that human experts provide.

Regulatory compliance is another fundamental pillar that underpins the cybersecurity plan. Organizations are subject to a wide array of legal and industry-specific requirements that mandate stringent security controls. Frameworks such as NIST SP 800-53, ISO/IEC 27001, and the CIS Controls offer structured guidance that helps organizations build comprehensive security programs. At the same time, industry-specific regulations— such as HIPAA for healthcare, PCI DSS for payment card security, and NERC CIP for critical infrastructure—impose additional layers of requirements. The cybersecurity plan must align with these standards, ensuring that all security measures are not only effective but also compliant with applicable laws and regulations. This alignment helps mitigate the risk of legal penalties and bolsters the organization's reputation by demonstrating a commitment to following best practices and maintaining high standards of security.

A vital component of the cybersecurity plan is its focus on continuous improvement. In a world where cyber threats evolve on a daily basis, a static security plan is inadequate. The plan must be treated as a living document—one that is continually reviewed, updated, and refined to incorporate new intelligence, technological advancements, and lessons learned from past incidents. Continuous monitoring, regular vulnerability assessments, and routine incident response exercises are essential for maintaining an up-to-date security posture. The insights gained from these activities feed back into the planning process, allowing the organization to adapt its defenses proactively. This iterative approach to security ensures that the cybersecurity plan remains relevant and effective over time, evolving in step with the changing threat landscape.

Ultimately, a cybersecurity plan is not merely a set of policies and procedures; it is the strategic heart of an organization's defense against cyber threats. It weaves together risk management, technical controls, incident response, regulatory compliance, and a culture of continuous improvement into a cohesive framework that protects the organization's digital and physical assets. It is a dynamic roadmap that guides every decision, every investment, and every action taken to safeguard sensitive data and maintain the integrity of critical systems. As cyber threats become increasingly sophisticated and pervasive, the importance of a well-crafted, adaptive cybersecurity plan cannot be overstated.

This plan stands as a testament to the organization's commitment to security—a commitment that begins with the simple yet profound truth that "you can't protect what you don't know you have." By developing a complete, accurate inventory of assets and rigorously assessing the risks they face, the organization lays the groundwork for every subsequent security measure. Each policy, procedure, and technical safeguard is built upon the knowledge of what exists within the environment, ensuring that every potential vulnerability is accounted for and addressed. The cybersecurity plan is the culmination of this understanding, translating it into a clear, actionable strategy that permeates every level of the organization.

As we look to the future, the challenges of cybersecurity will only grow more complex. New technologies will emerge, adversaries will continue to innovate, and the digital environment will become even more interconnected. In response, the cybersecurity plan must evolve, continually incorporating new insights and adapting to changing circumstances. Through this ongoing process of improvement and adaptation, organizations can build a resilient security posture that not only withstands the current threat landscape but also anticipates and counters future risks.

In the end, the cybersecurity plan is more than a document— it is a living, breathing framework that embodies the collective wisdom, experience, and dedication of the entire organization. It represents a shared commitment to protecting what is most valuable, ensuring that every asset is accounted for, every risk is managed, and every member of the organization understands their role in maintaining a secure environment. It is through the disciplined execution of this plan, coupled with a steadfast commitment to continuous improvement, that organizations can navigate the complexities of the digital age and build a secure, resilient future.

Important Note: Writing a Cyber Security Plan is a daunting and time consuming task. This is made more difficult as it is difficult to find fully formed non-proprietary templates that would be suitable to serve as a basis. Although dated and designed specifically for the nuclear power industry NRC RG 5.71 and NEI 08-09 are both good examples of fully-formed cyber security plans, particularly if you are in a heavily regulated sector. Note that these documents reflect the regulatory environment that US Nuclear Power Plants operate within, and controls considered to be applicable specifically to that industry. Remember, even if you find an example plan or plan template that you like, this is just the beginning of your work. The plan must reflect your organizational requirements, needs, capabilities and resources for it to be effective.

CHAPTER 10: CYBER SECURITY POLICIES

"Cybersecurity policies are the backbone of a resilient defense; without them, even the most advanced security technologies become ineffective."

— Adapted from common industry wisdom

This quote, widely attributed to Ed Amoroso and others, encapsulates a fundamental truth that has come to define modern approaches to digital defense: robust cybersecurity is achieved not by the mere acquisition of tools and technology, but through the disciplined, systematic application of well-designed policies, procedures, and practices. Cybersecurity policies form the backbone of an organization's security framework; they are the high-level directives that shape how technology is deployed, maintained, and monitored, ensuring that every security measure works in concert with others to protect critical assets, sensitive data, and infrastructure. Without clear, well-defined policies, even the most sophisticated security technologies can falter because they lack the guiding principles necessary to align with an organization's broader risk management and business objectives.

A cybersecurity plan lays out the strategic vision, providing a roadmap for identifying vulnerabilities, managing risks, and orchestrating an effective response to incidents. However, the cybersecurity policies derived from that plan are the detailed, formalized documents that spell out the "what" and "why" of an organization's security posture. They translate strategic objectives into specific requirements and standards that govern everyday practices. These policies ensure that security measures are not implemented haphazardly, but are carefully coordinated to address human behavior, regulatory compliance, and risk management in a holistic manner. In other words, policies ensure that every layer of a security system works together cohesively, transforming advanced technology into a resilient defense when governed by a structured, strategic approach.

Developing comprehensive cybersecurity policies begins with a deep understanding of risk. Every organization operates within a unique threat landscape; therefore, a thorough risk assessment is essential. This process involves identifying the assets that need protection, understanding the potential threats they face, and evaluating the vulnerabilities that could be exploited. Whether the risks stem from external sources like sophisticated hackers and malware, or from internal sources such as human error and insider threats, a detailed assessment allows an organization to prioritize its security efforts. It is only when the most critical vulnerabilities are clearly understood that resources can be allocated effectively, ensuring that high-value assets receive the strongest protections. Without such clarity, significant gaps may remain in the organization's defenses, leaving blind spots that attackers can easily exploit.

Risk is not a static concept; it evolves as new technologies are adopted, business processes change, and adversaries develop new tactics. For this reason, cybersecurity policies must be dynamic documents that are reviewed and updated regularly. Continuous monitoring, vulnerability scanning, and periodic audits ensure that any changes in the threat environment are quickly identified and addressed. This iterative process not only informs the development of technical controls such as firewalls, intrusion detection systems, and encryption protocols, but also shapes the administrative procedures that govern day-to-day operations. By integrating risk management into every aspect of the cybersecurity policy, organizations remain agile and responsive to emerging threats.

Once risks have been thoroughly assessed, the cybersecurity policies outline the strategies and measures that will be used to mitigate them. This involves a layered defense strategy that combines technical, administrative, and physical controls. Technical measures—such as advanced threat detection systems, secure access controls, and endpoint protection—form the first line of defense. Yet these measures alone are insufficient if they are not complemented by policies that dictate how they are implemented and managed. Administrative controls, which include the rules, guidelines, and procedures that dictate acceptable behavior, ensure that every member of the organization understands their responsibilities in maintaining security. Physical controls, such as secure facilities, surveillance systems, and access restrictions, further safeguard the tangible assets that form the foundation of the digital environment. Together, these controls create a comprehensive defense-in-depth strategy; if one layer fails, additional layers remain to protect critical assets and maintain operational continuity.

The role of incident response is central to the cybersecurity policies. No matter how effective preventive measures are, the reality is that breaches can and do occur. A robust cybersecurity plan must therefore include a well-defined incident response strategy. This strategy outlines clear steps for detecting, analyzing, containing, and eradicating threats, as well as for recovering from an incident with minimal damage. Effective incident response hinges on clearly delineated roles and responsibilities, ensuring that every team member—from front-line technicians to executive management—knows exactly what to do when an incident occurs. Detailed communication protocols are established to ensure that, in the event of an incident, internal stakeholders, customers, regulators, and law enforcement are informed promptly and accurately. Regular training sessions, simulations, and drills are critical in testing these protocols, so that the organization can respond swiftly and decisively, thereby limiting the impact of any breach.

The scope and complexity of cybersecurity policies must be tailored to the unique needs of the organization. For individuals and small organizations, a cybersecurity plan may focus primarily on personal security practices such as managing strong, unique passwords, utilizing antivirus software, and backing up important data. At the same time, small organizations must also secure business-critical systems even as they contend with resource constraints. For these organizations, cybersecurity policies typically emphasize practical measures—such as staff training to recognize phishing attempts, encryption of sensitive data both in transit and at rest, and the implementation of role-based access controls—to achieve a balance between effectiveness and feasibility. Often, small organizations rely on off-the-shelf solutions and external managed service providers to support their cybersecurity efforts, tailoring their policies to cover essential areas without overwhelming their limited resources.

In larger organizations, however, the scale and complexity of operations demand a far more comprehensive approach. Cybersecurity policies in large enterprises must address a wide range of threats, incorporate sophisticated risk management processes, and deploy advanced technical controls. Such organizations typically have dedicated cybersecurity teams led by a Chief Information Security Officer, supported by a Cybersecurity Steering Committee and specialized incident response teams. Their policies must be aligned with industry standards and regulatory requirements, drawing on frameworks such as NIST SP 800-53, ISO/IEC 27001, and the CIS Controls. In these environments, cybersecurity policies often differentiate between assets based on their criticality; high-value assets like sensitive customer data and proprietary information are subjected to more stringent controls than less critical systems. This tiered approach optimizes resource allocation and limits the potential impact of a breach by ensuring that the most sensitive areas are heavily fortified.

One of the key strengths of an effective cybersecurity framework is its emphasis on defense in depth. This approach involves implementing multiple, overlapping layers of security controls so that if one layer is compromised, additional layers remain to protect the organization's critical assets. For example, even if an attacker manages to bypass perimeter defenses such as firewalls or intrusion detection systems, they will still encounter internal safeguards such as network segmentation and strict access controls. In operational technology environments, particularly within industrial control systems, defense in depth is even more crucial, as a breach in these areas can have real-world consequences that go beyond data loss or service disruption. Here, policies must address both the technical aspects of security and the operational imperatives of maintaining system availability and safety. Measures such as unidirectional data flows enforced by data diodes, robust physical security controls, and dedicated monitoring solutions are often integrated into the overall cybersecurity strategy to ensure that every potential vulnerability is addressed comprehensively.

A fundamental component of any cybersecurity policy is its focus on clearly defined roles and responsibilities. Security is not solely the domain of IT professionals; every member of an organization has a role to play in safeguarding its digital assets. Cybersecurity policies establish the expectations and responsibilities for every individual, from the executive leadership that sets the strategic vision to the front-line employees who interact with systems daily. Senior leadership, such as the Chief Information Security Officer, is tasked with ensuring that the cybersecurity plan aligns with the organization's broader business objectives and that policies are consistently enforced. Meanwhile, specialized teams—such as the Cybersecurity Steering Committee, incident response teams, and compliance auditors—are responsible for the implementation and ongoing refinement of security practices. Clear communication channels and predefined escalation procedures are essential so that when an incident occurs, decisions are made rapidly and effectively. Regular training, simulated exercises, and cross-departmental reviews help to reinforce these roles and ensure that every employee understands their responsibilities.

The relationship between the overarching cybersecurity plan and the specific policies and procedures that stem from it is a critical one. The cybersecurity plan provides the strategic roadmap for protecting the organization's assets and managing risk, while the policies serve as the formal directives that implement that vision. For instance, if the cybersecurity plan identifies robust configuration management as a critical priority, the related policies will specify the exact controls, procedures, and guidelines that must be followed to ensure that systems remain secure. Cybersecurity procedures then translate these high-level policies into detailed, step-by-step instructions for everyday operations, ensuring that the plan is operationalized effectively. This layered approach—from plan to policy to procedure—creates a coherent and comprehensive security framework in which every element is aligned with the organization's long-term objectives and risk management strategies.

An important example of how cybersecurity policies function in practice can be seen in the context of supply chain management. Supply chain risks have become a major focus of cybersecurity efforts, as organizations increasingly depend on third-party vendors, suppliers, and contractors for critical goods and services. A well-crafted Supply Chain Management Policy sets forth a framework for evaluating and managing the cybersecurity risks associated with these external partners. Such a policy might require that, prior to entering into any contractual agreement, the organization conducts a thorough risk assessment of the potential vendor's cybersecurity posture. This assessment would include reviewing the vendor's security policies, incident response capabilities, and compliance with relevant industry standards such as ISO/IEC 27001 or NIST SP 800-53. The policy would also mandate that contracts with approved vendors include specific cybersecurity requirements —ranging from data protection measures and access control protocols to incident reporting and audit rights. By establishing a formal process for assessing and managing supply chain risks, the policy not only protects the organization's sensitive data and critical systems but also ensures that vendors are held to the same high security standards as the organization itself. An illustrative modification of such a policy might include the addition of continuous video surveillance in a receiving area, a targeted measure designed to detect tampering or unauthorized access in real time. This example underscores the flexibility of cybersecurity policies: while the overall cybersecurity plan may be difficult to modify due to regulatory constraints, individual policies can be updated more frequently to address emerging threats.

The creation and implementation of cybersecurity policies must be grounded in well-established frameworks and regulatory requirements. Standards such as NIST SP 800-53 provide comprehensive catalogs of security and privacy controls, while NIST SP 800-82 offers detailed guidance for securing industrial control systems. International standards like ISO/IEC 27001, along with the CIS Controls, offer further guidance and best practices that help ensure policies are both robust and adaptable. Moreover, industry-specific regulatory guides—such as NERC CIP for the energy sector, HIPAA for healthcare, and PCI DSS for payment card security—offer tailored insights that ensure policies address the unique challenges and compliance obligations of different sectors. By aligning cybersecurity policies with these frameworks, organizations create a structured, measurable approach to security that not only addresses technical vulnerabilities but also meets regulatory obligations and industry best practices.

Another critical dimension of cybersecurity policies is their role in fostering a culture of security within the organization. While the technical and administrative measures outlined in policies are essential, their true effectiveness is realized only when every member of the organization embraces the principles of cybersecurity. Regular training and awareness programs are crucial for educating employees about the latest threats, best practices, and their specific responsibilities. By ensuring that every employee understands the importance of cybersecurity policies and the reasons behind each control, organizations can reduce the likelihood of human error and cultivate a proactive, security-first mindset. This cultural transformation is vital because even the most advanced technical controls can be undermined by complacency or a lack of awareness. When security is viewed as a shared responsibility, every employee becomes an active participant in the defense strategy, reinforcing the organization's overall resilience.

In today's rapidly evolving digital landscape, the threat environment is in constant flux. New technologies emerge, attackers develop innovative tactics, and business processes evolve, all of which can introduce new vulnerabilities. For this reason, cybersecurity policies are not static documents; they must be living, breathing guidelines that are continuously reviewed, updated, and refined. Continuous monitoring and periodic vulnerability assessments are essential for ensuring that the policies remain relevant and effective in addressing current threats. Lessons learned from past incidents—whether minor breaches or major cyber attacks—must be integrated into policy revisions to improve incident response and overall risk management. This commitment to continuous improvement not only helps protect the organization against emerging threats but also demonstrates a proactive approach to cybersecurity that can reassure customers, regulators, and other stakeholders.

The role of technology in supporting and enforcing cybersecurity policies cannot be overstated. Automated tools for asset discovery, vulnerability scanning, and continuous monitoring provide critical data that informs policy development and updates. These technologies enable security teams to maintain real-time visibility into the organization's environment, quickly detect deviations from established baselines, and trigger alerts when potential threats are identified. However, technology alone is insufficient. The insights from these tools must be combined with human judgment and strategic planning to create a comprehensive defense strategy. It is the interplay between advanced technological solutions and the disciplined application of well-crafted policies that ultimately transforms a cybersecurity program from a reactive patchwork into a proactive, resilient system of defense.

Physical security is another indispensable element of a robust cybersecurity policy. While much of modern cybersecurity focuses on digital threats, the physical protection of assets remains a critical component of an organization's security posture. Unauthorized physical access to facilities, servers, or network devices can bypass even the most sophisticated digital controls, leading to data breaches, system tampering, or the installation of rogue devices. Cybersecurity policies must therefore integrate physical security measures such as controlled access to sensitive areas, surveillance systems, and environmental monitoring. These measures not only protect physical assets but also support the integrity of the digital systems housed within them. In environments where physical and digital security intersect—such as data centers or industrial control facilities—the policies must address both dimensions in a coordinated manner.

The process of drafting and refining cybersecurity policies is inherently iterative and requires input from multiple stakeholders. Senior leadership, including the Chief Information Security Officer and members of the Cybersecurity Steering Committee, must set the strategic vision and ensure that policies align with the organization's broader business objectives. At the same time, technical experts, compliance officers, and end users contribute their perspectives to ensure that the policies are practical, effective, and reflective of real-world operating conditions. Regular reviews and updates, informed by incident response exercises, audits, and evolving threat intelligence, ensure that the policies remain current and capable of addressing emerging risks. This collaborative approach fosters a sense of shared ownership and accountability, ensuring that cybersecurity policies are not merely abstract documents but practical tools that guide everyday operations.

In addition to internal collaboration, external resources and guidance play a vital role in shaping cybersecurity policies. Documents such as the "NIST Cyber Security Framework Policy Template Guide," published by The Center for Internet Security and the Multi-State Information Sharing and Analysis Center, provide standardized templates and best practices that can be tailored to the unique requirements of an organization. Similarly, policy references from organizations like SANS offer pre-written security policies that serve as valuable starting points. While these templates and examples are invaluable resources, they are only the beginning. Every organization must customize its policies to reflect its specific needs, operational environment, and regulatory obligations. It is through this process of adaptation and continuous refinement that cybersecurity policies become truly effective in safeguarding an organization's assets.

A particularly instructive example of the practical application of cybersecurity policies can be found in the area of supply chain management. Supply chain risks have emerged as one of the most significant challenges in modern cybersecurity, as organizations increasingly rely on third-party vendors, suppliers, and service providers for critical functions. A well-defined Supply Chain Management Policy establishes the framework for evaluating, managing, and monitoring the cybersecurity practices of these external partners. It mandates that, before entering into any contractual agreements, a thorough risk assessment is conducted to evaluate the vendor's security posture. This assessment includes a review of the vendor's policies, incident response capabilities, and compliance with industry standards. Contracts must then include specific cybersecurity requirements, such as data protection measures, access control protocols, and incident reporting procedures. An illustrative modification of such a policy might involve the addition of continuous video surveillance in the receiving area, a targeted measure designed to detect unauthorized access or tampering in real time. This example highlights the flexibility of cybersecurity policies, demonstrating how targeted updates can be implemented quickly to address emerging risks without disrupting the overall cybersecurity plan.

Ultimately, cybersecurity policies are the formalized embodiment of an organization's security strategy. They provide a structured, cohesive framework that guides every aspect of the security program—from risk assessment and incident response to daily operational practices and regulatory compliance. By clearly defining the roles, responsibilities, and expectations for every member of the organization, these policies create a foundation of accountability and transparency. They ensure that every layer of the organization's security architecture is aligned with the broader strategic vision and that each control, whether technical or administrative, is designed to mitigate specific risks.

As cyber threats continue to evolve in complexity and scope, the importance of robust cybersecurity policies becomes ever more pronounced. They are not static documents; rather, they must be living, breathing frameworks that evolve in response to new challenges, emerging technologies, and lessons learned from past incidents. Continuous improvement is the hallmark of a mature cybersecurity program—a program that recognizes that the landscape of threats is in constant flux and that security must be an ongoing, iterative process. By maintaining a commitment to regular reviews, updates, and training, organizations ensure that their cybersecurity policies remain effective, relevant, and capable of protecting their critical assets. The journey to effective cybersecurity is long and complex, but it is built on the simple truth that "you can't protect what you don't know you have." Through meticulous risk assessments, detailed planning, and the disciplined implementation of well-crafted policies and procedures, organizations build a resilient defense that can withstand the relentless tide of cyber threats. It is this comprehensive, strategic approach—integrating technology, human factors, regulatory compliance, and continuous improvement—that transforms cybersecurity from a reactive set of measures into a proactive, resilient system of defense.

In conclusion, cybersecurity policies are not merely an administrative burden; they are the strategic heart of an organization's security efforts. They translate a high-level vision into actionable directives that govern every aspect of security, from the configuration of systems and the management of risks to the coordinated response to incidents. By aligning these policies with established frameworks and regulatory requirements, and by fostering a culture of continuous learning and improvement, organizations can ensure that every asset is protected and every vulnerability is addressed. In an age where cyber threats are both pervasive and constantly evolving, the discipline and foresight embodied in well-crafted cybersecurity policies are essential to building a secure and resilient future.

Important Notes: The included policy is for illustrative purposes. For guidance on writing actual policies, please refer to a document titled: "NIST Cyber Security Framework Policy Template Guide" published by The Center for Internet Security, and MS-ISAC, the Multi-State Information Sharing and Analysis Center. This document is an invaluable resource for those involved in creating policies for their organization and is available in PDF format for free on the internet. This document, and the links contained therein, will provide you with standardized templates provided courtesy of the State of New York and the State of California and can easily be customized for use in creating organizational Policy. The Guide correlates the templates to 49 of the NIST CSF categories.

You may also want to visit the SANS website for policy references. SANS offers a set of pre-written security policies. These templates are also available in PDF format for free on the internet. Remember, even if you find an example policy or policy template that you like, this is just the beginning of your work. Policies must reflect your organizational requirements, needs, capabilities and resources for it to be effective.

CHAPTER 12: OPERATIONALIZING CYBERSECURITY – FROM MONITORING TO INCIDENT RESPONSE

"Cybersecurity is a continuous journey—not a destination."
- Anonymous

This truth underpins the transition from strategic planning to everyday practice in the realm of cybersecurity. After exploring the evolution of cyber threats, building robust security architectures, and formulating comprehensive cybersecurity plans in earlier chapters, this chapter delves into the dynamic process of operationalizing those plans. It explains how organizations can transform strategic intentions into daily actions that protect critical assets, weaving together technology, people, and process into a cohesive, responsive defense.

Operationalizing cybersecurity requires constant attention to detail and a relentless commitment to execution. It means taking the lofty goals defined in governance documents and translating them into routines, checklists, and reflexive habits that govern daily operations. This is where organizations begin to differentiate themselves—where the maturity of a cybersecurity program reveals itself not through words on a page but through actions taken at 2:00 AM on a Saturday when a critical alert fires. At that moment, success is defined not by the plan but by the ability of people and systems to follow through on that plan under stress. The alignment between high-level strategy and real-time operational decision-making becomes the true measure of a program's efficacy.

One such instance occurred at a regional bank, which had implemented a cybersecurity strategy that emphasized multifactor authentication and logging but failed to rehearse response coordination among its departments. When a phishing campaign successfully compromised a user account, an alert was triggered by their SIEM platform at 1:48 AM on a Sunday. The alert routed to a shared mailbox instead of triggering an incident response escalation. The IT administrator on call checked it hours later and did not notify security staff, believing it to be a routine logon anomaly. By the time security investigated, threat actors had used the access to pivot laterally and begin reconnaissance. In the aftermath, the bank developed a clear alert handling procedure, built a rotating on-call schedule, and tied alert priority levels directly to escalation thresholds. The updated system included automatic escalation via paging software for any after-hours event involving privileged accounts or lateral movement indicators. What emerged from this incident was not just a technical fix, but a cultural change in how cybersecurity incidents were handled. Planning alone did not save the organization—execution did.

Many organizations discover that while their cybersecurity plan looks comprehensive on paper, operationalizing that plan exposes gaps—particularly in coordination and execution. Teams may not know who is responsible for a specific step, tools may not be configured correctly, or procedures may be outdated or poorly understood. These challenges become evident during incidents but can often be traced back to day-to-day practice, or lack thereof. Take, for example, a logistics firm that built an impressive cybersecurity strategy centered around advanced detection tools and a cloud-native security stack. But during a ransomware incident that exploited a vulnerable third-party plugin, the company struggled to determine the scope of affected systems and could not verify backup integrity. The reason? They lacked a consistent operational routine for logging, asset inventory reconciliation, and backup restoration drills. The result was a longer recovery time and a greater financial impact—despite a well-articulated plan.

An effective cybersecurity operation starts with monitoring. It is not enough to deploy security tools; those tools must be calibrated, maintained, and operationally integrated. Monitoring begins with visibility—knowing what assets exist, what data flows through them, and which users access them. In practice, this means configuring telemetry across endpoints, networks, applications, and cloud platforms, then funneling that data into an environment where it can be correlated and analyzed.

At the heart of operational cybersecurity lies the Security Operations Center (SOC), the nerve center where technology and human expertise converge to safeguard the organization around the clock. A well-established SOC is much more than a collection of monitoring tools—it is an ecosystem designed to detect, analyze, and respond to threats as they unfold in real time. Within this dynamic environment, advanced systems continuously monitor network traffic, system logs, and user activities, capturing a wealth of data that is then analyzed for any signs of suspicious behavior. This process begins with state-of-the-art Security Information and Event Management (SIEM) systems, which collect and correlate data from a variety of sources, transforming disparate streams of information into actionable intelligence.

The true strength of a SOC comes from the dedicated team that operates it. Cybersecurity professionals working within the SOC are trained not only to recognize technical anomalies but also to interpret the broader context in which these anomalies occur. Their expertise allows them to distinguish between false alarms and genuine threats, ensuring that alerts are swiftly validated and acted upon. In practice, the SOC team functions as a modern-day command center where analysts, incident responders, and threat hunters work in concert to maintain situational awareness and mitigate risks.

They continuously scrutinize incoming data, analyze alerts, and initiate investigations that delve deep into the causes of suspicious activity.

Establishing an effective SOC requires careful planning and a significant investment in both technology and talent. Organizations must ensure that their SOC is equipped with the latest detection tools, seamlessly integrated into a comprehensive monitoring framework that enhances the speed and accuracy of threat detection. This integration provides a holistic view of the organization's security posture, enabling the team to rapidly pinpoint vulnerabilities and potential breaches while contextualizing every alert within the broader network environment.

Moreover, the SOC is not an isolated unit—it serves as a central communication hub that interfaces with various departments across the organization. Whether coordinating with IT teams to implement remedial measures, briefing executive leadership on emerging threats, or liaising with external partners such as law enforcement and cybersecurity vendors, the SOC orchestrates a unified response to incidents. Regular drills, cross-functional collaboration, and comprehensive reporting protocols are integral to its operation, ensuring that the organization remains agile and prepared for any eventuality.

Beyond the SOC, operational cybersecurity demands a meticulously crafted incident response strategy. Even the most fortified organizations cannot guarantee complete immunity from cyberattacks. A well-prepared incident response plan is essential to minimize damage, preserve crucial evidence, and accelerate recovery. This plan begins long before any incident occurs, with detailed playbooks that define roles and responsibilities, establish communication protocols, and provide guidelines for a swift, coordinated response.

The Incident Response Team includes a designated incident response manager to lead the effort, technical analysts who can swiftly interpret system logs and network data, and forensic experts capable of conducting deep-dive investigations into the breach. Equally important are communications specialists who manage internal and external messaging during a crisis, legal advisors to navigate regulatory and compliance implications, and representatives from public relations who help protect the organization's reputation. In many organizations, leaders from various departments—ranging from operations and finance to human resources and engineering—are also incorporated into the team. Their involvement ensures that decisions consider the broader organizational impact and that every department is aligned during a crisis. In environments that include Operational Technology (OT) and Industrial Control Systems (ICS), the incident response team further expands to include specialized engineers with deep knowledge of OT/ICS systems. These engineers are critical for understanding the unique technical constraints and safety considerations inherent in OT/ICS environments, ensuring that response measures do not compromise essential industrial processes or safety protocols. Together, this multidisciplinary team ensures that every facet of an incident—from technical resolution to stakeholder communication—is addressed with precision and expertise.

When a threat is detected, rapid analysis of logs and network behavior becomes critical in identifying the scope and nature of the breach. Immediate actions—such as isolating compromised networks and disabling affected user accounts—are taken to contain the threat. Following containment, the organization focuses on eradication by removing all traces of malicious activity and then on recovery, restoring systems from secure backups and applying necessary updates.

A critical component of an effective incident response strategy is the regular practice of response procedures. Organizations must conduct detailed practice sessions that simulate a wide variety of attack scenarios, ranging from tabletop exercises to full-scale simulations. These sessions are designed to replicate real-world conditions, allowing the response team to experience the pressures and complexities of an actual incident in a controlled environment. During these rehearsals, every phase of the response—from detection and analysis to containment, eradication, and recovery—is executed as if the incident were real. Such practices not only reinforce technical procedures but also stress-test communication channels, decision-making processes, and cross-departmental coordination. Following each exercise, comprehensive debriefings are held to evaluate performance, identify areas for improvement, and update the incident response playbooks accordingly. In many cases, these practice sessions extend beyond the internal team to involve external partners such as cybersecurity vendors and law enforcement agencies, further ensuring that all stakeholders are aligned and prepared to act swiftly in the face of a genuine threat.

Continuous monitoring is the backbone of a proactive cybersecurity posture, providing organizations with a constant, real-time pulse on their digital environment. In today's fast-paced threat landscape, relying solely on scheduled audits or sporadic manual checks leaves too many gaps—gaps that can be exploited by determined adversaries. Instead, continuous monitoring involves deploying a suite of automated tools that constantly scan networks, endpoints, applications, and data flows for signs of unusual or potentially malicious behavior. At its core, continuous monitoring collects vast amounts of data from across the organization's infrastructure, including system logs, network traffic, user activities, and application behaviors, all of which are funneled into advanced analytical systems like SIEM platforms. These platforms not only aggregate information but also correlate it in meaningful ways, quickly separating benign activity from suspicious deviations. The ability to instantly detect departures from established patterns enables security teams to act before minor anomalies evolve into significant breaches.

This process is deeply integrated with threat intelligence feeds that bring in external data about emerging vulnerabilities, new malware variants, and evolving tactics used by cyber adversaries. By merging internal data with external insights, organizations can assign risk levels to alerts more accurately, prioritize responses, and even anticipate potential attack vectors before they manifest within their own networks. This dual perspective creates a layered, dynamic defense system that adapts as the threat environment changes. Beyond automated alerting and analysis, continuous monitoring also supports proactive threat hunting, whereby security professionals actively search for hidden threats that might have evaded conventional detection mechanisms. This proactive approach not only mitigates risks in real time but also provides valuable feedback to continuously refine overall security strategies.

Moreover, the benefits of continuous monitoring extend to incident response. When an incident does occur, the real-time data provided by monitoring tools allows for a swift and informed response. Detailed logs and performance metrics help responders quickly assess the scope of a breach, identify affected systems, and determine appropriate containment and remediation steps, thereby accelerating the entire incident response process and minimizing potential damage.

A robust corrective actions program is essential to transforming lessons learned into lasting improvements. This program should be established as an integral component of the organization's culture, where every infraction—even the smallest deviation from established security protocols—is recorded, tracked, and analyzed. By documenting minor oversights alongside major incidents, organizations can develop comprehensive metrics that reveal trends, highlight recurring vulnerabilities, and ultimately inform targeted employee training and policy refinements.

The corrective actions program operates as a continuous feedback mechanism that monitors the efficacy of all security measures. When an infraction or vulnerability is identified—whether through routine audits, simulated exercises, or live incidents—it is promptly logged in a centralized system. Here, root causes are analyzed and corrective measures are formulated with clear guidelines for reporting, assigning responsibility, and setting remediation deadlines. Over time, this data forms a rich source of metrics that can pinpoint systemic issues and shape future training programs and security policies.

Furthermore, recurring events—whether they are minor infractions or repeated system anomalies—can trigger an "extent of condition" investigation. When similar incidents occur repeatedly, they signal that there may be broader systemic issues that require a comprehensive review. Such investigations delve deeply into the underlying causes and measure the full scope and impact of the problem. By understanding these recurring patterns, organizations can develop targeted metrics that not only drive corrective actions but also enhance employee training and inform policy adjustments. This proactive approach transforms isolated incidents into opportunities for systemic learning and continuous improvement, reinforcing a culture where accountability and vigilance are paramount.

This iterative process is further enhanced by establishing structured feedback loops within the organization. After every incident, audit, or corrective action, comprehensive debriefings are conducted with all relevant stakeholders—ranging from IT teams to executive leadership—to evaluate what went well and what could be improved. These sessions facilitate open discussions about emerging threats and evolving vulnerabilities, ensuring that lessons learned are effectively translated into actionable improvements. Additionally, the data collected from the corrective actions program directly informs ongoing education and training initiatives. Regular workshops, simulations, and refresher courses are designed based on identified trends and weaknesses, ensuring that every employee —from frontline staff to senior management—remains current on best practices and emerging threats.

A commitment to regular audits and continuous improvement is the final pillar of this operational framework, ensuring that an organization's defenses never remain static but evolve to meet new challenges. Routine audits, both internal and external, verify that security controls function as intended and that the organization complies with ever-evolving industry standards and regulatory requirements. Vulnerability assessments and penetration testing are integral components of these audits. By simulating attack scenarios and probing for weaknesses, these evaluations reveal potential vulnerabilities before they can be exploited by malicious actors.

The insights gained from audits and testing are not merely documented and stored; they drive a cycle of continuous improvement. Each audit, each vulnerability scan, and each simulated attack becomes an opportunity for the organization to refine its strategies and bolster its defenses. Findings are meticulously analyzed, and corrective actions are promptly initiated to address any identified gaps. A well-structured corrective actions program ensures that issues are tracked, root causes are identified, and remediation measures are implemented effectively. This program provides a systematic approach for verifying that corrective measures have been successfully applied and that vulnerabilities do not recur, thereby reinforcing the overall cybersecurity posture.

In essence, operationalizing cybersecurity is the critical bridge between strategic planning and effective defense. It transforms a static blueprint into a dynamic, continuously evolving practice capable of adapting to emerging threats and minimizing damage when breaches occur. By investing in a capable SOC, developing a resilient incident response plan with a well-rounded team and regular practice sessions, leveraging continuous monitoring and threat intelligence, and embracing a culture of regular review, corrective actions, and systemic improvement—including thorough investigations of recurring events—organizations can convert their cybersecurity strategies from theoretical plans on paper into practical, real-world defenses. This chapter is a call to action for organizations to commit fully to this ongoing journey, ensuring that cybersecurity remains an active, adaptive, and integral part of daily operations in an increasingly digital world.

CHAPTER 13: GOVERNANCE, RISK MANAGEMENT, AND COMPLIANCE

"Effective governance is the cornerstone of a resilient organization; it transforms strategy into action, ensures accountability, and empowers every level of leadership to drive success."
— Unknown

This quote encapsulates how vital governance is to an organization by highlighting its role in turning high-level strategic goals into tangible outcomes, fostering accountability, and empowering leaders throughout the organization. Governance isn't just about policy; it is about operationalizing intent. It is about ensuring that what is planned is actually executed in a measurable and effective way. For cybersecurity, this concept is even more crucial. A single point of failure due to lack of oversight or unclear accountability can become the foothold for catastrophic breaches. As digital risk becomes a boardroom topic, governance must evolve to encompass not only the oversight of business strategy but the strategic and operational oversight of cyber risk as well.

Cybersecurity does not exist in isolation. As organizations mature their defenses and operational practices, it becomes imperative to embed cybersecurity into the broader framework of corporate governance. In this chapter, we explore how establishing robust governance, risk management, and compliance (GRC) practices can provide a solid foundation for an effective cybersecurity strategy. This holistic approach ensures that security measures align with organizational objectives, adhere to regulatory requirements, and continuously evolve to meet emerging threats. By integrating these elements into the organizational fabric, companies create a resilient posture that not only mitigates risks but also supports long-term strategic goals. Consider the case of a global manufacturing firm that suffered a ransomware attack that halted operations for a week. A post-incident investigation revealed that while technical controls were in place, the lack of a unified governance structure led to delayed decision-making and inadequate response coordination. Embedding GRC earlier could have prevented the operational and financial impact.

Cybersecurity governance structures can vary widely depending on the size, industry, and maturity of the organization. Some adopt a centralized model where cybersecurity authority is consolidated under a CISO or security office, ensuring consistency and centralized oversight. Others implement a federated model that distributes security responsibilities among business units, with central governance providing standards and oversight. Each model presents benefits and trade-offs. Centralized models offer tighter control and uniform enforcement, ideal for highly regulated industries such as finance or defense. Federated models allow for flexibility and business-specific customization, often favored in multinational corporations or diversified enterprises. The key is ensuring that governance structures—regardless of model—are clearly defined, supported by leadership, and reinforced through repeatable processes.

At its core, cybersecurity governance is about establishing clear roles, responsibilities, and accountability for protecting the organization's digital assets. It begins with the active involvement of executive leadership—leaders who not only set the tone from the top but also ensure that cybersecurity is integrated into the strategic vision of the enterprise. Senior leaders, including board members and C-suite executives, must understand that cybersecurity is not just a technical issue; it is a fundamental business risk that can affect every part of the organization. By creating dedicated oversight committees and appointing leaders such as a Chief Information Security Officer (CISO), organizations can build a command structure that drives the development, implementation, and ongoing evaluation of security policies and practices. As one insightful saying goes, "Effective governance is the cornerstone of a resilient organization; it transforms strategy into action, ensures accountability, and empowers every level of leadership to drive success." This structured approach ensures that decisions related to cybersecurity receive the appropriate attention and resources from the highest levels of the organization. In sectors such as energy or finance, regulatory bodies often require evidence of board-level cybersecurity oversight—a mandate that reflects the broader recognition that governance drives accountability. Boards increasingly request cybersecurity metrics, such as maturity scores, threat trend summaries, and coverage ratios, to inform their oversight role. Dashboards designed for executive comprehension—mapping risk to business impact—are becoming indispensable tools in boardroom conversations.

The effective management of GRC is best achieved by a dedicated, multidisciplinary team rather than by a single individual. Executive buy-in is essential for the success of a GRC group. When senior leadership fully supports the initiative, they provide not only the necessary resources and authority but also a clear signal that cybersecurity is a top priority across the organization. This commitment from the top helps ensure that GRC policies are enforced uniformly, that cross-departmental collaboration is fostered, and that all employees understand the importance of their roles in maintaining a secure environment. Take, for instance, the transformation seen in healthcare systems following HIPAA enforcement actions. Institutions that once viewed compliance as a bureaucratic checkbox began forming cross-functional GRC teams that included IT, legal, clinical operations, and patient services—leading to improved outcomes and incident reduction. However, cross-functional dynamics are not always harmonious. Conflicts can arise between legal departments prioritizing risk avoidance and IT teams focused on operational uptime. Successful GRC teams navigate these tensions through strong facilitation, shared metrics, and escalation paths that align with strategic goals.

The makeup of a successful GRC team is inherently multidisciplinary, drawing from a wide array of skills and perspectives. This group typically includes technical experts who understand the intricacies of cybersecurity threats and defense mechanisms, compliance specialists who ensure adherence to industry standards and regulatory requirements, and risk management professionals who can assess and mitigate potential vulnerabilities. Additionally, legal advisors contribute critical insights regarding data protection laws and contractual obligations, while representatives from various business departments—such as finance, operations, and human resources—ensure that cybersecurity policies align with broader organizational objectives. By assembling a team with such diverse expertise and ensuring strong executive support, organizations can create a robust, proactive GRC function that not only safeguards digital assets but also drives strategic decision-making across the enterprise. The ability to quickly evaluate new regulatory risks, such as updates to international data residency laws, becomes feasible only when such multidisciplinary coordination is established.

Effective cybersecurity governance requires that policies and strategies are clearly documented and communicated throughout the organization. Detailed cybersecurity frameworks, guidelines, and procedures should be developed and disseminated so that every employee understands their specific roles and responsibilities. This clarity not only aids in swift decision-making during a security incident but also creates a sense of shared responsibility across the entire workforce. Regular reporting to the board, transparent risk assessments, and measurable performance indicators allow leaders to track progress and adjust strategies as needed. In this way, governance becomes a continuous process rather than a one-time setup, with periodic reviews ensuring that cybersecurity remains aligned with evolving business objectives and external threats. Organizations often leverage frameworks such as NIST Cybersecurity Framework or ISO/IEC 27001 to codify this process, making governance auditable and repeatable. Governance also benefits from internal maturity models like CMMI or custom scorecards that help organizations benchmark progress and communicate improvements in terms stakeholders understand.

Effective governance extends into risk management, which is the systematic process of identifying, assessing, and mitigating potential threats. Rather than relying on periodic risk assessments alone, organizations must foster a dynamic approach that continuously monitors and evaluates risks in real time. Risk management encompasses not only the technical dimensions of cybersecurity—such as vulnerability assessments and threat intelligence—but also the broader impact on business processes and strategic objectives. This holistic view allows organizations to prioritize risks based on potential impact and likelihood, enabling them to make informed decisions about resource allocation and strategic investments. For example, real-time risk scoring platforms can integrate inputs from threat intelligence feeds, vulnerability scans, and user behavior analytics to generate a living risk profile that evolves as the threat landscape changes. To support these efforts, many organizations are turning to structured risk analysis methodologies such as the FAIR model (Factor Analysis of Information Risk), which quantifies risk in financial terms. This allows security leaders to communicate more effectively with executive stakeholders and prioritize investments based on potential loss exposure.

A robust risk management framework also involves scenario planning and stress testing. Organizations conduct regular risk assessments that simulate potential cyber incidents, evaluate the effectiveness of existing controls, and project the financial and operational consequences of breaches. These exercises help to identify gaps in the current security posture and prompt the development of targeted mitigation strategies. By integrating risk management into the daily operations and strategic planning, companies can respond quickly to emerging threats and adjust their priorities accordingly. This proactive approach not only minimizes the impact of potential breaches but also creates a culture of preparedness and agility throughout the organization. Consider the example of a financial institution that conducts red team exercises quarterly. These exercises simulate adversary tactics and test detection and response capabilities in a controlled environment. As a result, the institution improves its mean-time-to-detect (MTTD) and mean-time-to-respond (MTTR), key metrics that directly correlate to operational resilience.

Compliance is another cornerstone of the GRC framework, ensuring that cybersecurity practices align with legal, regulatory, and industry-specific standards. In an era of increasingly stringent data protection regulations, organizations must ensure that their cybersecurity measures meet or exceed these external requirements. Compliance is not simply about avoiding penalties; it is a strategic tool that enhances trust among customers, partners, and regulators. By rigorously adhering to standards such as GDPR, HIPAA, PCI DSS, and other relevant frameworks, organizations can demonstrate their commitment to protecting sensitive data and upholding ethical practices in all aspects of their operations. Furthermore, compliance often serves as the baseline from which more advanced and tailored security practices are developed, allowing organizations to go beyond minimal standards. Some firms have used superior compliance as a market differentiator, marketing their adherence to industry-leading standards to attract privacy-conscious clients or to streamline third-party audits during M&A activities or vendor onboarding.

Embedding compliance into everyday operations involves regular audits, continuous monitoring, and thorough documentation of all cybersecurity activities. Organizations must maintain detailed records of their security policies, incident response actions, and remediation efforts. This documentation not only facilitates external audits and regulatory reviews but also serves as a valuable resource for internal assessments and training initiatives. When compliance is woven into the fabric of daily operations, it becomes a proactive measure rather than a reactive response, ensuring that security practices evolve in tandem with both regulatory changes and emerging threats. In the case of multinational corporations, compliance becomes a logistical challenge due to varying regional requirements. Organizations that develop a centralized compliance management system with localized adaptations can better manage this complexity. Increasingly, automation platforms are used to manage compliance tasks, reduce human error, and create real-time dashboards for compliance officers and external assessors.

Central to the success of the GRC framework is the emphasis on continuous education and training programs. In today's rapidly evolving threat landscape, regular training is essential to ensure that all employees—from frontline staff to executive leadership—are equipped with the knowledge and skills to recognize and respond to cybersecurity risks. Training programs must be dynamic and responsive, informed by data collected from the corrective actions program. By analyzing recurring incidents and feedback from audits, organizations can tailor training content to address specific vulnerabilities and emerging threats. Oversight of these training programs is a key responsibility of the GRC team, ensuring that the curriculum remains current, effective, and aligned with both organizational policies and regulatory requirements. This approach not only strengthens the overall security posture but also fosters a culture where every employee views cybersecurity as a shared responsibility. Leading organizations often implement gamified training platforms and phishing simulation campaigns, which significantly improve engagement and retention of best practices. In one well-documented case, a regional government agency reduced successful phishing attempts by over 60% within six months of launching a dynamic, role-specific training program based on simulated attack feedback.

A mature GRC framework weaves these elements together into an integrated system that supports decision-making at every level of the organization. Regular board meetings, detailed risk reports, and comprehensive audits are used to continuously evaluate the organization's security posture. Feedback from these processes informs policy updates and training programs, ensuring that cybersecurity practices remain agile and effective. Moreover, the GRC framework extends beyond internal operations to include third-party relationships, where suppliers and partners are held to the same rigorous security standards. This holistic approach not only protects the organization's internal environment but also reinforces the security of the entire supply chain, reducing vulnerabilities that could arise from external connections. Vendor risk management platforms and contract clauses requiring cyber insurance and breach notification protocols are examples of how organizations extend their GRC reach. Advanced approaches now include software bill of materials (SBOM) requirements, real-time API-based third-party monitoring, and tiered onboarding workflows based on risk classification.

Embedding cybersecurity governance into the organizational fabric requires a cultural shift that permeates every level of the company. It means fostering an environment where every employee understands their role in maintaining security and where reporting potential vulnerabilities is both encouraged and rewarded. When cybersecurity is seen as a shared responsibility, employees are more likely to adhere to established policies and engage in proactive behaviors that protect the organization. Continuous training and open communication channels ensure that all staff, from frontline employees to senior management, remain informed about the latest threats and best practices. This collective commitment strengthens the organization's overall resilience and transforms cybersecurity from a siloed initiative into a core element of the company's strategic vision. Achieving this cultural shift is often the most difficult aspect of GRC implementation, requiring persistent leadership, internal champions, and reinforcement through both policy and practice.

In essence, Governance, Risk Management, and Compliance form the backbone of a resilient cybersecurity strategy. They ensure that security is not merely a technical endeavor but a core business function that is integrated into every aspect of the organization. By establishing clear governance structures, continuously monitoring and mitigating risks, rigorously adhering to compliance standards, and prioritizing robust training programs under the oversight of the GRC team, organizations can create a secure, agile, and trustworthy digital environment. This chapter invites leaders to view cybersecurity through a broader lens—one where proactive governance and integrated risk management are key drivers of sustainable success in an increasingly complex digital world.

CHAPTER 14: BUILDING A SECURITY CULTURE AND MEASURING CYBER RESILIENCE

"A strong security culture is the bedrock of effective cybersecurity —without every employee embracing security as their personal responsibility, even the best technical defenses can crumble."
— Unknown

This quote underscores a critical truth: technology alone cannot shield an organization from cyber threats. The real strength lies in the collective commitment of every employee. When security is woven into the very fabric of the workplace, it transforms cybersecurity from a set of isolated technical measures into a comprehensive, resilient strategy. Each team member's vigilance and adherence to best practices ensure that vulnerabilities are swiftly identified and addressed, reinforcing the overall defense posture of the organization.

In today's digital landscape, technology alone cannot safeguard an organization—people and processes play an equally critical role. Building a robust security culture means embedding cybersecurity awareness into the daily fabric of the organization, where every employee feels responsible for protecting digital assets and is equipped with the knowledge to recognize and respond to threats. This chapter explores how organizations can foster a proactive security culture and leverage data-driven metrics to measure and improve their cyber resilience over time.

A security-aware culture begins at the top. Executives must set the tone by clearly communicating that cybersecurity is not just an IT issue but a core business priority that affects every aspect of operations. When leadership openly discusses cybersecurity risks, allocates necessary resources, and visibly participates in security initiatives, it sends a powerful message throughout the organization. Employees, seeing their leaders take security seriously, are more likely to adopt best practices in their everyday work. This top-down approach creates an environment in which cybersecurity is woven into the strategic vision of the company rather than being viewed as an afterthought.

The value of tone-from-the-top leadership cannot be overstated. When board members and senior executives regularly attend cybersecurity briefings, receive tailored threat intelligence reports, and include cyber risk in enterprise risk management discussions, it signals institutional prioritization. Some organizations formalize this involvement by designating cybersecurity champions on the board or incorporating CISO performance into executive compensation plans. Such mechanisms institutionalize accountability, shifting cybersecurity from a support function to a strategic pillar.

Yet, leadership engagement is only part of the equation. Behavioral psychology plays an integral role in shaping a sustainable security culture. Cognitive biases like the optimism bias—where employees believe breaches won't happen to them —or habituation to frequent alerts can dull vigilance. To counteract this, organizations are increasingly using behavioral nudges: subtle environmental or procedural cues that guide users toward secure behavior without mandating it. Examples include just-in-time security warnings, color-coded risk prompts in email systems, or system defaults that encourage multi-factor authentication.

Equally important is the establishment of open communication channels. Regular briefings, town hall meetings, and transparent reporting systems help disseminate critical security information throughout the organization. When employees are informed about current threats and the organization's response strategies, they become active participants in the security process. This transparency not only builds trust but also encourages employees to report suspicious activities without fear of reprimand, thereby enabling a faster, collective response to potential incidents. Organizations with mature reporting cultures often supplement formal reporting systems with anonymous hotlines, security ambassador programs, and internal threat hunting competitions to keep awareness high.

Changing culture is not without its challenges. Employees may resist new security protocols due to perceived inconvenience, lack of understanding, or fear of making mistakes. Others may believe security isn't part of their job. Successful transformations employ change management principles: clear communication of the "why," gradual rollouts, feedback loops, and strong internal advocates who model the desired behaviors. Storytelling is especially powerful—anonymized case studies or internal "war stories" can personalize the impact of breaches and galvanize support.

One of the most persistent cultural challenges is shadow IT—when employees adopt unauthorized software or hardware to bypass perceived limitations in corporate systems. While often rooted in good intentions (e.g., improving productivity), shadow IT introduces serious risks by circumventing governance and visibility. Instead of relying solely on punitive controls, leading organizations engage with these behaviors to understand unmet needs, offering secure alternatives or safe zones for innovation. Solutions such as cloud access security brokers (CASBs) and zero trust network access (ZTNA) can enable visibility and control without stifling innovation.

Training plays a pivotal role in cultivating a security culture. Cybersecurity training programs must be dynamic, continually evolving to address the latest threats and informed by real-world data collected through corrective actions and incident feedback. For instance, if phishing attempts increase in frequency, specialized training modules that simulate realistic phishing scenarios can be introduced to enhance employee vigilance. It is critical that regular training becomes a mandatory job requirement for all employees. This ensures that cybersecurity awareness isn't treated as an optional add-on, but as an essential part of every role within the organization.

Advanced organizations implement differentiated training plans tailored to job roles. Technical staff might receive in-depth content on secure coding or vulnerability management, while finance teams learn about business email compromise. Gamification—through badges, leaderboards, and simulation-based learning—also boosts engagement. A well-structured training program can transform cybersecurity from a compliance burden into a competitive advantage, especially when clients and regulators inquire about workforce readiness.

Furthermore, every employee should be encouraged to participate actively in the corrective actions program. Whether by individually reporting security incidents or by engaging in post-incident reviews, employees play a crucial role in identifying vulnerabilities. For example, imagine an employee who finds a non-company issued USB memory stick lying on the floor—a clear violation of the media protection requirements outlined in the cybersecurity plan. Without a formal report through the corrective actions process, this might be dismissed as an isolated oversight. However, by reporting it, the organization can determine if similar incidents have occurred elsewhere, triggering an extent of condition investigation or prompting adjustments in training to emphasize media policies. Such participation transforms individual observations into actionable data that fuels continuous improvement across the enterprise.

Insider threats—whether malicious, negligent, or accidental—remain a major concern. A culture that promotes psychological safety can reduce the likelihood of insider incidents by encouraging open dialogue, peer accountability, and a sense of shared mission. Case studies such as Edward Snowden or the Tesla employee accused of sabotage highlight how trust breakdowns and misalignment between employees and leadership can lead to catastrophic outcomes. Conversely, organizations that emphasize inclusion, transparency, and respect for ethical concerns are better equipped to detect and mitigate insider risks.

Beyond incident reporting, organizations can empower employees by integrating them into cyber exercises. Tabletop exercises, purple team simulations, and phishing response drills allow staff to experience security events in controlled environments. These interactions increase readiness and instill a shared sense of mission. Some sectors, particularly critical infrastructure and defense, now require periodic involvement of business units in full-scope incident response exercises, reflecting the critical role of the workforce in overall security posture.

Security should also be embedded across the employee lifecycle—from onboarding to offboarding. New hires should be introduced to cybersecurity expectations from day one, with clear messaging that security is everyone's responsibility. Access should be role-based and reviewed regularly, and departing employees must be promptly deprovisioned. High-performing organizations create visible cultural touchpoints: security newsletters, recognition for best practices, or even cybersecurity awareness weeks. Reinforcing secure behavior through performance evaluations and promotion criteria further embeds security into the organizational identity.

Measuring cyber resilience is equally critical for understanding the effectiveness of security initiatives and for guiding future investments. Organizations must establish a robust framework of key performance indicators (KPIs) and metrics that provide real-time insights into their security posture. Examples of such KPIs include the frequency of security incidents, the mean time to detect and respond to breaches (MTTD/MTTR), and the success rates of remediation efforts.

For example, a company might set a goal to reduce the MTTR from 24 hours to 12 hours or to achieve a remediation rate of 95% for critical vulnerabilities within 30 days. Other KPIs might track employee engagement in training programs—such as the percentage of staff completing mandatory cybersecurity training—and the rate of reported incidents, which can indicate how actively employees participate in the corrective actions program. These metrics provide tangible benchmarks that inform management about the current state of cybersecurity and help prioritize improvements.

A mature measurement framework often includes both leading and lagging indicators. Leading indicators, such as patch cadence or phishing test success rates, help predict future performance. Lagging indicators, like breach cost or unplanned downtime, assess outcomes after incidents. Balanced scorecards incorporating both types offer a more complete view. In regulated industries, measurement is also critical for demonstrating compliance, especially under evolving frameworks like NIST CSF 2.0 or the EU's NIS2 directive.

Organizations are increasingly adopting security culture maturity models (SCMM) to assess and benchmark cultural progress. These models define levels of maturity—ranging from unaware to embedded—based on employee behaviors, attitudes, and alignment with organizational values. Maturity assessments often include surveys, focus groups, and behavioral audits, providing qualitative and quantitative data that complement technical KPIs. By measuring culture itself, organizations can identify not just what's being done, but how and why it's being done.

An integrated approach to measurement creates a continuous feedback loop between security performance and training programs. For example, if data reveals that phishing incidents are on the rise despite existing training efforts, the GRC team can refine training content and adjust awareness campaigns accordingly. Similarly, recurring vulnerabilities may prompt a reassessment of patch management processes or investments in advanced threat detection tools. This feedback loop not only helps address immediate vulnerabilities but also drives strategic decision-making to improve long-term cyber resilience.

Emerging technologies, such as artificial intelligence and machine learning, further enhance measurement capabilities by processing vast amounts of security data in real time. These technologies excel at identifying subtle anomalies that might otherwise go unnoticed by traditional monitoring systems. For example, machine learning algorithms can learn the normal behavioral patterns of network traffic and user activity, enabling them to detect deviations that may signal an ongoing or impending breach. As these systems continuously refine their models based on new data, they become increasingly adept at predicting potential vulnerabilities and flagging suspicious events before they escalate.

Beyond anomaly detection, artificial intelligence is revolutionizing the way organizations analyze and respond to security incidents. AI-powered systems can quickly correlate events across disparate sources—ranging from log files and user activity records to threat intelligence feeds—and prioritize alerts based on the calculated risk level. This not only accelerates incident response but also improves the accuracy of threat assessments. For instance, an AI system might automatically classify an unusual login attempt as benign during off-peak hours but escalate similar activity during critical business periods, ensuring that human analysts focus their attention where it's most needed.

Moreover, emerging technologies are enabling a more proactive and strategic approach to cybersecurity. Blockchain, for example, offers a decentralized and tamper-proof method of recording security events and maintaining the integrity of digital identities. While still an emerging application in cybersecurity, blockchain can be used to create immutable logs for audit trails, ensuring that historical security data remains unaltered and reliable. This can be particularly useful for regulatory compliance and forensic investigations. Similarly, homomorphic encryption and confidential computing are being explored to protect data in use, enabling secure analytics without compromising privacy—a growing concern in industries handling sensitive personal information.

Cyber resilience also encompasses supply chain and third-party dynamics. An organization's security posture is only as strong as its weakest link. Metrics must be extended to assess the cyber hygiene of vendors and partners. This may include tracking the number of third-party assessments completed, the percentage of vendors meeting minimum security standards, or the average time taken to remediate findings. These measurements inform procurement strategies and contractual safeguards, driving better security outcomes across the ecosystem.

Culture also shapes how an organization communicates during a crisis. The quality and speed of incident communication can influence public trust, employee confidence, and legal exposure. Companies like Maersk have been praised for transparent communication following major breaches, while others, such as Equifax, faced backlash for delayed or opaque disclosures. Regular crisis simulations that include communications personnel can ensure that messaging aligns with security realities and public expectations.

Global organizations must also contend with cultural variability across geographic regions. The interpretation and implementation of security culture can vary widely depending on local customs, regulatory expectations, and attitudes toward authority. A security message that resonates in Germany may fall flat in Brazil or India. Successful multinational organizations localize training content, adjust communication styles, and empower regional security champions who understand local nuances while reinforcing universal principles.

This cultural adaptation ensures that security culture is inclusive and consistent without being prescriptive.

Human Resources plays a pivotal role in embedding security culture. As the custodian of onboarding, training compliance, policy enforcement, and disciplinary frameworks, HR departments are natural allies to the security function. Organizations that integrate cybersecurity expectations into job descriptions, performance reviews, and promotion criteria signal that secure behavior is a baseline professional standard. Likewise, HR systems can help track participation in training, enforce policy attestations, and mediate employee concerns related to surveillance or monitoring.

Leadership transitions present a unique threat to cultural continuity. Even organizations with strong cyber cultures may experience setbacks when key champions depart. Embedding cybersecurity values into institutional memory—through documented charters, culture manifestos, and cross-functional governance boards—helps maintain momentum. Some firms link executive scorecards to culture health metrics, or require successor onboarding programs that include a deep dive into existing cybersecurity values and metrics.

Boards and CFOs are increasingly interested in quantifying the return on investment (ROI) of cultural initiatives. While culture may seem intangible, its effects are measurable. Reduced security incidents, fewer regulatory fines, improved audit outcomes, lower insurance premiums, and higher trust from clients and partners all correlate with a robust security culture. Organizations that articulate these benefits in financial terms are more likely to secure ongoing funding and board support.

Security culture also intersects with Environmental, Social, and Governance (ESG) efforts. Investors and stakeholders are beginning to view digital resilience as a proxy for strong governance. Cybersecurity disclosures are appearing in sustainability reports, and third-party ESG rating agencies are evaluating data privacy practices, breach histories, and board-level oversight. A mature security culture demonstrates ethical stewardship of customer and employee data—positioning the organization as a responsible actor in the digital economy.

Finally, organizations with mature cultures are not merely compliant—they are innovative. Employees who understand risks and feel empowered are more likely to suggest security improvements, flag anomalies early, and champion initiatives that strengthen defenses. Some companies host internal hackathons, reward "best security idea" submissions, or create cross-functional working groups that tackle emerging challenges. In these environments, security becomes a catalyst for creativity, not a constraint.

Despite all the positive reinforcement, it's important to acknowledge the psychological toll that persistent cybersecurity demands can place on employees. Constant vigilance, simulated phishing campaigns, and surveillance technologies can erode morale, especially when not coupled with clear explanations or empathetic leadership. "Security fatigue"—a state of desensitization to security messages—can undermine even the best cultural programs. Leaders must balance awareness with empowerment, avoiding a culture of fear and instead promoting one of shared responsibility and resilience. Periodic pulse surveys, wellness check-ins, and feedback channels help ensure that security culture supports, rather than stifles, the workforce.

Ultimately, the true test of a security culture is not its slogans or training modules, but its lived experience during moments of stress. Whether facing a phishing campaign, a ransomware outbreak, or an insider breach, organizations with strong cultures respond cohesively, communicate clearly, and recover quickly. Culture, more than any single control or product, is what determines whether cybersecurity is an enabler of trust—or a silent vulnerability waiting to be exploited.

CHAPTER 15: INCIDENT RESPONSE, RECOVERY, AND CRISIS MANAGEMENT

"Failing to plan is planning to fail."
— Benjamin Franklin

In the rapidly evolving digital landscape, cyberattacks are no longer a matter of *if*—they are a matter of *when*. No matter how advanced an organization's security measures are, attackers continuously adapt and refine their methods to find new vulnerabilities. A single successful breach can disrupt critical systems, expose sensitive data, and damage an organization's financial stability and reputation. In this high-stakes environment, the ability to respond swiftly and effectively to a security incident is just as important as preventing it in the first place.

Incident response, the incident response team, and incident response training are critical components that should be clearly defined within an organization's cyber security plan. A well-structured incident response framework ensures that the organization can quickly identify, contain, and mitigate security breaches, minimizing potential damage and recovery time. The incident response team should have clearly defined roles and responsibilities, ensuring that all team members are prepared to respond effectively to various types of security incidents. Additionally, regular incident response training is essential to keep the team updated on the latest threats, response techniques, and communication protocols. Establishing specific policies and procedures around these topics strengthens the organization's ability to respond swiftly and efficiently to cyber threats, reduces downtime, and protects sensitive data and critical systems from compromise.

Incident response (IR) is the structured process that organizations follow to detect, contain, mitigate, and recover from cybersecurity breaches and threats. A well-crafted incident response plan (IRP) enables security teams to act quickly and decisively, minimizing damage and restoring normal operations as soon as possible. Effective incident response requires preparation, coordination, and a continuous feedback loop that strengthens future defenses. A strong response strategy not only mitigates immediate damage but also ensures that the organization can learn from incidents, making future attacks less likely to succeed.

Incident response is not a single event—it's a continuous process that evolves alongside the threat landscape. The National Institute of Standards and Technology (NIST) defines a structured incident response lifecycle consisting of five phases: preparation, detection, containment, eradication, and recovery. Each phase plays a critical role in ensuring that the organization can manage an incident effectively and minimize its impact.

The foundation of any effective incident response strategy begins with preparation. Without a clear plan in place, an organization's response to an incident will likely be chaotic and ineffective. Preparation involves developing a comprehensive incident response plan that defines the roles and responsibilities of each team member. This plan should outline the steps for identifying, containing, and eradicating threats, as well as the protocols for communicating with stakeholders and regulators. Without these predefined guidelines, confusion and miscommunication can severely hamper response efforts when time is of the essence.

A comprehensive and up-to-date inventory of assets is one of the most critical components of an effective incident response strategy. During a security incident, the ability to quickly identify which systems, applications, and data have been affected—or are at risk—is essential for a fast and targeted response. Without a clear understanding of the organization's assets, incident response teams are forced to work blindly, increasing the time it takes to detect, contain, and eradicate threats. A well-maintained inventory provides the foundation for incident scoping, impact assessment, and recovery, ensuring that no affected systems are overlooked and that the response is both thorough and efficient.

An effective inventory includes detailed information on all hardware, software, data, and network components within the organization. This means maintaining an accurate record of servers, endpoints, virtual machines, cloud resources, applications, databases, and even connected Internet of Things (IoT) devices. Each asset should be classified based on its criticality to business operations and the sensitivity of the data it handles. For example, customer databases, financial systems, and intellectual property repositories should be categorized as high-priority assets requiring immediate attention in the event of an incident. This classification allows the incident response team to prioritize efforts, focusing on the most critical systems first to minimize business disruption and data loss.

During the detection and analysis phase of incident response, a well-organized inventory allows the team to quickly identify which systems or data have been compromised. For example, if network monitoring systems detect suspicious activity on a specific IP address, the team can consult the inventory to determine which server is associated with that IP, the applications running on it, and the data it stores. This enables a faster diagnosis of the attack's scope and impact. Furthermore, knowing which systems are connected to the affected asset through network diagrams or dependency maps helps the team anticipate lateral movement and isolate vulnerable areas before the attack spreads.

In the containment and eradication phases, having a detailed inventory allows the team to isolate affected systems more effectively. For example, if a compromised server needs to be taken offline, the team can use the inventory to understand which business processes will be disrupted and determine whether failover or backup systems are available. This ensures that containment efforts are surgical, minimizing downtime without causing unnecessary business disruption. Additionally, during the eradication process, understanding the exact configuration of affected systems helps the team ensure that all traces of the threat are removed without damaging critical infrastructure.

Finally, during the recovery and post-incident review phases, a well-maintained inventory helps confirm that all affected systems have been restored and are functioning correctly. It also provides valuable insight into potential vulnerabilities and misconfigurations that contributed to the incident, guiding improvements to security controls and incident response protocols. An up-to-date inventory is also essential for compliance and reporting, as regulatory frameworks like GDPR and HIPAA require organizations to demonstrate that they have a clear understanding of the systems and data affected by a breach.

A well-structured Incident Response Team (IRT) is essential for executing an effective response plan. The IRT should be composed of individuals from different functional areas within the organization to ensure a comprehensive approach to managing security incidents. At the core of the IRT is the Incident Leader, who oversees the entire response effort, makes key decisions, and ensures that the response follows the established incident response plan. The Incident Leader acts as the primary point of contact for executive leadership and coordinates communication between the various response teams.

Supporting the Incident Leader are several specialized roles. Security Analysts are responsible for identifying and analyzing threats, monitoring security alerts, and conducting forensic analysis to understand how the attack occurred. Network Engineers work to isolate affected systems, restore network functionality, and prevent lateral movement of the attack within the infrastructure. Forensics Specialists are tasked with gathering and preserving evidence for both internal investigation and potential legal action. They help determine the attack's entry point, the scope of the compromise, and the attacker's methods.

If the environment includes Operational Technology (OT) or Industrial Control Systems (ICS), the IRT should also include OT/ICS Engineers. These specialists have deep knowledge of the organization's industrial systems, including SCADA (Supervisory Control and Data Acquisition) systems, programmable logic controllers (PLCs), and other connected devices that control physical processes. OT/ICS environments are often more sensitive to disruptions than traditional IT systems, and improper handling of an incident could lead to operational downtime, equipment damage, or even safety risks. OT/ICS Engineers help isolate affected systems, assess potential operational impacts, and implement recovery strategies that minimize downtime and maintain safety.

The IRT should also include a Legal and Compliance Officer, who ensures that the organization complies with regulatory requirements during and after an incident. This includes reporting breaches to authorities, notifying affected parties, and managing legal exposure. A Public Relations Officer handles external communication, including media inquiries and customer updates. This role is critical for preserving the organization's reputation and managing stakeholder confidence.

In larger organizations, the IRT may also include HR representatives (in the case of insider threats), third-party vendors (such as incident response consultants or cybersecurity firms), and law enforcement liaisons (if the attack involves criminal activity). Having a multidisciplinary team ensures that the response is well-coordinated, technically sound, and aligned with the organization's broader operational and reputational goals.

An effective IRT operates with clear lines of authority and communication, and team members should undergo regular training and simulation exercises to remain prepared. The ability of the IRT to respond quickly and efficiently often determines the overall impact of the incident and the speed at which the organization can recover.

Training plays a critical role in preparation. All employees —not just the security team—should receive regular training on identifying and reporting potential threats. For example, phishing simulations can help employees recognize suspicious emails and prevent attackers from gaining an initial foothold. Simulated attacks, such as red-team/blue-team drills, allow security teams to practice their response in a controlled environment, improving reaction times and coordination. The more realistic and thorough the training, the better prepared the team will be when faced with a real-world attack.

A comprehensive training program should involve a variety of exercises to test the readiness of the incident response team under different scenarios. Tabletop exercises are particularly useful for evaluating the decision-making process in a simulated environment. During these exercises, the team discusses how they would respond to a hypothetical attack, identifying gaps in the response plan and improving communication channels. Live-fire exercises, where real attacks are simulated in a controlled setting, allow teams to test their technical capabilities under pressure. Red-team/blue-team drills pit offensive security teams (red team) against defensive teams (blue team), exposing weaknesses in the organization's defenses and improving response times.

Cross-functional training is also important for ensuring that the entire organization is aligned during an incident. Legal, public relations, and compliance teams should be involved in training to understand their roles and responsibilities. For example, the public relations team should be prepared to issue timely and accurate statements, while the legal team should be ready to assess regulatory obligations and potential liabilities. Ensuring that every team member understands the broader context of incident response improves coordination and minimizes delays.

Additionally, training should cover new and emerging threats. Cyberattack techniques evolve rapidly, and response teams must stay current on the latest tactics used by threat actors. Threat intelligence briefings, workshops, and participation in industry forums help keep the team updated on the evolving threat landscape.

A culture of continuous improvement and learning is essential for maintaining readiness. After every incident, the team should conduct a thorough post-mortem analysis to assess what worked, what didn't, and how the response can be improved. Lessons learned should be incorporated into updated training programs and response plans, ensuring that the organization becomes more resilient over time.

Threat modeling and risk assessment are also essential parts of preparation. Understanding the organization's most valuable assets and identifying the most likely attack vectors allows security teams to focus their efforts where they are needed most. This involves mapping out the organization's network infrastructure, identifying critical systems and data, and assessing the potential impact of various attack scenarios. Threat modeling should account for insider threats, supply chain vulnerabilities, and external attacks, providing a comprehensive view of the organization's threat landscape.

Risk assessments should be conducted regularly to identify new vulnerabilities and evaluate the effectiveness of existing controls. Penetration testing and vulnerability scans can help uncover weak points in the organization's defenses. Security teams should prioritize addressing high-risk vulnerabilities and strengthening the most frequently targeted attack surfaces. This process helps allocate resources effectively and ensures that the most significant risks are addressed first.

Monitoring systems and automated detection tools should be tested regularly to ensure they are functioning correctly and capable of detecting real-world threats. Anomalous behavior, such as unusual login attempts, suspicious data transfers, or changes in system configurations, should trigger immediate alerts. Security Information and Event Management (SIEM) systems can help aggregate and analyze these alerts, allowing security teams to respond quickly to potential threats.

Furthermore, organizations need to establish secure communication channels for coordinating the response effort. If normal communication systems are compromised during an attack, backup methods such as encrypted messaging platforms or out-of-band communication lines should be in place. Ensuring that communication remains intact during a crisis is critical for coordinating response efforts and preventing further damage.

Threat modeling and risk assessment are ongoing processes that should be integrated into the organization's broader security strategy. As the threat landscape evolves, security teams must continuously reassess their risk posture and update their models and controls to reflect new threats and vulnerabilities. Regular updates to threat models and risk assessments ensure that the organization remains one step ahead of potential attackers.

Even with thorough preparation, no organization can prevent every attack. Therefore, the next critical phase of incident response is detection. The sooner an organization detects a breach, the better positioned it is to contain the threat before significant damage occurs. Successful detection depends on monitoring the organization's systems and networks for unusual activity that could signal an attack.

Security Information and Event Management (SIEM) systems, endpoint detection tools, and network monitoring solutions play a crucial role in this phase. These tools analyze system logs and network traffic for anomalies, such as repeated failed login attempts, unauthorized access attempts, and unusual data transfer patterns. For instance, if a user account is logging in from an unusual geographic location or at odd hours, that could indicate that the account has been compromised. Suspicious file modifications, unexpected reboots, and unauthorized software installations are other common indicators of compromise (IOCs).

Establishing baseline system behavior is key to improving detection. By defining what "normal" looks like, security systems can more easily identify deviations that may signal an attack. Automated alerts allow security teams to respond quickly to anomalies, and real-time monitoring systems ensure that suspicious activity is flagged as soon as it occurs. Effective detection minimizes the time between the initial breach and the organization's response, which can mean the difference between a minor disruption and a catastrophic data breach.

Once an incident is detected, containment becomes the top priority. Containment is the process of limiting the spread of the attack and preventing the attacker from gaining further access to the system. This phase requires swift decision-making, as a delayed response can give attackers more time to escalate their privileges, exfiltrate data, and compromise additional systems.

Containment strategies generally fall into two categories: short-term and long-term. Short-term containment focuses on isolating affected systems and cutting off the attacker's access. For example, disconnecting compromised devices from the network, blocking malicious IP addresses, and disabling affected user accounts can prevent further spread of the attack. Immediate containment efforts aim to stabilize the situation and prevent additional damage.

Long-term containment involves restoring affected systems and implementing changes to prevent the attack from recurring. This may include patching vulnerabilities that were exploited, increasing network segmentation, and improving access controls. For example, if an attacker gained access through a compromised user account, implementing multi-factor authentication 1about stopping the immediate threat—it's about ensuring that the same attack cannot happen again.

After containment, the next phase of incident response is eradication. It's not enough to stop the immediate threat—organizations must ensure that the attacker's presence is completely removed from the environment. Eradication involves identifying the root cause of the incident and eliminating any malicious code, backdoors, or compromised user accounts left behind by the attackers.

Thorough system scans and forensic analysis are essential during eradication. Simply removing the malware is not enough—security teams must ensure that any underlying vulnerabilities have been patched and that no persistence mechanisms remain in place. Attackers often create hidden access points or leave behind tools for future exploitation, so careful analysis is required to identify and remove these threats.

Restoring affected systems from clean backups may be necessary to ensure that no malicious code remains. However, security teams need to verify that the backups themselves are not compromised before restoring them. Once eradication is complete, security teams should continue monitoring the environment closely to confirm that the threat has been fully neutralized.

With the threat eradicated, the focus shifts to recovery. Recovery involves restoring affected systems and returning to normal operations without reintroducing vulnerabilities or allowing the attack to resume. Organizations should proceed carefully during this phase, as rushing the recovery process can lead to further complications.

Systems should be restored from clean backups, and security teams should conduct thorough testing to confirm that the restored systems are functioning properly. Continuous monitoring should remain in place to detect any signs of lingering compromise. If the attack exposed sensitive customer data or disrupted business operations, transparent communication with customers and stakeholders is essential for rebuilding trust.

The recovery process may also include legal and regulatory responses. For example, if customer data was exposed, the organization may need to notify regulators or affected individuals under data protection laws like the General Data Protection Regulation (GDPR) or the California Consumer Privacy Act (CCPA). Many regulations have specific timelines for reporting incidents, such as the GDPR's requirement to notify authorities within 72 hours of becoming aware of a breach. Failure to meet these deadlines can result in substantial fines and legal penalties.

In addition to notifying regulators, organizations may be required to provide specific details about the nature of the breach, the types of data involved, the potential impact on affected individuals, and the steps being taken to mitigate future risks. Some regulations also require organizations to offer identity protection or credit monitoring services to affected individuals.

Industry-specific regulations, such as the Health Insurance Portability and Accountability Act (HIPAA) for healthcare organizations or the Payment Card Industry Data Security Standard (PCI DSS) for financial institutions, may impose additional requirements. These could include forensic analysis, evidence preservation, and enhanced monitoring to ensure compliance.

Organizations should work closely with legal and compliance teams to understand the specific reporting obligations that apply to their industry and geographic location. Establishing a clear process for identifying and addressing these requirements during the recovery phase helps mitigate legal exposure and protects the organization's reputation.

Finally, once recovery is complete, it is essential to learn from the incident. Conducting a post-mortem analysis allows organizations to identify what worked and what didn't during the response process. Security teams should document the entire incident, including the initial attack vector, the containment measures taken, and the eradication process. Identifying gaps in the response plan or failures in detection systems allows organizations to strengthen their defenses.

The Post-Incident Review (PIR) is a critical phase of the incident response process that focuses on learning from the incident to strengthen future defenses and improve the overall security posture. Once an incident has been contained, eradicated, and systems have been restored, conducting a thorough post-incident review allows the organization to identify the root cause of the attack, evaluate the effectiveness of the response, and implement corrective actions to prevent similar incidents in the future. This phase transforms the incident into a learning opportunity, ensuring that the organization becomes more resilient to future threats.

A comprehensive post-incident review involves gathering all key stakeholders involved in the response process, including the incident response team, IT staff, executive leadership, and relevant business units. The review should begin with a detailed timeline of events, starting from the initial detection of the incident to the final resolution. This timeline helps identify gaps or delays in the response process and provides insight into how the attack unfolded. For example, if it took an unusually long time to detect the attack, this could indicate a need to improve monitoring capabilities or enhance staff training. Similarly, if containment efforts were delayed due to unclear decision-making, the response plan might require better-defined roles and escalation procedures.

One of the primary objectives of the post-incident review is to conduct a thorough root cause analysis (RCA). Understanding how the incident occurred—whether through a phishing email, unpatched vulnerability, or misconfigured system—allows the organization to address the underlying weaknesses that enabled the attack. For example, if the root cause was a failure to patch a known vulnerability, the organization might need to strengthen its patch management program. If the attacker exploited weak employee passwords, enhancing password policies and implementing multi-factor authentication (MFA) could be recommended. By addressing the root cause, the organization reduces the likelihood of the same type of incident recurring.

The post-incident review should also assess the effectiveness of the response. This includes evaluating whether the incident response team followed the established incident response plan, whether communication channels were effective, and whether decision-making was efficient. Any deviations from the plan should be documented and analyzed to determine whether they were justified or indicative of a flaw in the plan. For instance, if containment was delayed because the team lacked the authority to shut down a critical system, the organization might need to revise decision-making protocols to give the incident manager greater autonomy during critical events.

Finally, the post-incident review should result in a list of corrective actions and lessons learned. These could include updating the incident response plan, enhancing employee training, strengthening monitoring tools, or improving network segmentation. All corrective actions should be assigned to specific teams or individuals, with clear deadlines for implementation. This ensures that the lessons learned from the incident are actively integrated into the organization's security strategy rather than being forgotten. Additionally, follow-up exercises such as tabletop simulations or red team exercises should be scheduled to test the effectiveness of the revised response plan.

The post-incident review is not just about understanding what went wrong—it's about using that knowledge to build a stronger, more adaptive security framework. Cyber threats are constantly evolving, and a mature incident response program is one that treats every incident as an opportunity to improve. By conducting a thorough post-incident review and implementing the lessons learned, organizations can minimize the impact of future incidents and improve their overall cyber resilience.

Lessons learned should be incorporated into updated security policies and training programs. Regular reviews of incident response plans ensure that they remain relevant as the threat landscape evolves. Conducting follow-up training sessions based on the findings from the incident also helps to reinforce security awareness and improve future responses.

Metrics and performance indicators should also be tracked to measure the effectiveness of the incident response program. Tracking factors like time to detect, time to contain, and time to recover can help highlight areas for improvement. By continually assessing performance and adapting to new threats, organizations can strengthen their overall security posture and reduce the impact of future incidents.

Root Cause Analysis (RCA) is a critical step in the incident response process that focuses on identifying the underlying cause of a security incident rather than just addressing its symptoms. While containing and eradicating a threat may resolve the immediate problem, failing to identify and correct the root cause leaves the organization vulnerable to repeat attacks and similar breaches. Conducting a thorough RCA ensures that the organization understands exactly how the incident occurred, what vulnerabilities were exploited, and what changes are necessary to prevent a recurrence.

RCA begins by collecting and analyzing all available data related to the incident, including system logs, network traffic, endpoint activity, and user actions. The goal is to piece together a timeline of events that led up to the incident and trace the attacker's actions from initial access to compromise. For example, if the incident involved malware, the RCA would aim to determine how the malware entered the network—whether through a phishing email, a misconfigured firewall, or a compromised third-party application. Understanding the attack vector helps the response team determine which controls failed and where gaps in the organization's security framework exist.

One of the most effective methods for performing RCA is the "Five Whys" technique, where the team repeatedly asks "why" until the fundamental cause is identified. For example:

1. Why did the system get infected? → Because an employee opened a malicious attachment.

2. Why was the attachment not flagged by the email security gateway? → Because the gateway's malware definitions were outdated.

3. Why were the definitions outdated? → Because the automatic update function was disabled.

4. Why was it disabled? → Because of a misconfiguration during a recent software update.

5. Why was the misconfiguration not detected? → Because system audits were not being conducted regularly.

This process helps move beyond surface-level explanations and exposes deeper systemic issues that need to be corrected. RCA also involves identifying any contributing factors that may have amplified the impact of the incident. For example, if a successful phishing attack was made worse by a lack of multi-factor authentication (MFA) or poor user training, those weaknesses would need to be addressed as part of the remediation process.

RCA also plays a crucial role in evaluating the effectiveness of security controls and identifying gaps in the organization's security posture. If an attacker exploited an unpatched vulnerability, RCA would help the team determine whether the patch management process failed, whether endpoint protection tools were misconfigured, or whether the vulnerability was a zero-day attack that required more sophisticated detection capabilities. If insider activity was involved, RCA would assess whether access controls, monitoring, and user behavior analysis tools were sufficient to detect and prevent unauthorized actions.

Once the root cause has been identified, the next step is to implement corrective actions. This might include updating security configurations, deploying additional monitoring tools, enhancing employee training, or revising access controls. All corrective actions should be documented and assigned to specific teams or individuals, with clear deadlines and follow-up reviews to ensure proper implementation.

Ultimately, root cause analysis helps organizations transition from a reactive to a proactive security posture. By understanding how and why an incident occurred, organizations can address the structural and procedural gaps that allowed the breach to happen, reducing the likelihood of future incidents and improving overall resilience against evolving threats.

The incident debrief is a structured meeting conducted after the resolution of a security incident to review the response process, identify strengths and weaknesses, and ensure that valuable insights are captured for future improvement. Unlike the broader post-incident review, which involves a detailed analysis of the incident's root cause and long-term corrective actions, the debrief focuses on the immediate response—what happened, how the team handled it, and how the response could have been faster or more effective. A well-executed debrief ensures that all involved parties are aligned, informed, and better prepared for future incidents.

An effective debrief should involve all key members of the incident response team (IRT), including technical staff, security analysts, communication officers, legal representatives, and business leaders. This ensures that the discussion covers not only the technical aspects of the incident but also the business, legal, and reputational impact. The debrief should take place as soon as possible after the incident is resolved—preferably within 24 to 48 hours—while the events and actions are still fresh in the minds of the responders. The goal is to create a clear and accurate picture of how the response unfolded and where improvements can be made.

The debrief should follow a structured format to keep the discussion focused and productive. It typically begins with a timeline reconstruction, where the team walks through each phase of the incident—detection, containment, eradication, and recovery. Each participant should describe their role, the actions they took, and any challenges they encountered. This helps identify bottlenecks, miscommunications, or decision-making delays that could have been avoided. For example, if containment was delayed because the incident manager couldn't reach the network administrator, the team might conclude that alternative contact methods or a backup response chain is needed.

The team should also assess the effectiveness of communication during the incident. Were the right people notified promptly? Were escalation paths followed correctly? Were decisions made quickly and with enough information? If there were gaps in communication or confusion over roles and responsibilities, those issues should be addressed in the incident response plan. For instance, if confusion arose because team members weren't clear on who had the authority to shut down a compromised server, the escalation protocols should be clarified and reinforced through additional training.

Another key element of the debrief is discussing the tools and technologies used during the response. Did the SIEM system provide timely and accurate alerts? Were the endpoint detection and response (EDR) tools effective in identifying and isolating the threat? If any tools failed or underperformed, the team should investigate whether they need to be replaced, updated, or better configured. If manual processes caused delays, opportunities for automation should be explored to improve response times.

The debrief should conclude with a list of immediate takeaways and actionable improvements. These could include updating the incident response plan, improving specific tools, refining communication protocols, or conducting additional training. Each action item should be assigned to a specific person or team with a clear deadline to ensure accountability. The team should also discuss whether additional tabletop exercises or simulated attacks are needed to test the revised response plan.

Ultimately, the incident debrief is about creating a feedback loop that continuously strengthens the incident response process. By systematically reviewing the response, identifying areas for improvement, and applying lessons learned, organizations can build a more resilient security posture and improve their ability to respond swiftly and effectively to future incidents.

An Incident Response Plan is only effective if it remains current, relevant, and aligned with the evolving threat landscape. Cyber threats are constantly changing, with attackers developing new techniques, exploiting novel vulnerabilities, and adjusting to enhanced security measures. After every incident, the incident response plan should be carefully reviewed and updated to reflect the lessons learned and to close any gaps identified during the incident response and post-incident review. Keeping the plan updated ensures that the organization is prepared to respond effectively to future threats, minimizing damage and improving recovery times.

The process of updating the IRP should begin with insights gained during the post-incident review and root cause analysis.

These reviews often reveal gaps in the response process, such as delays in communication, unclear roles and responsibilities, or ineffective containment strategies. For example, if an incident response team struggled to isolate a compromised server because the escalation process was unclear, the IRP should be revised to outline clear decision-making protocols. Additionally, if containment efforts were hindered by a lack of proper tools, the revised IRP may include improved guidance on the deployment of detection and isolation technologies.

One of the key drivers for updating the incident response plan is the insight gained from the root cause analysis (RCA) and post-incident review. If the RCA reveals that the attack was enabled by poor patch management, outdated endpoint protection, or ineffective employee training, the IRP should be updated to include new or revised processes to address those weaknesses. For example, the plan may need to establish stricter patch management policies, mandate more frequent vulnerability assessments, or update employee training programs to cover new social engineering tactics. Similarly, if communication delays during the incident were identified as a weakness, the IRP might need to clarify escalation procedures or introduce new communication tools to streamline information sharing.

The incident response plan should also be adjusted to account for new threats and attack vectors. For instance, if the incident involved a supply chain attack, the plan should be updated to strengthen vendor risk assessments, implement stricter third-party access controls, and establish protocols for monitoring supply chain activity. Likewise, if the attack targeted a cloud-based system or exploited a misconfigured remote work setup, the IRP should be revised to include specific response playbooks for cloud and remote environments. Threat intelligence from industry sources and government agencies should also be incorporated into the plan to anticipate emerging threats and refine defensive measures. Regularly consulting frameworks like the MITRE ATT&CK model can provide valuable insights into emerging attack techniques and ensure the IRP is aligned with modern threat landscapes.

Role assignments and responsibilities within the incident response team should also be reviewed and updated regularly. If the post-incident review identifies confusion over roles or decision-making authority during the response, the IRP should clarify team member responsibilities and escalation protocols. Any personnel changes—such as staff turnover, new hires, or role reassignments—should be reflected in the plan to ensure that the right people are notified and empowered to act when an incident occurs. Updating the plan should also include verifying that all contact information for team members, stakeholders, and external partners (e.g., law enforcement, third-party security providers) is accurate and up to date.

Testing and simulation exercises are critical to ensuring that updates to the incident response plan are effective. Once the plan has been updated, the organization should conduct tabletop exercises and red team/blue team drills to validate the new procedures and identify any remaining weaknesses. These exercises help ensure that all team members understand their roles and that the new protocols are practical and effective under real-world conditions. Continuous testing also helps build muscle memory among the response team, improving their ability to act quickly and decisively during an actual incident.

Another key area for improvement is training and awareness. The updated IRP should outline plans for educating staff on new threats, revised containment strategies, and improved response processes. Conducting regular tabletop exercises and live simulations ensures that the updated IRP is well-understood by all relevant personnel. These exercises also provide an opportunity to evaluate whether new processes are effective and to refine them further if necessary.

Ultimately, the incident response plan should be treated as a living document that evolves alongside the organization's business operations, technology infrastructure, and threat environment. Regular updates—ideally conducted at least annually or after any significant incident—help ensure that the plan remains aligned with industry best practices and regulatory requirements. By maintaining an adaptive and well-practiced incident response plan, organizations can improve their ability to contain and mitigate incidents, reduce downtime, and protect sensitive data and business operations from evolving cyber threats.

Incident response is not just a technical challenge—it is a strategic imperative. A well-defined and tested incident response plan protects an organization's assets, reputation, and operational continuity. Organizations that invest in preparation, training, and continuous improvement are better equipped to handle even the most sophisticated attacks. The ability to respond effectively to an incident defines not only an organization's resilience but also its long-term success in an increasingly hostile digital environment.

CHAPTER 16: THREAT HUNTING AND PROACTIVE DEFENSE

"If you wait until you're attacked to respond, you're already losing the battle."

— Dmitri Alperovitch

Dmitri Alperovitch's quote underscores the fundamental shift in modern cybersecurity strategy from a reactive to a proactive approach. Traditional security measures—such as firewalls, antivirus software, and intrusion detection systems —are designed to respond to threats *after* they have already penetrated a system or network. While these defensive tools are essential, they are inherently limited because they rely on the detection of known attack patterns or signatures. This means that attackers who use novel techniques or exploit zero-day vulnerabilities (which lack a known signature) can bypass these defenses altogether.

Alperovitch's statement reflects the strategic disadvantage of relying solely on reactive security. Once an attack is underway, the damage has likely already begun. Attackers may have already gained access to sensitive data, established backdoors, or moved laterally through the network by the time security teams detect the breach. The longer an attacker remains undetected (known as dwell time), the more damage they can inflict—whether it's data exfiltration, sabotage, or ransomware deployment.

The quote highlights the core weakness of reactive security: attackers only need to succeed once to cause significant harm, but defenders need to be successful every time to prevent it. This asymmetry creates an environment where waiting for an attack to be detected effectively gives the advantage to the attacker.

Alperovitch's solution to this problem is embedded in the idea of threat hunting. By shifting from a reactive to a proactive defense model, organizations no longer passively wait for an alert or incident report to indicate a breach. Instead, they actively search for signs of compromise before an attack becomes visible. This includes analyzing network traffic for unusual patterns, investigating suspicious endpoint activity, and using threat intelligence to anticipate attack methods based on the behavior of known adversaries.

In essence, the quote challenges the defensive status quo. It reflects the reality that waiting to respond until after an attack is discovered is too late—the damage has already begun, and the attacker may have already established persistence within the network. True cybersecurity resilience comes from the ability to anticipate, detect, and neutralize threats before they reach a critical stage. This requires the development of a threat-hunting capability that combines human analysis, artificial intelligence, and behavioral pattern recognition to uncover hidden threats.

Alperovitch's statement is not merely a warning—it's a call to action. It reflects the broader shift in modern cybersecurity from static, defensive postures toward dynamic, intelligence-driven security strategies. By adopting a proactive stance, organizations can close the gap between attack and detection, reducing the window of opportunity for attackers and reclaiming the strategic advantage in an increasingly hostile digital landscape.

In the evolving landscape of cybersecurity, reactive defense is no longer enough. Traditional security measures—firewalls, antivirus software, and intrusion detection systems (IDS)—are essential, but they often operate passively, waiting for an attack to happen. This creates a dangerous gap in protection because modern adversaries are constantly refining their techniques to evade detection. Waiting for an alert to sound before acting gives attackers an advantage—time. Threat hunting fills this gap by adopting a proactive mindset. Rather than waiting for signs of an attack, threat hunting involves actively searching for indicators of compromise (IoCs) and anomalies that might indicate an undetected breach or ongoing infiltration.

Threat hunting transforms cybersecurity from a reactive process into a strategic, intelligence-driven effort. It's not about waiting for threats to appear—it's about finding them before they can cause harm. Organizations that embrace threat hunting gain an advantage by reducing the dwell time of attackers, identifying vulnerabilities before they're exploited, and improving the overall resilience of their security posture.

Reactive defense is no longer sufficient. Traditional security measures—firewalls, antivirus software, and intrusion detection systems (IDS)—are designed to detect and respond to known threats. They rely on established signatures, threat models, and predefined rules to identify malicious activity. However, cyber attackers have evolved. They now use sophisticated techniques, including fileless malware, living-off-the-land (LOTL) tactics, and advanced persistent threats (APTs) that are specifically designed to bypass traditional defenses. As a result, security teams are often left blind to ongoing attacks, even as threat actors move freely within a network.

Threat hunting addresses this gap by shifting from a reactive to a proactive security strategy. Instead of waiting for an alert to signal that an attack has already occurred, threat hunting involves actively searching for signs of compromise or suspicious behavior within a network. It is a deliberate, hypothesis-driven process that relies on human intuition, pattern recognition, and threat intelligence to uncover hidden threats that automated systems might miss.

Threat hunting has become a critical component of modern cybersecurity because reactive defense is no longer enough. Traditional security measures like firewalls, antivirus software, and intrusion detection systems (IDS) were designed to detect and respond to known threats. They rely on established signatures, threat models, and predefined rules to identify malicious activity. But cyber attackers have evolved. They now use sophisticated techniques like fileless malware, living-off-the-land (LOTL) tactics, and advanced persistent threats (APTs) that are specifically designed to bypass traditional defenses. This creates a dangerous blind spot in security posture, leaving organizations vulnerable to subtle, undetected breaches.

Reactive defense creates a dangerous lag between the moment an attacker breaches a system and the moment the attack is discovered. This period, known as dwell time, is when the most damage occurs. Industry research shows that the average dwell time for a cyberattack can range from 30 to 120 days. During this time, attackers can exfiltrate sensitive data, create backdoors, establish persistence, and compromise additional systems. The longer an attacker remains undetected, the more damage they can inflict.

The problem lies in how traditional security tools function. Most are designed to recognize known patterns of malicious behavior. Antivirus software relies on malware signatures, and SIEM (Security Information and Event Management) systems use predefined rules to flag suspicious activity. If an attacker uses a new type of malware or modifies existing code, signature-based detection will fail. Attackers have also learned to exploit trusted system tools to carry out malicious activity. LOTL attacks, for example, use legitimate tools like PowerShell and Windows Management Instrumentation (WMI) to move laterally within a network without triggering alarms. Polymorphic malware presents another challenge—it constantly modifies its code to evade detection. This means that even the most advanced detection tools can be blind to attacks that deviate from known patterns.

Threat hunting addresses this fundamental weakness by shifting from a reactive to a proactive security model. Instead of waiting for an attack to happen, threat hunting involves actively searching for signs of compromise or suspicious behavior within a network. Threat hunters create hypotheses based on threat intelligence and behavioral analysis, then investigate those leads by analyzing network traffic, endpoint activity, and system behavior. They focus on identifying patterns and anomalies rather than relying on known attack signatures. This allows them to detect threats that are subtle or previously unknown.

The process of threat hunting begins with forming a hypothesis. For example, if state-sponsored actors have been targeting financial institutions with fileless malware, a threat hunter might investigate whether similar activity is occurring within their network. Threat hunters rely on threat intelligence reports and frameworks like MITRE ATT&CK to guide these hypotheses. They study known adversary tactics, techniques, and procedures (TTPs) and apply that knowledge to their specific environment. The goal is to think like an attacker—to anticipate their next move before they strike.

Once a hypothesis is established, the next step is data collection. Threat hunters analyze a wide range of information, including network logs, endpoint behavior, user activity, and threat intelligence feeds. They look for deviations from normal activity. Unusual login attempts, suspicious outbound traffic, and unexpected privilege escalations are all red flags. Unlike traditional security tools, which rely on static rules, threat hunting focuses on behavior. An attacker using PowerShell to execute commands will not be detected by antivirus software, but their behavior—such as executing commands at odd hours or accessing restricted systems—can raise suspicions.

Pattern recognition and anomaly detection are at the core of threat hunting. Threat hunters study the data for signs of lateral movement, unauthorized file access, and command-and-control (C2) traffic. Lateral movement is especially concerning because it indicates that the attacker is expanding their reach within the network. Threat hunters also look for privilege escalation attempts, where an attacker tries to gain administrative control over a system. These behavioral patterns often reveal the presence of an attacker even when no malware signature is detected.

When a threat is identified, threat hunters move quickly to contain and neutralize it. They may isolate compromised endpoints, terminate malicious processes, and revoke compromised credentials. Removing the threat is only part of the solution. Threat hunters also work to understand how the breach occurred and how to prevent similar incidents in the future. This might involve patching a software vulnerability, adjusting firewall rules, or updating security policies. Threat hunting is not just about stopping an attack—it's about strengthening overall resilience.

The benefits of threat hunting are clear. First, it reduces dwell time. By actively searching for threats, organizations can detect attacks earlier and minimize damage. Second, it allows organizations to uncover unknown threats. Signature-based tools only detect known threats, but threat hunting reveals novel attacks based on behavior. Third, threat hunting improves the quality of threat intelligence. Findings from threat hunting operations feed back into threat intelligence platforms, improving future detection capabilities. Finally, threat hunting strengthens the entire security posture. It helps identify weak points in network architecture, allowing organizations to improve configurations and close security gaps.

Threat hunting has already proven its value in real-world cases. In one instance, a financial institution's threat hunting team discovered unusual network traffic to an IP address in Eastern Europe. Further investigation revealed that the traffic originated from a compromised workstation. The attacker had used PowerShell commands to exfiltrate data, bypassing the company's traditional security defenses. Without threat hunting, the attack might have continued for weeks or months, causing significant financial and reputational damage. In another case, a healthcare provider's threat hunting team identified a backdoor hidden in a newly installed software package. Left undetected, the backdoor could have been used to deploy ransomware, potentially compromising patient data and disrupting medical services.

The rise of sophisticated, stealthy cyberattacks means that threat hunting is no longer optional. Modern attackers are innovative and adaptive. They exploit the smallest gaps in network security, use social engineering to bypass defenses, and employ advanced evasion techniques to remain undetected. Threat hunting gives defenders the ability to anticipate, identify, and neutralize these threats before they escalate.

Threat hunting represents a fundamental shift in cybersecurity strategy. It transforms security from a reactive function into an active, intelligence-driven effort. Instead of relying on automated alerts and signature-based detection, threat hunting puts human intuition and analysis at the forefront of defense. Cyber attackers are constantly evolving, but threat hunting ensures that defenders stay one step ahead. In a world where waiting for an attack to happen is no longer an option, threat hunting is not just a tactical advantage—it's a strategic necessity.

Threat hunting has already proven its value in both IT and OT/ICS environments, where attackers are constantly refining their techniques to evade detection. In one notable case, a major financial institution's threat hunting team identified an attack that would have bypassed traditional defenses. The security team noticed a series of encrypted packets being sent to an IP address in Eastern Europe at irregular intervals. Automated security tools didn't flag the activity because it didn't match known threat signatures, but the pattern was suspicious enough for a threat hunter to investigate. They traced the traffic back to a senior financial officer's workstation and discovered that the attacker was using legitimate system tools like PowerShell to exfiltrate data—an example of a living-off-the-land (LOTL) attack. The attacker had gained initial access through a compromised VPN credential. Because the threat was identified early, the security team was able to isolate the workstation, cut off the connection, and prevent any significant data loss.

A similar case occurred in the healthcare sector, where threat hunting exposed a backdoor hidden in a newly installed software package. During routine network analysis, a threat hunter noticed that the software was making unexpected outbound connections to an IP address in Eastern Europe. While the package had passed initial security checks, the unusual network behavior raised red flags. Further investigation revealed that the package contained malicious code designed to install ransomware upon receiving a command from an external server. The threat hunter's proactive response allowed the security team to isolate the affected systems, remove the backdoor, and prevent a large-scale ransomware attack that could have compromised patient data and disrupted medical services.

Threat hunting has also played a critical role in protecting OT/ICS environments, where the consequences of an attack can extend beyond financial damage to physical harm and infrastructure disruption. In one case, a utility company's threat hunting team detected an attempt to breach the power grid. The attackers were using stolen VPN credentials to attempt remote logins at odd hours from suspicious geographic locations. While the logins were blocked due to multi-factor authentication, the pattern suggested that the attackers were mapping the network infrastructure and probing for vulnerabilities. Further analysis revealed that the attackers had installed a backdoor on an engineering workstation connected to the SCADA (Supervisory Control and Data Acquisition) network. The backdoor would have allowed remote command execution on critical infrastructure, including circuit breakers and transformers. The threat hunting team quickly isolated the workstation, revoked the compromised credentials, and closed the attack vector before any operational disruption occurred.

Another example involved a U.S.-based water treatment

facility, where threat hunting uncovered an attempt to alter chemical levels in the water supply. Operators noticed a brief but unexplained spike in sodium hydroxide (lye) levels during a routine system check. A threat hunter investigated and discovered that an attacker had gained access through a poorly secured RDP (Remote Desktop Protocol) connection. The attacker issued direct commands to increase the concentration of sodium hydroxide to dangerous levels. Fortunately, automated safety controls corrected the imbalance before it became hazardous. The threat hunter traced the breach to compromised administrator credentials and a misconfigured RDP setting. The security team responded by revoking the compromised credentials, introducing multi-factor authentication for remote access, and segmenting the network to prevent future incidents.

Threat hunting also proved essential in a manufacturing environment where attackers attempted to disrupt production lines by modifying programmable logic controllers (PLCs). A manufacturing company specializing in automotive parts experienced a series of unexplained disruptions in its production processes. The security team initially suspected mechanical failures, but threat hunters discovered malicious code embedded in the PLCs controlling the production lines. The attackers had gained access through a compromised third-party contractor's VPN connection and used the access to introduce slight variations in machine operation, resulting in defective products and increased waste. The threat hunters quickly isolated the affected PLCs, restored them from backup, and closed the compromised VPN connection. The company also strengthened its vendor access controls and implemented deeper monitoring of PLC activity to prevent future breaches.

These examples highlight the unique challenges and importance of threat hunting in both IT and OT/ICS environments. IT networks are often dynamic and complex, with large volumes of unpredictable traffic and rapidly changing user behavior. This was demonstrated in the case of the financial institution, where the attackers used encrypted data streams and legitimate system tools to avoid detection, and in the healthcare case, where malicious code was hidden within a seemingly legitimate software package. In contrast, OT systems are highly structured and stable, which makes deviations from normal patterns more obvious—but only if the threat hunter knows where to look. The power grid attack demonstrated how suspicious login attempts from unexpected geographic locations signaled a threat, while the water treatment facility case exposed the danger of compromised remote access controls. The manufacturing plant case showed how even subtle disruptions in machine performance could signal malicious activity within industrial control systems. Whether in the unpredictable landscape of IT or the more rigid environment of OT, threat hunting relies on understanding baseline system behavior and recognizing even the smallest deviations.

Threat hunting in IT and OT/ICS environments requires a blend of technical expertise and operational awareness. In IT environments, threat hunters must understand complex network architectures, user behavior, and emerging attack techniques. The attackers in the financial institution case exploited stolen VPN credentials and LOTL tactics to bypass security controls, while the healthcare attackers embedded a backdoor in legitimate software to evade detection. In OT/ICS environments, threat hunters need specialized knowledge of industrial protocols, control systems, and operational processes. The attackers in the power grid case used compromised VPN credentials to infiltrate the SCADA network, while the water treatment facility breach involved direct manipulation of chemical dosing systems through insecure RDP access. In the manufacturing plant case, the attackers exploited a contractor's compromised VPN connection to modify PLC settings and disrupt production. These incidents illustrate that adversaries are adapting their methods to exploit the unique characteristics of both IT and OT systems. Successful attacks on IT networks can lead to data breaches, financial losses, and reputational damage, while attacks on OT systems can result in physical damage, safety hazards, and critical infrastructure failures. Proactive threat hunting allows organizations to identify and neutralize these threats before they escalate, protecting both digital assets and the physical infrastructure that underpins modern society.

CHAPTER 17: THREAT INTELLIGENCE AND THREAT MODELING

"Knowing your enemy is the first step in defeating them."
— *Sun Tzu*, The *Art of War*

Sun Tzu's words, though written over two thousand years ago, remain profoundly relevant in the realm of cybersecurity. Threat intelligence and threat modeling embody this principle by shifting the focus from mere defense to understanding the adversary's tactics, motivations, and vulnerabilities. In cybersecurity, knowledge is power. Reactive security measures, such as firewalls and antivirus software, can only go so far in protecting an organization from modern threats. To truly defend a network, security teams must anticipate how an attacker might operate and adapt their defenses accordingly. Threat intelligence provides the insight into who the attackers are, how they behave, and what tools they are using, while threat modeling applies this understanding to predict and prevent future attacks. Just as a general cannot expect to win a battle without understanding the enemy's strategy and objectives, a security team cannot mount an effective defense without intelligence and foresight. Sun Tzu's advice underscores the fact that knowing how an adversary operates is not just an advantage—it's a necessity.

Threat intelligence and threat modeling are natural extensions of threat hunting, providing the strategic foundation needed to anticipate and neutralize future attacks. While threat hunting focuses on identifying and stopping ongoing threats, threat intelligence seeks to understand the broader context behind those threats—who the attackers are, what their motivations might be, and how they are likely to operate in the future. Threat modeling takes this intelligence and applies it systematically to anticipate and mitigate future attacks by identifying vulnerabilities, predicting attack vectors, and strengthening defenses before an incident occurs. Together, threat intelligence and threat modeling transform a reactive security posture into a proactive, adaptive strategy.

Threat intelligence involves collecting and analyzing information about potential and existing threats to an organization. Unlike basic network monitoring, which looks for anomalies in real time, threat intelligence focuses on gathering data from a wide range of sources to build a comprehensive understanding of the threat landscape. Sources of threat intelligence include open-source intelligence (OSINT), such as security blogs and research papers; commercial intelligence platforms that aggregate and analyze global threat data; and internal sources, such as data from threat hunting and incident response activities. Threat intelligence also benefits from information-sharing networks like Information Sharing and Analysis Centers (ISACs), which allow industries and government agencies to pool insights about emerging threats and vulnerabilities.

Raw data alone isn't enough to create effective threat intelligence. The real value comes from analysis—identifying patterns, correlating different data points, and turning that information into actionable insights. For example, if an intelligence feed reports increased use of a specific remote access trojan (RAT) by state-sponsored attackers, an organization can create specific hunting playbooks to search for indicators of compromise (IoCs) related to that trojan. Threat intelligence also helps to identify the tactics, techniques, and procedures (TTPs) used by known adversaries. By mapping these TTPs against frameworks like MITRE ATT&CK, security teams can anticipate how an attacker might operate and adjust their defenses accordingly.

Threat intelligence enhances not only defensive measures but also the effectiveness of threat hunting. A threat hunter who knows that a particular threat group often uses fileless malware executed through PowerShell can adjust their hypothesis and investigative approach to focus on memory analysis and script execution patterns. Intelligence also informs response strategies—knowing that an attacker has a history of deploying ransomware after initial infiltration allows the security team to prioritize isolating affected systems and securing backups. Effective threat intelligence shortens response times, improves detection accuracy, and helps security teams stay ahead of emerging threats.

Threat modeling builds on this intelligence by providing a structured approach to identifying and addressing potential threats. Instead of reacting to threats as they emerge, threat modeling allows organizations to think like an attacker and anticipate how they might exploit vulnerabilities. It begins by mapping out the organization's attack surface—everything from exposed internet-facing servers to employee endpoints and third-party connections. Each potential entry point represents a possible attack vector. By evaluating these vectors against known TTPs, security teams can create models that predict how an attacker might attempt to compromise the system.

Threat modeling is a structured process used to identify, evaluate, and mitigate potential threats before attackers can exploit them. It's essentially a way of thinking like an attacker —analyzing a system's design and implementation to uncover vulnerabilities and predict how an adversary might attempt to exploit them. Unlike reactive security measures, which focus on responding to attacks after they've occurred, threat modeling allows security teams to anticipate and neutralize threats before they can cause damage. This transforms a passive security posture into an active, predictive strategy that reduces risk and strengthens overall defenses.

The process begins with defining the scope and objectives of the threat model. The scope could include an entire network, a specific application, or even a single industrial control system (ICS). For example, in an IT environment, the goal might be to protect customer financial data stored in a cloud-based database. In an OT/ICS environment, the focus could be on securing the control systems for a power grid or water treatment facility. Clearly defining the scope ensures that security efforts are focused on the most critical assets and attack surfaces. A well-defined scope also helps the security team avoid wasting time and resources on areas that represent low strategic value to an attacker.

Once the scope is defined, the next step is to map out the system architecture and data flow. This involves creating a detailed diagram that shows how data moves through the system, how different components interact, and where security boundaries exist. The diagram includes network segments, external interfaces, authentication mechanisms, firewalls, and sensitive data flows. For instance, in a SCADA network, mapping the system might reveal that sensitive operational data is passing through an unsecured external connection, creating an opportunity for an attacker to intercept or manipulate that data. By visually representing the system, security teams can identify weak points, potential entry points for attackers, and any misconfigurations that could be exploited. This process helps establish a baseline of normal activity, making it easier to spot anomalies or suspicious behavior later on.

Identifying threats is the next step in the process. Threat modelers use established frameworks to systematically analyze the system for different types of vulnerabilities and attack methods. One widely used framework is STRIDE, which evaluates threats based on six categories: spoofing, tampering, repudiation, information disclosure, denial of service, and elevation of privilege. In the context of a financial institution, spoofing could involve an attacker pretending to be a legitimate employee to gain unauthorized access to customer records. Tampering could involve modifying transaction data in transit. In an OT environment, elevation of privilege might involve an attacker gaining administrative access to a programmable logic controller (PLC) and changing operational settings. The STRIDE framework helps security teams anticipate how an attacker might target different parts of the system and what impact a successful attack would have on business operations.

Another framework used in threat modeling is DREAD, which assigns a risk score to each identified threat based on five factors: damage, reproducibility, exploitability, affected users, and discoverability. This approach helps security teams prioritize mitigation efforts by focusing on the most dangerous and easily exploitable threats first. For example, a threat that could be easily discovered and exploited by an attacker, and which could cause widespread operational damage, would be assigned a higher priority than a low-impact vulnerability that would be difficult for an attacker to identify. The goal is to maximize the impact of security efforts by addressing the most serious and exploitable threats first.

After identifying threats, the next step is to analyze how an attacker might exploit them. This involves tracing the possible attack paths and entry points into the system. Attackers often use multiple stages to compromise a target, starting with initial access through phishing or stolen credentials, followed by lateral movement to higher-privilege systems, and finally executing their objective—whether that's data exfiltration, system disruption, or financial fraud. For example, in the power grid case, the attack path involved stolen VPN credentials, which allowed the adversary to bypass external defenses and plant a backdoor on an engineering workstation. Once inside the network, the attacker could have moved laterally to other systems, manipulated circuit breakers, and caused widespread power outages. Identifying and understanding these attack paths allows security teams to block or contain them before they can reach critical assets.

Choke points—strategic locations where multiple attack paths converge—are especially valuable in threat modeling. Strengthening security at these points can significantly reduce the overall risk of an attack. For example, network segmentation between IT and OT environments serves as a choke point, limiting the attacker's ability to pivot from the IT network into the ICS environment. By reinforcing access controls and monitoring activity at these critical intersections, security teams can prevent attackers from expanding their reach within a network.

Once threats and attack paths have been identified, the next step is to prioritize and mitigate them. Threats are ranked based on their severity and likelihood of exploitation, with the most critical threats addressed first. Mitigation strategies might include patching known vulnerabilities, improving authentication controls, segmenting networks to limit lateral movement, and enhancing monitoring and detection capabilities. In the water treatment facility case, for example, the highest priority was closing the compromised remote desktop protocol (RDP) connection and implementing multi-factor authentication for all remote access. Additional measures included tightening segmentation between the IT and OT networks and increasing real-time monitoring of operational commands to detect future manipulation attempts. By focusing on high-impact threats and addressing them systematically, security teams can strengthen their overall security posture.

Validating the threat model is the final step in the process. This involves testing the model through red team exercises, penetration testing, and tabletop exercises. Red team exercises simulate real-world attacks to see if the threat model holds up under pressure. Penetration testing involves attempting to exploit identified vulnerabilities to determine whether mitigation efforts are effective. Tabletop exercises simulate attack scenarios with the security team to test response capabilities and identify any weaknesses in the threat response plan. The results of these tests are used to refine the threat model, ensuring that it remains effective as the threat landscape evolves. Threat modeling is not a one-time activity—it's a continuous process that must adapt to new technologies, evolving business operations, and emerging threats.

Threat modeling is most effective when integrated into the broader security strategy. Threat hunting provides real-time insights into how attackers operate, while threat intelligence informs security teams about emerging trends and adversary tactics. Threat modeling takes these insights and applies them in a structured, predictive manner—strengthening defenses before an attack occurs. For example, in the healthcare case, threat intelligence would have helped the security team recognize the indicators of compromise associated with the backdoor hidden in the software package. Threat modeling would have highlighted the supply chain as a potential attack vector, prompting the organization to conduct more thorough security audits of third-party vendors. Similarly, in the power grid case, threat modeling would have identified the engineering workstation and VPN connection as high-risk entry points, allowing the security team to tighten access controls before the attack occurred.

Threat modeling provides security teams with a roadmap for defending against future attacks. It transforms threat intelligence from raw data into actionable strategy and ensures that defenses are tailored to the specific risks and vulnerabilities of the organization. By continuously refining threat models based on new intelligence and hunting data, organizations can stay ahead of the evolving threat landscape. The combination of threat hunting, threat intelligence, and threat modeling creates a dynamic security posture—one that allows security teams to anticipate, detect, and neutralize threats before they escalate.

A common threat modeling framework is STRIDE, which stands for Spoofing, Tampering, Repudiation, Information Disclosure,

Denial of Service, and Elevation of Privilege. This framework helps security teams systematically evaluate different types of threats and vulnerabilities. For example, in the context of an ICS (Industrial Control System) network, spoofing could involve an attacker pretending to be a legitimate device on the network, while elevation of privilege could involve exploiting a misconfigured PLC (Programmable Logic Controller) to gain administrative access. By analyzing these potential scenarios, threat modeling allows security teams to prioritize risks based on both the likelihood of an attack and the potential impact on business operations.

Threat modeling is not a one-time exercise—it is a continuous process that evolves with the threat landscape. As new threat intelligence emerges, the models are updated to reflect the latest tactics and vulnerabilities. For instance, after the discovery of the SolarWinds supply chain attack, many organizations revised their threat models to account for the risk of compromised software updates and hidden backdoors. Threat modeling also helps to strengthen defenses by identifying gaps in existing security controls. If a threat model reveals that an attacker could exploit a lack of network segmentation to move laterally between IT and OT systems, security teams can implement additional firewall rules and network monitoring to close that gap.

The real-world value of threat intelligence and threat modeling becomes clear when they are integrated into security operations. In the financial institution case, threat hunting uncovered a LOTL attack involving encrypted data exfiltration through PowerShell. Threat intelligence would have helped the security team recognize that this technique is commonly used by certain state-sponsored groups, allowing them to anticipate additional stages of the attack and adjust their response accordingly. Threat modeling could have revealed that the VPN credential used in the attack represented a critical vulnerability, prompting the team to implement additional authentication requirements and monitor privileged account activity more closely.

In the healthcare example, threat intelligence would have helped the security team recognize the indicators of compromise (IoCs) associated with the backdoor hidden in the software package. Threat modeling would have highlighted the supply chain as a potential attack vector, prompting the organization to conduct more thorough security audits of third-party vendors. Similarly, in the power grid case, threat intelligence would have provided early warning about the tactics used by state-sponsored actors targeting critical infrastructure. Threat modeling would have identified the engineering workstation and VPN connection as high-risk entry points, allowing the security team to tighten access controls before the attack occurred.

Threat intelligence and threat modeling are not separate from threat hunting—they are complementary. Threat hunting provides real-time insights into how attackers are operating, while threat intelligence transforms those insights into a strategic understanding of the threat landscape. Threat modeling takes it a step further by applying that understanding to predict how future attacks might unfold and strengthening defenses accordingly. Together, they create a feedback loop: threat hunting uncovers new tactics, threat intelligence analyzes and classifies them, and threat modeling strengthens the overall security posture based on that analysis.

In a modern threat environment where attackers are constantly evolving, reactive security is no longer enough. Threat intelligence and threat modeling provide the strategic foundation needed to anticipate, identify, and mitigate threats before they escalate. Organizations that integrate these practices into their security operations gain a significant advantage—they are no longer just defending against known threats, but actively preparing for the next wave of attacks. By combining the tactical insights of threat hunting with the strategic foresight of threat intelligence and threat modeling, security teams can stay one step ahead in the ongoing battle against cyber threats.

CHAPTER 18:
CYBERSECURITY
FRAMEWORKS AND
COMPLIANCE

"Compliance is not security—but security without compliance is unsustainable."

This quote reflects the delicate balance between compliance and true security. Compliance refers to the process of adhering to specific laws, regulations, and industry standards, which are often reactive responses to known threats and vulnerabilities. Security, on the other hand, is a proactive and comprehensive effort to protect an organization's assets, systems, and data from all forms of threats, both known and unknown. The distinction lies in the fact that an organization can be compliant with regulations yet still vulnerable to attacks if its security controls are not robust enough to address emerging threats. Conversely, a well-secured organization that ignores compliance requirements risks legal penalties, reputational damage, and financial loss. This quote underscores the reality that compliance alone does not guarantee security, but a lack of compliance can undermine even the most sophisticated security programs. Compliance creates a baseline for security practices, while security builds resilience beyond those baseline requirements.

In the complex and ever-evolving world of cybersecurity, protecting digital assets requires more than just deploying firewalls, intrusion detection systems, and endpoint security solutions. Effective cybersecurity depends on a structured and strategic approach that aligns with industry standards and legal requirements. Cybersecurity frameworks provide organizations with a structured, repeatable, and measurable way to implement and improve security controls. Compliance, on the other hand, ensures that these controls meet legal, regulatory, and industry-specific requirements. While compliance alone does not guarantee security, aligning security practices with recognized frameworks strengthens an organization's overall security posture and reduces risk exposure.

Cybersecurity frameworks are blueprints that guide how organizations develop and maintain security programs. They create a consistent foundation for identifying, assessing, and managing cyber risks. A well-designed framework helps establish consistent security policies and procedures, aligns security efforts with business objectives, improves risk management, and facilitates communication between technical teams, management, and regulatory bodies. Most importantly, it provides a structured approach to preventing, detecting, responding to, and recovering from security incidents. The value of a cybersecurity framework lies in its ability to turn complex security challenges into manageable processes that organizations can adapt to their unique environments.

One of the most widely recognized frameworks is the NIST Cybersecurity Framework (NIST CSF), developed by the U.S. National Institute of Standards and Technology. Originally created to strengthen the security posture of critical infrastructure sectors, the NIST CSF has since been adopted across industries due to its flexibility and adaptability. The framework organizes security efforts into five core functions: Identify, Protect, Detect, Respond, and Recover. These functions reflect the lifecycle of an effective cybersecurity program. The Identify function focuses on understanding the business environment, assets, risks, and legal obligations. Protect refers to the implementation of safeguards to prevent security incidents. Detect involves monitoring systems to identify breaches as quickly as possible. Respond focuses on executing response plans to contain and mitigate incidents, and Recover ensures that systems and data are restored while lessons learned are incorporated into future improvements. The strength of the NIST CSF lies in its flexibility—it can be customized to fit the size and complexity of any organization, making it suitable for both small businesses and global enterprises.

NIST 800-53 and NIST 800-82 are two specialized publications within the broader NIST framework that provide detailed, tactical guidance for implementing security controls. While the NIST Cybersecurity Framework (NIST CSF) serves as a high-level strategic guide for building and maintaining a cybersecurity program, NIST 800-53 and NIST 800-82 dive deeper into the technical and operational details of how to secure different types of systems and environments. Together, they extend the core NIST framework by offering concrete steps for implementing the broader guidance outlined in the CSF.

NIST 800-53, titled *Security and Privacy Controls for Federal Information Systems and Organizations*, is one of the most comprehensive and widely adopted security standards in existence. It was initially developed to provide mandatory security controls for U.S. federal agencies, but its relevance has expanded to the private sector, government contractors, and state and local governments. Over time, it has become the gold standard for implementing security controls in IT environments. NIST 800-53 defines over 1,000 security and privacy controls that cover all aspects of information security, including access control, risk assessment, incident response, and system monitoring. These controls are organized into families that address different dimensions of security, such as protecting network communications, managing user identities, detecting threats, and ensuring business continuity.

What makes NIST 800-53 particularly valuable is its flexibility. Organizations can select and customize controls based on their specific operational and regulatory requirements. For example, a healthcare provider subject to HIPAA might adopt controls focused on data encryption and user access, while a financial institution might focus more on fraud detection and transaction integrity. The strength of NIST 800-53 lies in its ability to translate the high-level strategic goals of the NIST CSF into actionable measures. If the CSF calls for an organization to improve its ability to "Detect" potential security incidents, NIST 800-53 provides detailed instructions on how to implement real-time monitoring, log analysis, and automated threat detection tools. The CSF sets the direction, while NIST 800-53 defines the path.

While NIST 800-53 focuses primarily on traditional IT environments, NIST 800-82 addresses the unique security challenges of operational technology (OT) and industrial control systems (ICS). Operational technology includes the systems that control physical processes in industries such as energy, water treatment, manufacturing, and transportation. Unlike traditional IT systems, which prioritize confidentiality, ICS systems are primarily concerned with integrity and availability. A disruption to an industrial control system could have catastrophic consequences—blackouts, chemical spills, or transportation failures—that far exceed the impact of a typical data breach.

NIST 800-82, titled *Guide to Industrial Control Systems (ICS) Security*, recognizes these unique risks and provides specific guidance for securing operational environments. It emphasizes the importance of network segmentation, ensuring that ICS networks are isolated from traditional IT networks to prevent lateral movement of threats. It also focuses on securing legacy systems that cannot be easily updated or patched without interrupting operations. Unlike IT systems, which can often tolerate temporary downtime during updates or repairs, many ICS systems operate continuously and cannot be easily taken offline. NIST 800-82 addresses this challenge by recommending alternative controls such as strict access controls, physical security measures, and real-time intrusion detection systems.

A key distinction between securing IT and OT systems lies in the prioritization of availability over confidentiality. In an industrial setting, ensuring that a power plant or water treatment facility remains operational is often more important than securing the data that flows through it. For this reason, NIST 800-82 places significant emphasis on operational continuity, incident response, and disaster recovery. For example, if an industrial control system is compromised, the priority is not necessarily to prevent data theft but to ensure that the physical process remains stable and operational while the breach is contained.

The relationship between NIST 800-53, NIST 800-82, and the broader NIST Cybersecurity Framework reflects a layered and integrated approach to security. The CSF provides the overarching strategic framework, defining the core functions of an effective cybersecurity program—Identify, Protect, Detect, Respond, and Recover. NIST 800-53 expands on these functions by providing specific controls that organizations can adopt to meet the strategic goals outlined in the CSF. If the CSF calls for an organization to "Protect" its data, NIST 800-53 will provide detailed options for encryption, network segmentation, and endpoint protection. On the other hand, if the CSF calls for improving "Response" capabilities, NIST 800-53 outlines procedures for incident containment, forensic analysis, and recovery.

NIST 800-82 complements this structure by applying the same core principles to operational technology. If the CSF calls for an organization to "Detect" security incidents, NIST 800-82 will recommend implementing real-time monitoring systems tailored to ICS environments, such as deep packet inspection for control signals or specialized malware detection tools for programmable logic controllers (PLCs). The alignment of IT and OT security under a single, unified framework enables organizations to develop consistent and comprehensive security strategies across their entire operational landscape.

Many organizations, particularly those in critical infrastructure sectors like energy and transportation, adopt both NIST 800-53 and NIST 800-82 simultaneously. A power company, for example, might use NIST 800-53 to secure its customer billing systems, employee email infrastructure, and corporate network while applying NIST 800-82 to protect its grid control systems and generation facilities. The ability to integrate both frameworks under the broader guidance of the NIST CSF allows organizations to harmonize their security strategies, ensuring that both digital and physical systems are protected.

In practice, the two frameworks reinforce one another. If an organization applies NIST 800-53 to protect its IT infrastructure, it can extend similar protections to its ICS systems using the guidelines in NIST 800-82. For example, access controls and authentication mechanisms implemented under NIST 800-53 can be adapted for ICS environments by using jump hosts, secure network gateways, and role-based access controls. Likewise, insights gained from monitoring ICS traffic under NIST 800-82 can inform broader threat intelligence and detection strategies in the IT environment.

The integration of NIST 800-53 and NIST 800-82 under the NIST CSF creates a cohesive and scalable security architecture. The CSF defines the strategic objectives, NIST 800-53 provides the detailed controls for traditional IT systems, and NIST 800-82 tailors those controls for operational technology and industrial environments. This layered approach enables organizations to manage both IT and OT risks in a coordinated and efficient manner, strengthening their overall resilience against evolving cyber threats.

By adopting this combined strategy, organizations can create a unified security posture that spans both the digital and physical domains. The strategic guidance of the NIST CSF, the tactical depth of NIST 800-53, and the operational focus of NIST 800-82 together form a comprehensive defense strategy that enables organizations to anticipate, prevent, and respond to threats across their entire operational ecosystem. This integrated approach not only ensures compliance with regulatory requirements but also enhances the organization's ability to withstand and recover from increasingly sophisticated cyberattacks.

In addition to the comprehensive guidance provided by the NIST Cybersecurity Framework, NIST 800-53, and NIST 800-82, several industry-specific frameworks have emerged to address the unique challenges faced by critical infrastructure sectors such as energy, nuclear power, and telecommunications. These frameworks, including NERC CIP (North American Electric Reliability Corporation Critical Infrastructure Protection) and NRC Regulatory Guide 5.71 (along with the more widely used NEI 08-09), build on the foundational principles of NIST but are tailored to the operational realities and regulatory requirements of their respective industries. While the NIST frameworks establish broad guidelines for building security programs, industry frameworks like NERC CIP and NEI 08-09 provide detailed, sector-specific requirements that reflect the complex and high-stakes nature of securing critical infrastructure.

NERC CIP is one of the most influential and strictly enforced industry frameworks, focusing on the protection of the North American bulk electric system. The bulk electric system includes high-voltage transmission networks, power generation facilities, and key control systems that ensure the stable operation of the electric grid. Given the interconnected and interdependent nature of the power grid, a failure or breach in one part of the system can have cascading effects across the entire network, leading to widespread blackouts, infrastructure damage, and even threats to national security. Recognizing this vulnerability, NERC developed the CIP standards to mandate a comprehensive approach to securing critical assets within the electric grid.

The NERC CIP standards are structured around a set of mandatory requirements that cover both technical and procedural controls. These include strict access controls to limit who can interact with control systems, network segmentation to prevent lateral movement of threats, and real-time monitoring to detect and respond to anomalies in system behavior. NERC CIP also mandates detailed incident response and recovery planning, requiring operators to demonstrate that they have the capacity to restore grid stability in the event of a cyberattack or operational failure. One of the unique aspects of NERC CIP is its focus on personnel training and background checks. The framework recognizes that insider threats—whether intentional or accidental—represent a significant risk to grid stability. As a result, NERC CIP requires that all personnel with access to critical systems undergo rigorous background screening and cybersecurity training.

Compliance with NERC CIP is not optional for electric utilities—it is a legal requirement enforced by the Federal Energy Regulatory Commission (FERC). Non-compliance can result in significant fines, reputational damage, and even operational sanctions. The framework is updated regularly to reflect emerging threats and technological advancements, ensuring that utilities remain capable of defending against increasingly sophisticated cyberattacks. NERC CIP's strength lies in its ability to balance operational resilience with security, recognizing that the electric grid must remain functional even while under attack. Unlike traditional IT frameworks, which may prioritize data confidentiality over system uptime, NERC CIP places a higher value on system availability and integrity. The failure of a power grid is not just a technical issue—it is a national security threat, and the NERC CIP framework reflects the gravity of that reality.

In the nuclear power sector, the Nuclear Regulatory Commission (NRC) has established its own set of cybersecurity requirements through Regulatory Guide 5.71. This framework addresses the unique risks associated with securing nuclear power plants and related infrastructure. While a cyberattack on an IT network might result in data loss or financial damage, a successful attack on a nuclear power facility could lead to catastrophic physical and environmental consequences. Regulatory Guide 5.71 recognizes this heightened level of risk and mandates strict security controls to protect against both digital and physical threats.

Regulatory Guide 5.71 provides a structured approach to securing nuclear power systems, emphasizing the importance of network isolation, physical security barriers, and continuous monitoring. It requires nuclear operators to implement strong access controls, including multi-factor authentication and role-based permissions, to ensure that only authorized personnel can access sensitive systems. The framework also mandates robust incident detection and response capabilities, including the ability to isolate compromised systems and maintain operational control even under attack.

One of the key principles of Regulatory Guide 5.71 is defense in depth—the idea that security must be implemented in multiple layers to prevent a single point of failure. This means that even if an attacker breaches an external perimeter, additional barriers will exist to slow down or contain the intrusion. For example, the framework requires that control networks be physically and logically separated from business networks, ensuring that a breach in an administrative system cannot be used to access reactor control systems. This layered approach reflects the understanding that in a high-risk environment like a nuclear power plant, redundancy and compartmentalization are essential for maintaining safety and stability.

While Regulatory Guide 5.71 sets the baseline requirements for nuclear cybersecurity, the industry has widely adopted a more flexible and practical framework known as NEI 08-09. Developed by the Nuclear Energy Institute (NEI), NEI 08-09 was designed to provide nuclear operators with a clear and actionable guide for implementing the requirements of Regulatory Guide 5.71. The NRC officially endorsed NEI 08-09 as a means of demonstrating compliance with Regulatory Guide 5.71, making it the de facto standard for nuclear cybersecurity.

NEI 08-09 streamlines the more complex and prescriptive elements of Regulatory Guide 5.71, offering a more practical approach to implementing cybersecurity controls in a nuclear environment. It focuses on establishing secure boundaries between networks, implementing role-based access controls, and ensuring that critical safety systems remain protected from unauthorized access. NEI 08-09 also emphasizes the importance of continuous monitoring and regular testing, requiring nuclear operators to conduct penetration tests and red team exercises to identify and address vulnerabilities before they can be exploited.

A key strength of NEI 08-09 is its adaptability. While Regulatory Guide 5.71 provides a rigid set of requirements, NEI 08-09 allows nuclear operators to tailor their security programs based on the specific design and operational needs of their facilities. This flexibility is particularly important in the nuclear sector, where plants may rely on legacy systems that cannot easily be modified or replaced. NEI 08-09 enables operators to implement compensating controls—alternative security measures that achieve the same protective effect—when standard technical solutions are not feasible.

The alignment between NEI 08-09 and Regulatory Guide 5.71 creates a balanced approach to nuclear cybersecurity. Regulatory Guide 5.71 establishes the regulatory floor, while NEI 08-09 offers a practical and operationally focused framework for meeting those requirements. This structure allows nuclear operators to maintain compliance while developing security programs that reflect the unique challenges and risks of their operational environments.

The relationship between NERC CIP, Regulatory Guide 5.71, and NEI 08-09 highlights the evolving nature of industry-specific frameworks. While the NIST frameworks provide a broad foundation for cybersecurity best practices, industry frameworks tailor those principles to the specific needs and threat landscapes of critical infrastructure sectors. NERC CIP's focus on grid stability and operational resilience reflects the interconnected nature of the power grid, where even a small disruption can have far-reaching consequences. Regulatory Guide 5.71 and NEI 08-09 address the heightened risks associated with nuclear operations, where safety and containment are as important as digital security.

Together, these frameworks demonstrate that effective cybersecurity is not a one-size-fits-all solution. Each sector faces unique risks and operational constraints, requiring tailored strategies and specialized controls. By integrating industry frameworks with the broader guidance provided by NIST, organizations can build layered and resilient security programs that address both strategic and operational threats. This alignment ensures that critical infrastructure remains secure and operational even in the face of increasingly sophisticated cyberattacks. The success of this approach lies in understanding that security is not static—it is a continuous process of adaptation, improvement, and alignment with both industry standards and emerging threats.

Another influential framework is ISO/IEC 27001, an international standard for information security management systems (ISMS). Unlike NIST, which provides broad guidance, ISO/IEC 27001 offers a systematic, certifiable approach to managing sensitive information and ensuring its confidentiality, integrity, and availability. The framework emphasizes a risk-based approach, requiring organizations to conduct risk assessments, define how risks will be treated, and continuously monitor and improve security processes. ISO/IEC 27001's focus on governance and accountability makes it particularly valuable for organizations that face complex regulatory environments or need to demonstrate compliance with international standards.

The Center for Internet Security (CIS) Controls offers a more tactical framework, focused on specific defensive actions that address common cyber threats. The CIS Controls consist of 18 prioritized security actions, including inventorying and controlling hardware and software assets, managing administrative privileges, and establishing secure network configurations. The appeal of the CIS Controls lies in their practicality—they provide step-by-step recommendations that even small and mid-sized organizations can implement without requiring extensive resources or specialized expertise.

COBIT (Control Objectives for Information and Related Technologies) is another widely adopted framework, but it focuses on governance and business alignment. Developed by ISACA, COBIT helps organizations integrate their IT and cybersecurity strategies with business goals. It emphasizes meeting stakeholder needs, enabling a holistic approach to governance, and separating management from governance. COBIT's strength lies in its ability to bridge the gap between technical teams and executive leadership, ensuring that security becomes a strategic priority rather than a purely operational concern.

Payment security has its own set of standards through the Payment Card Industry Data Security Standard (PCI DSS). Developed by major credit card companies, PCI DSS outlines specific requirements for securing cardholder data and payment systems. Organizations that handle credit card transactions are required to encrypt cardholder data, restrict access to sensitive information, and maintain strong monitoring and testing protocols. PCI DSS is not just a recommendation—it's a mandate. Organizations that fail to comply with PCI DSS can face fines, reputational damage, and even the loss of the ability to process credit card transactions.

While frameworks provide guidance for building and managing security programs, compliance ensures that organizations meet legal and regulatory requirements. In recent years, data privacy and protection laws have become more stringent, reflecting the growing recognition that personal information is one of the most valuable assets in the digital economy. The General Data Protection Regulation (GDPR) in the European Union is one of the most comprehensive privacy laws in existence. It gives EU citizens control over their personal data and imposes strict requirements on how businesses collect, store, and use that data. Violations of GDPR can result in fines of up to 4% of a company's annual revenue, making compliance a business-critical issue.

In the United States, the Health Insurance Portability and Accountability Act (HIPAA) regulates the protection of health information, while the California Consumer Privacy Act (CCPA) grants California residents greater control over their personal information. The Sarbanes-Oxley Act (SOX) establishes financial reporting and data security requirements for public companies, while the Federal Information Security Management Act (FISMA) mandates security requirements for federal agencies and government contractors.

Maintaining compliance with these regulations presents several challenges. First, the regulatory landscape is constantly evolving. New regulations are introduced regularly, and existing ones are updated to reflect changes in technology and emerging threats. Global organizations face additional complexity because they must navigate overlapping and sometimes conflicting regulations across different countries and jurisdictions. The cost of compliance can be significant, particularly for small and mid-sized businesses with limited resources. Compliance requirements also place a heavy operational burden on organizations. Conducting audits, maintaining documentation, and preparing for regulatory reviews can strain internal resources and distract from other business priorities.

Despite these challenges, compliance and security frameworks are not mutually exclusive—they are complementary components of a comprehensive security strategy. While compliance focuses on what organizations must do to meet legal obligations, frameworks provide the how by offering structured guidance for building security programs. Organizations that adopt a recognized framework such as NIST or ISO/ IEC 27001 are better positioned to demonstrate compliance with GDPR, HIPAA, PCI DSS, and other regulations. Aligning compliance efforts with established frameworks reduces audit fatigue by consolidating overlapping requirements, improves efficiency, and enhances resilience by embedding continuous improvement into security processes.

The key to success lies in recognizing that compliance is not enough. An organization can meet the minimum legal requirements and still suffer a breach if its security controls are weak or poorly implemented. True security comes from adopting a framework that not only ensures compliance but also enhances the organization's ability to anticipate, prevent, and respond to threats.

The relationship between cybersecurity frameworks and compliance is symbiotic. Frameworks provide the foundation for building effective security programs, while compliance ensures that those programs meet external requirements. By integrating both into a cohesive strategy, organizations can protect their digital assets, maintain customer trust, and avoid costly penalties and reputational damage. In a world where cyber threats are constantly evolving and regulatory scrutiny is increasing, a strong, adaptable security framework combined with a proactive approach to compliance is essential for long-term success. Effective cybersecurity requires not only meeting minimum compliance standards but also building a resilient and adaptive defense strategy grounded in industry best practices.

CHAPTER 19 – TAILORING CYBER SECURITY CONTROLS

"The only secure computer is the one that's unplugged, locked in a safe, and buried 20 feet under the ground. But even then, I'm not completely confident."
— Gene Spafford

This quote by Gene Spafford captures the inherent challenge in achieving absolute security. In the modern digital landscape, no system can be completely immune to threats, but organizations can significantly improve their security posture by tailoring cybersecurity controls to their specific environment and risks. Spafford's statement highlights the balance that organizations must strike between securing their systems and maintaining operational functionality. Effective security is not about achieving an unattainable state of perfect protection, but about adapting and customizing controls to counter the most pressing threats while ensuring that business operations remain smooth and efficient.

Once security requirements are defined, organizations can select and modify controls based on established frameworks such as the NIST Cybersecurity Framework, ISO/IEC 27001, and the Center for Internet Security (CIS) Controls. Tailoring involves adjusting the scope and depth of controls according to the value of assets and the severity of threats. It may also require modifying configuration settings to align with existing infrastructure and business processes. After selecting and customizing controls, the next step is to implement them systematically, ensuring that they function as intended and integrate smoothly with the existing technological ecosystem. Testing and validation are essential to confirm that controls effectively mitigate identified risks.

Cybersecurity is not a static field, and tailored controls must evolve alongside emerging threats. Continuous monitoring and improvement are crucial to maintaining an effective security posture. Leveraging threat intelligence and participating in information-sharing networks enable organizations to stay informed about new attack techniques and potential vulnerabilities. By adopting a dynamic approach to tailored controls, organizations can respond quickly to changing threats and minimize the impact of security incidents.

Tailoring cybersecurity controls involves balancing security and usability. Overly strict controls can impede operational efficiency and frustrate users, while lax controls can expose systems to attacks. Finding the right balance requires engaging stakeholders from different business units to ensure that tailored controls support business objectives without introducing unnecessary complexity. Automation plays a key role in improving efficiency and consistency in cybersecurity operations. Automated controls for threat detection, incident response, and log analysis reduce human error and enhance response times.

Despite its advantages, tailoring cybersecurity controls presents certain challenges. Resource constraints, particularly in small and mid-sized organizations, can limit the ability to develop and implement customized controls. Partnering with managed security service providers (MSSPs) can help bridge this gap by providing specialized expertise and scalable solutions. Complexity and compatibility issues may also arise when modifying controls within an existing IT ecosystem. Careful planning, phased deployment, and thorough compatibility testing are essential to avoid operational disruptions. Keeping pace with evolving threats is another challenge, as cybercriminals continually develop new tactics. Organizations can address this challenge by leveraging threat intelligence platforms and collaborating with industry groups to stay ahead of emerging threats.

The National Institute of Standards and Technology (NIST) Special Publication 800-53, which is widely considered one of the most comprehensive cybersecurity frameworks, illustrates the complexity and scale of security control implementation. NIST 800-53 provides a catalog of over 1,000 controls and control enhancements across 20 control families, covering a broad range of security domains, including access control, incident response, risk assessment, system integrity, and data protection. These controls are designed to provide a structured and systematic approach to managing security risks in federal information systems and critical infrastructure, but their sheer number and complexity present significant implementation challenges.

Control enhancements add another layer of complexity. Each base control in NIST 800-53 is often accompanied by multiple control enhancements that extend or refine the control's function. For example, the access control family includes not only basic measures for limiting access to authorized users but also a range of enhancements for multifactor authentication, remote access, session management, and privileged access monitoring. The complexity increases when enhancements require integration with other controls, such as encryption, monitoring, and audit logging, creating interdependencies that must be carefully managed.

The feasibility of implementing all NIST 800-53 controls with their enhancements is highly limited for most organizations, even large and well-resourced enterprises. Implementing every control enhancement would require substantial financial resources, technical expertise, and operational capacity. Moreover, some controls and enhancements may not be relevant to every organization's threat environment or operational model. For instance, controls designed for classified government systems may not be practical or necessary for a small healthcare provider or a private sector business.

This challenge reinforces the importance of tailoring. Instead of attempting to implement all controls uniformly, organizations should focus on conducting a comprehensive risk assessment to identify which controls and enhancements are most relevant to their specific threat landscape and business needs. By prioritizing high-impact controls and those that address critical vulnerabilities, organizations can achieve a more effective security posture without overburdening their resources. Tailoring allows organizations to allocate security investments strategically, ensuring that the most critical risks are addressed while maintaining operational efficiency and scalability.

Ultimately, NIST 800-53 serves as a valuable foundation for building a robust security program, but its successful application depends on thoughtful customization and risk-based prioritization. Organizations that attempt to implement all controls and enhancements without considering their unique context are likely to face resource exhaustion, operational bottlenecks, and diminishing returns on their security investments. Tailoring enables organizations to focus on the most relevant and effective controls, striking a balance between comprehensive security and practical feasibility.

Tailoring cybersecurity controls is a critical approach to enhancing the protection of organizational information systems against evolving threats. In an increasingly interconnected and digital world, organizations face a wide range of cyber threats, including data breaches, ransomware attacks, state-sponsored espionage, and insider threats. While the need for robust cybersecurity measures is widely recognized, applying generic security frameworks without considering the specific context of an organization often leads to ineffective protection and resource inefficiencies. A tailored approach to cybersecurity involves customizing security controls to match an organization's unique operational environment, risk profile, and regulatory requirements, thereby improving both security effectiveness and operational resilience.

Tailoring controls from NIST 800-53 is a practical and essential step in building an effective cybersecurity framework that aligns with an organization's unique operational environment, risk profile, and business goals. NIST 800-53 provides a comprehensive catalog of controls and control enhancements designed to cover a wide range of security domains, including access control, incident response, data protection, and system integrity. However, implementing every control and its associated enhancements is neither practical nor necessary for most organizations. Tailoring allows an organization to focus resources on the most critical risks while maintaining operational efficiency and meeting compliance requirements.

The process of tailoring controls begins with defining the scope and context of the security program. This includes understanding the organization's mission and objectives and how security supports them, identifying the systems, data, and processes that require protection, and assessing the threat landscape to identify the most likely and damaging threats. Regulatory requirements, such as HIPAA or PCI-DSS, must also be factored in to ensure that mandatory controls are incorporated. Equally important is defining the organization's risk tolerance—how much risk the organization is willing to accept and which types of threats are most important to mitigate. For example, a healthcare provider handling sensitive patient data will have a different control focus than a retail business primarily concerned with point-of-sale security.

A tailored control strategy is most effective when guided by a comprehensive risk assessment. This includes identifying threats and vulnerabilities, evaluating the potential impact of a security breach on business operations, reputation, and financial health, and calculating the likelihood of different threat scenarios. The results of this assessment help guide the prioritization of controls. Controls that address high-impact, high-likelihood threats should be prioritized over those that address low-impact or unlikely risks.

Once critical risks and assets have been identified, the next step is to select and modify base controls from NIST 800-53. The framework divides controls into 20 control families, such as Access Control, System Integrity, and Incident Response. After identifying the relevant control families, the next task is to determine which base controls are applicable to the organization's specific threat environment and operational model. Not all controls will apply to every organization. For example, controls related to classified data might not be relevant for a small business but are critical for government contractors. Controls should also be evaluated for business impact. While some controls provide strong protection, they might introduce operational friction that reduces efficiency or affects user experience. Adjustments to control implementation should be made to match operational realities. A small business, for example, might not have the resources to build an in-house Security Operations Center (SOC) but could outsource monitoring to a managed security provider.

Tailoring also requires evaluating and applying control enhancements. Enhancements in NIST 800-53 extend the functionality of base controls, adding additional layers of protection or fine-tuning security mechanisms. However, not all enhancements are necessary or practical. Enhancements should be implemented when they provide a meaningful reduction in risk or address specific vulnerabilities, and when the operational impact of the enhancement is manageable. Enhancements may not be necessary when the threat is unlikely or has minimal impact, when alternative controls provide equivalent or better protection, or when the enhancement introduces unacceptable complexity or cost. For example, if Account Management (AC-2) is selected as a base control, it includes several enhancements such as automated account management, account lockout, and role-based access control (RBAC). In a small business with minimal administrative staff, implementing automated account management and account lockout might be essential for managing security risks. However, implementing RBAC might not be practical due to limited staff and system complexity.

Organizations vary greatly in terms of size, industry, technological infrastructure, and regulatory obligations. A multinational financial institution, for instance, will encounter a different set of threats and compliance requirements than a small healthcare provider or a government agency. This diversity makes a one-size-fits-all approach to cybersecurity inadequate. The threat landscape itself is constantly changing as cybercriminals become more sophisticated and innovative. New vulnerabilities emerge regularly, and tailored controls allow organizations to respond to these changes more effectively. Additionally, industries such as healthcare, finance, and defense are subject to stringent regulatory requirements, including frameworks like HIPAA, PCI-DSS, and NIST guidelines. Customizing controls ensures that these specific compliance mandates are met without compromising operational efficiency.

Tailoring cybersecurity controls requires a structured, risk-based approach. The process begins with a comprehensive risk assessment to identify critical assets, evaluate threats, and determine the potential impact of a security breach. By understanding where the greatest vulnerabilities lie, an organization can define its security requirements and align them with business objectives and risk tolerance. This process helps prioritize security measures that will have the highest impact on mitigating threats while minimizing disruptions to operations.

A common misconception in risk-informed decision-making is the idea that certain controls can be disregarded simply because other controls are already in place. For example, an organization might conclude that passwords are unnecessary for an internal asset because it is protected behind a firewall and cannot be accessed externally. While this logic may seem reasonable on the surface, it overlooks the principle of defense in depth and the broader range of potential attack vectors that could bypass or compromise the initial layer of protection.

Defense in depth is a foundational concept in cybersecurity that emphasizes the use of multiple overlapping controls to protect assets. It is based on the understanding that no single control is foolproof. While a firewall may effectively block external access, it does not protect against insider threats, physical breaches, or lateral movement within the network. If an attacker gains access to the internal network through phishing, a compromised endpoint, or even a misconfigured VPN, the absence of password protection would leave the asset completely exposed.

Furthermore, assets are rarely exposed to a single type of access or vulnerability. An asset behind a firewall may still be accessed through remote maintenance protocols, internal administrative interfaces, or wireless access points. Physical access also presents a significant risk. If an attacker or malicious insider gains access to the facility, they could connect directly to the network or manipulate hardware to bypass the firewall altogether.

Less obvious scenarios can also lead to breaches when a defense-in-depth strategy is ignored. For example, supply chain attacks have become increasingly common, where compromised software updates or embedded malicious code in third-party hardware provide an entry point into the network. If passwords or other internal access controls are removed under the assumption that the firewall is sufficient, an attacker who bypasses the firewall through a supply chain attack would face no further barriers to accessing sensitive data or systems.

This is why layering controls is essential. A firewall may reduce the likelihood of an external attack, but passwords and authentication protocols limit the damage that can be done if the firewall is bypassed. Similarly, encryption, network segmentation, monitoring, and endpoint detection create multiple barriers that an attacker must overcome. Even if one layer fails, others remain in place to limit exposure and mitigate damage.

Risk-informed decision-making should focus on understanding how controls interact with one another rather than treating them as independent or redundant. Removing one control because another is in place ignores the reality that attackers often exploit combinations of weaknesses. A well-designed defense-in-depth strategy ensures that even if an attacker penetrates the outer defenses, they still face significant barriers at multiple levels, making it more difficult to move laterally or escalate privileges.

Ultimately, effective cybersecurity relies not on a single strong defense, but on the strategic layering of multiple controls that address different types of threats and access vectors. By maintaining overlapping layers of security, organizations can reduce the likelihood of a successful attack and minimize the damage if an attacker does manage to breach one layer. Ignoring this principle by eliminating controls under the assumption that others will compensate for them increases risk and weakens overall security posture.

The benefits of tailoring cybersecurity controls are significant. Customized controls enhance the overall security posture by addressing specific vulnerabilities and threats more effectively. Improved operational efficiency results from focusing security efforts where they are most needed, reducing resource wastage. Tailored controls also simplify compliance with industry-specific regulations, minimizing the risk of penalties and improving audit performance. Perhaps most importantly, tailored security controls increase an organization's resilience, enabling faster recovery and reduced downtime in the event of a security incident.

Real-world examples illustrate the value of tailored

cybersecurity controls. A global financial institution, for example, conducted a thorough threat assessment and implemented customized access controls, anomaly detection, and encryption standards. These changes led to a 40% reduction in data breach incidents over two years. A mid-sized healthcare provider improved its security posture by tailoring controls to meet HIPAA requirements. Multi-factor authentication, endpoint security, and encryption of electronic health records reduced unauthorized access and improved overall data protection. Similarly, a federal government agency used the NIST Cybersecurity Framework to tailor its controls, implementing automated threat detection and a segmented network architecture. This approach reduced the impact of cyberattacks by 30% within one year.

Once a core set of controls has been determined to be mandatory, the next step is to formally integrate them into the organization's cybersecurity framework. These controls should be documented and cataloged in the organization's cybersecurity plan, which serves as a central reference for managing security posture and ensuring consistent implementation. A well-developed cybersecurity plan provides a clear blueprint for how security controls are applied, maintained, and monitored across the organization. It establishes a foundation for consistency and accountability, helping to ensure that security measures are not only in place but also actively managed and improved over time.

The cybersecurity plan should detail the specific controls that have been selected, including their objectives, scope, and implementation requirements. For example, if multi-factor authentication (MFA) is selected as a core control under the Access Control (AC) family, the plan should outline which systems and user roles require MFA, how the authentication process will be managed, and how exceptions (if any) will be handled. The plan should also identify dependencies between controls and how they work together to create defense in depth.

If encryption is listed as a core control, the plan should specify which data types must be encrypted, the encryption standards to be used, and how encryption keys will be managed and rotated.

Once the controls are documented in the cybersecurity plan, they should be supported by both policies and procedures to ensure consistent application and enforcement. Policies define the organization's expectations and rules for implementing controls, while procedures provide step-by-step guidance on how to execute them. For instance, an access control policy might state that all privileged accounts must use multi-factor authentication, while the associated procedure would describe how to configure the MFA system, enroll users, and handle lockouts or system failures. Supporting documentation should also include guidelines for monitoring and auditing compliance with the established controls.

Establishing well-defined policies and procedures ensures that security controls are implemented consistently and uniformly across the organization. This consistency strengthens the overall security posture and reduces the risk of gaps or misconfigurations that could be exploited by attackers. Additionally, clear policies and procedures empower staff to understand their roles and responsibilities in maintaining security, fostering a culture of accountability and awareness. By cataloging core controls in the cybersecurity plan and reinforcing them with strong policies and procedures, organizations create a structured and resilient defense against evolving cyber threats.

Tailoring cybersecurity controls is not a one-time effort— it is an ongoing process that requires continuous evaluation, adjustment, and improvement. As the threat landscape evolves and business operations change, the controls cataloged in the cybersecurity plan should be regularly reviewed and updated to ensure they remain effective and aligned with the organization's risk profile. New threats, technological advancements, and shifts in regulatory requirements may necessitate the addition of new controls or the modification of existing ones. A flexible and adaptive approach to tailoring controls allows an organization to stay ahead of emerging threats while maintaining operational efficiency and compliance.

Ultimately, the strength of a tailored cybersecurity framework lies in its ability to balance security and practicality. By cataloging a core set of mandatory controls in the cybersecurity plan and reinforcing them with well-defined policies and procedures, an organization creates a resilient and structured defense. Defense in depth—where multiple layers of security controls work together to protect against a wide range of threats —ensures that even if one control fails, others remain in place to mitigate risk and limit the impact of a breach. A tailored approach allows organizations to focus their resources where they are most effective, ensuring that security measures are not only comprehensive but also sustainable over the long term. This strategic alignment of controls, policies, and procedures creates a cohesive security posture that can adapt to future challenges while maintaining the integrity, confidentiality, and availability of critical systems and data.

CHAPTER 20 – ENSURING EFFECTIVENESS OF CYBER SECURITY CONTROLS

"To secure peace is to prepare for war."
— Carl Von Clausewitz

Carl Von Clausewitz's quote highlights a core truth about cybersecurity: effective protection requires more than passive defense—it demands constant readiness and strategic preparation. Modern cyberattacks, especially those launched by Advanced Persistent Threats (APTs), are highly adaptive and strategic. Attackers carefully study their targets, exploit human psychology through social engineering, and use stealthy techniques to bypass even the most sophisticated technical controls. Therefore, securing a network requires not only strong defenses but also the ability to detect and respond to threats in real-time.

The effectiveness of cybersecurity controls is not measured solely by whether they prevent breaches but by how well they enable an organization to detect, contain, and recover from attacks. Firewalls, encryption, and multi-factor authentication provide important protection, but they cannot stop an attacker who gains access through compromised credentials or a trusted vendor. Strategies like Zero Trust Architecture (ZTA), which assumes no user or device should be trusted by default, and privileged access management (PAM), which limits administrative access, reduce the impact of an initial breach.

Threat intelligence and active defense are essential for improving control effectiveness. Platforms like MITRE ATT&CK provide insights into attacker tactics, helping organizations anticipate and adjust their defenses proactively. Red team exercises, where security teams simulate real-world attacks, help identify weaknesses and refine response strategies. Automated response systems and behavioral analytics improve the speed and precision of threat containment, reducing the damage caused by successful attacks.

Clausewitz's quote underscores that true security comes from constant preparation and adaptation. The key to maintaining peace in cybersecurity is not just building strong defenses but continuously monitoring and testing the effectiveness of those controls. Regular threat assessments, penetration testing, and real-time performance monitoring ensure that controls remain effective as threats evolve. Just as military success depends on adapting to battlefield conditions, cybersecurity success depends on adjusting defenses based on ongoing threat intelligence and attack patterns. Effective security is not static—it requires continuous evaluation and improvement.

The next logical step after tailoring and implementing cybersecurity controls is to evaluate their effectiveness. Once a core set of controls has been cataloged in the cybersecurity plan and supported with policies and procedures, it becomes essential to determine whether these controls are functioning as intended and providing the expected level of protection. A tailored security framework is only as strong as its ability to respond to real-world threats, so regular monitoring and assessment are necessary to ensure that controls remain aligned with the organization's threat landscape and operational environment. This ongoing evaluation process helps to identify weaknesses, measure performance, and adapt controls to changing threats and business needs.

To evaluate the effectiveness of cybersecurity controls, organizations must first define what success looks like. Success criteria should be based on measurable outcomes such as reduced incident response times, improved detection rates, or fewer unauthorized access attempts. For example, if multi-factor authentication has been implemented as a control, success could be measured by tracking the number of unauthorized login attempts that were blocked as a result of the additional authentication layer. Defining clear, measurable goals ensures that control performance can be objectively evaluated rather than relying on subjective assessments.

Continuous monitoring plays a crucial role in measuring control effectiveness. Security Information and Event Management (SIEM) systems and automated monitoring tools allow organizations to track security events in real time, providing immediate visibility into how controls are functioning. For example, an intrusion detection system might generate alerts when suspicious activity is detected on the network, allowing security teams to respond quickly and analyze whether the implemented controls successfully mitigated the threat. Continuous monitoring not only helps to detect threats in real time but also generates valuable data that can be used to evaluate control performance over time.

Testing and validation are also important components of assessing control effectiveness. Penetration testing, red team exercises, and simulated attacks provide valuable insight into how controls perform under pressure. For instance, if an access control system is supposed to prevent unauthorized entry, a red team exercise could attempt to bypass those controls using various attack techniques. If the red team is able to exploit a weakness, it indicates that the control is not functioning as intended and needs to be adjusted or reinforced. Regular testing helps identify vulnerabilities and provides a feedback loop for improving the security framework.

Performance metrics are a valuable tool for measuring the success of tailored controls. Organizations should track key performance indicators (KPIs) such as the number of detected threats, the mean time to detect and respond (MTTD/MTTR), and the rate of user compliance with security policies. These metrics provide a quantifiable way to measure how well controls are performing and whether they are contributing to a stronger

THE CYBERSECURITY BLUEPRINT

security posture. For example, if the average time to detect a threat decreases after implementing a new threat detection system, it provides evidence that the control is working effectively. On the other hand, if the number of successful phishing attempts remains unchanged despite implementing email filtering controls, it suggests that the control may need to be adjusted or supplemented with additional measures such as employee training.

Incident analysis is another key aspect of evaluating control effectiveness. When a security incident occurs, a post-incident analysis should be conducted to determine whether control failures contributed to the breach. If an unauthorized user accessed sensitive data despite having multi-factor authentication in place, the analysis might reveal that user accounts were not properly configured or that a bypass vulnerability existed in the authentication process. Lessons learned from incident analysis should be used to refine controls and close security gaps.

Adaptation and improvement are essential for maintaining an effective cybersecurity framework. Cyber threats are constantly evolving, and controls that were effective a year ago may no longer provide adequate protection against new attack techniques. Organizations should regularly reassess their controls and make adjustments based on new threat intelligence, technological advancements, and changes in business operations. For example, as remote work becomes more common, additional controls such as endpoint protection and secure VPN configurations may need to be added to address the increased attack surface. Similarly, if threat actors develop new techniques for bypassing multi-factor authentication, organizations may need to implement more sophisticated identity verification measures.

Evaluating control effectiveness is not a one-time event—it is an ongoing process that requires regular monitoring, testing, and adjustment. Tailored controls may seem effective on paper, but without real-world validation, they may fail to provide adequate protection. A successful cybersecurity program combines defense in depth with continuous improvement, ensuring that controls remain effective even as threats evolve.

Evaluating the effectiveness of cybersecurity controls should not only focus on how well the controls are performing but also on verifying that they were properly implemented in the first place and that they remain in place over time. Even the most well-designed control framework can lose its effectiveness if controls are inadvertently removed, misconfigured, or bypassed due to system changes, human error, or evolving operational requirements. Regular verification helps ensure that the intended controls are not only operational but also functioning as designed.

Periodic verification is essential because controls can degrade or become ineffective over time due to a variety of factors. Software updates, infrastructure changes, and evolving user behavior can all impact the performance of a control. For example, a firewall rule that was initially set to block traffic from certain geographic regions may become misconfigured after a system update, leaving the organization exposed to new threats. Similarly, an access control policy requiring multi-factor authentication may be accidentally bypassed during a user account provisioning process. Without routine verification, these issues could persist unnoticed, creating security gaps that could be exploited by attackers.

For many controls, verification can be conducted through automated systems. Security Information and Event Management (SIEM) platforms and automated monitoring tools can track whether certain controls are in place and functioning properly. For example, an automated system could verify that encryption settings remain active, that login attempts requiring multi-factor authentication are being processed correctly, and that firewall rules are properly applied traffic across boundaries. Automated verification reduces the burden on security teams and allows for more frequent checks, ensuring that controls remain consistently enforced.

However, not all controls can be verified through automation alone. Some controls require empirical data and direct observation to confirm that they remain in place and are functioning effectively. For example, incident response procedures can be tested through tabletop exercises and simulated attacks to confirm that staff are following the established protocols and that the process functions as expected. Physical security controls, such as badge access to restricted areas, may require direct observation and testing to ensure that access points are properly secured and that badges are being validated correctly.

One effective strategy for ensuring consistent control verification is to implement a control checklist that can be used during regular system maintenance and audits. A control checklist provides a structured way to verify that key controls are in place and functioning as intended. For example, the checklist could include confirmation that encryption settings are correctly configured, that backup processes are running on schedule, that endpoint protection software is active and up to date, and that access control policies are being consistently applied. The checklist should be tailored to the organization's specific controls and updated periodically to reflect changes in the threat environment and operational requirements.

A control checklist serves as both a validation tool and a training aid for security teams. It ensures that no critical control is overlooked during routine maintenance and provides a clear reference for assessing the overall health of the security framework. The use of a checklist also helps to identify patterns of control failure, such as recurring misconfigurations or policy violations, which can signal the need for deeper investigation or corrective action. Over time, data gathered from the checklist can inform broader security improvements, helping to refine policies and strengthen defense-in-depth strategies.

By combining automated monitoring with empirical testing and structured verification through control checklists, organizations can create a comprehensive evaluation process that not only measures control effectiveness but also ensures that controls are consistently implemented and maintained. This layered approach to verification strengthens overall security posture by addressing both technical and procedural gaps, ensuring that the cybersecurity framework remains robust and resilient even as threats and operational conditions change.

By defining success criteria, continuously monitoring performance, conducting regular testing, and adapting controls based on lessons learned, organizations can build a resilient security framework that is capable of withstanding both current and future threats. This process reinforces the idea that cybersecurity is not a static goal but a dynamic and iterative practice that requires constant attention and adaptation.

CHAPTER 22: ADVANCED THREATS AND APTS

"Amateurs hack systems; professionals hack people."
— Bruce Schneier

Bruce Schneier's quote highlights a fundamental truth about modern cyberattacks: the most dangerous and effective breaches are not necessarily technical—they are human. While early hackers focused on exploiting weaknesses in software and systems, today's most sophisticated threat actors, particularly those behind Advanced Persistent Threats (APTs), recognize that human behavior is the weakest link in cybersecurity. Schneier's observation underscores how professional threat actors, including state-sponsored operatives and organized cybercriminal groups, have shifted their focus from merely hacking systems to manipulating human psychology.

Social engineering, which includes tactics such as phishing, pretexting, and impersonation, has become a cornerstone of modern cyberattacks because it bypasses even the most robust technical defenses. Firewalls and encryption protocols can protect networks and data, but they cannot prevent a well-crafted phishing email from deceiving an employee into handing over login credentials. Schneier's insight reflects the reality that while technology continues to advance, human error remains a consistent vulnerability that professional attackers are skilled at exploiting.

Social engineering remains one of the most effective weapons in an attacker's arsenal because it targets human psychology rather than technical systems. Phishing emails disguised as legitimate messages from trusted sources are a common method of infiltration, but attackers have expanded their tactics to include vishing (voice phishing), smishing (SMS phishing), and deepfake impersonation. Attackers can use information gathered from social media profiles, leaked databases, and publicly available records to personalize their attacks, making them more convincing. A well-crafted spear-phishing email might include specific references to a recent business transaction or a trusted colleague, increasing the likelihood that the recipient will comply with a malicious request. More sophisticated APT groups even engage in long-term social engineering campaigns, gradually building trust with targets over weeks or months before initiating an attack. This calculated approach allows attackers to bypass technological defenses and exploit the natural human tendency to trust familiar sources.

Advanced threats are often not about brute force; they are about subtlety and deception. APT actors spend time studying their targets, understanding behavioral patterns, and crafting convincing narratives to manipulate insiders into granting access. This type of psychological manipulation allows attackers to establish an initial foothold without raising alarms, after which they can escalate their access and move laterally within the network.

Advanced threats and Advanced Persistent Threats (APTs) represent a new frontier in cybersecurity—a battlefield where the stakes are higher, the tactics more sophisticated, and the consequences more far-reaching than ever before. Unlike conventional cyberattacks that rely on quick strikes and opportunistic weaknesses, APTs are methodical, highly organized, and strategically motivated. These threats are not random acts of cybercrime; they are calculated campaigns led by well-funded and highly skilled adversaries, often linked to nation-states or powerful criminal organizations. Their goal is not just to steal information or cause temporary disruption —it is to infiltrate, control, and exploit their targets over an extended period, often for political, economic, or strategic gain.

What makes an advanced threat truly dangerous is not

just the complexity of the attack but the persistence and adaptability of the attacker. Traditional cybercriminals may launch a phishing attack or deploy malware in hopes of a quick payout, but APT actors take a different approach. They spend months, sometimes years, studying their targets. They map out network infrastructures, analyze employee behavior, and gather intelligence on operational weaknesses. When they strike, it is not with brute force but with surgical precision. APTs use custom-built malware, zero-day vulnerabilities, and advanced encryption techniques to bypass conventional defenses. Their methods are subtle—they mimic legitimate system activity, avoid triggering alerts, and often leave no obvious signs of intrusion.

APTs are defined by their strategic intent. Financial gain is rarely the primary objective. More often, these attacks target national security infrastructure, government agencies, defense contractors, and multinational corporations. The attackers aim to steal state secrets, intellectual property, or sensitive financial data—or, more dangerously, to sabotage critical infrastructure. The 2010 Stuxnet attack on Iran's nuclear program was a chilling demonstration of how cyberweapons could be used to disrupt physical systems. Stuxnet was designed to infect Siemens PLCs used in uranium enrichment centrifuges. By subtly altering their operating speeds, the malware caused physical damage to the centrifuges while reporting normal activity to monitoring systems—an elegant and devastating example of how cyberattacks can be weaponized.

An advanced attack begins long before the first line of malicious code is executed. It starts with reconnaissance. Attackers meticulously research their targets, gathering information from open-source intelligence (OSINT), social media, and even public databases. They identify key personnel, network architecture, and potential vulnerabilities. Social engineering often plays a role in this phase. An attacker might create a convincing spear-phishing email, posing as a trusted contact and encouraging the target to download a file or click on a link. Once the link is clicked, the attacker has gained a foothold.

Initial compromise is just the beginning. APT actors are patient. They use the initial breach as a staging ground, installing backdoors and rootkits that allow them to maintain access even if security teams detect and close the initial point of entry. They escalate privileges, seeking out administrative credentials that give them deeper access to the network. From there, they move laterally through the system, looking for high-value targets —sensitive files, customer databases, intellectual property, or strategic intelligence. The attackers exfiltrate this data slowly and stealthily, often breaking it into small, encrypted packets that blend in with normal network traffic to avoid detection.

What sets advanced threats apart is not just their ability to infiltrate but their ability to remain hidden. APT actors are masters of disguise. They cover their tracks by altering system logs, masking their activity as routine administrative traffic, and deploying malware that automatically deletes itself after a certain period. They establish multiple points of entry so that even if one is discovered and closed, others remain operational. The goal is not simply to get in—it is to stay in.

The SolarWinds attack in 2020 is one of the most striking examples of an APT in action. Attackers infiltrated the software development process of SolarWinds, a widely used IT management platform. By inserting malicious code into a legitimate software update, they gained access to the networks of more than 18,000 organizations, including U.S. government agencies and Fortune 500 companies. The attack went undetected for months, during which time the attackers were able to monitor communications, steal sensitive data, and potentially manipulate systems at the highest levels of government and industry. What made SolarWinds so dangerous was not just the initial breach—it was the stealth and persistence of the attackers. Even after the breach was discovered, security teams had to assume that multiple backdoors remained in place.

The 2015 Office of Personnel Management (OPM) breach was another example of a devastating APT. Chinese-linked hackers infiltrated the U.S. government's human resources database and stole personal information from over 22 million federal employees, including security clearance records and fingerprint data. The attackers used a combination of spear-phishing and credential harvesting to gain access, then moved laterally within the network, exfiltrating data over an extended period without detection. The breach exposed sensitive information about intelligence officers and government personnel, creating long-term security risks.

Defending against advanced threats requires a fundamental shift in cybersecurity strategy. Traditional perimeter-based defenses—firewalls, antivirus programs, and signature-based detection systems—are inadequate against adversaries that operate with this level of sophistication. APT actors are not deterred by locked doors; they find the hidden keys or create their own. This is why modern defense strategies focus on zero-trust architecture—never assume that any user or device is trustworthy, even if they are inside the network. Access should be granted based on identity, behavior, and risk assessment, not on location or credentials alone.

Defending against Advanced Persistent Threats (APTs) requires a multi-layered and adaptive approach that combines technological defenses, strategic planning, and human resilience. Unlike traditional cyberattacks, which may rely on single-entry points or isolated vulnerabilities, APTs are designed to evade detection, establish long-term presence, and escalate privileges over time. This means that a static or perimeter-focused defense strategy is insufficient. Effective protection against APTs requires continuous monitoring, intelligence-based threat detection, and rapid incident response.

One of the most effective strategies for defending against APTs is the Zero Trust Architecture (ZTA) model. Under Zero Trust principles, no user, device, or system is trusted by default—even those within the network perimeter. Access to resources is granted based on continuous verification of identity, behavior, and security posture, rather than location or network credentials alone. ZTA employs techniques such as multifactor authentication (MFA), least privilege access, and microsegmentation to restrict the lateral movement of attackers within a network. If an attacker gains initial access, the compartmentalized nature of a Zero Trust environment makes it difficult for them to escalate privileges or access sensitive systems.

Threat intelligence and behavioral analysis are critical components of an APT defense strategy. Traditional signature-based detection methods are ineffective against sophisticated APTs, which often use custom malware and fileless attack techniques. Behavioral analysis tools, powered by artificial intelligence (AI) and machine learning, monitor patterns of activity across the network and endpoints. By establishing a baseline of normal behavior, these tools can detect anomalies indicative of an attack—such as unusual login times, irregular data transfers, or unexpected access to administrative functions. Threat intelligence platforms, such as MITRE ATT&CK, provide insights into known adversary tactics, techniques, and procedures (TTPs), allowing security teams to anticipate and counter APT activity before it escalates.

Endpoint Detection and Response (EDR) and Extended Detection and Response (XDR) systems are essential for identifying and containing APT activity at the device level. EDR solutions continuously monitor endpoint activity, capturing detailed forensic data and analyzing it for signs of compromise. When suspicious activity is detected, automated response mechanisms can isolate affected endpoints, terminate malicious processes, and prevent lateral movement. XDR platforms extend this visibility and response capability beyond endpoints to include network traffic, cloud infrastructure, and application activity, providing a unified view of potential threats.

Network segmentation and micro-segmentation are effective measures for limiting the impact of an APT breach. By dividing the network into isolated segments and restricting access based on the principle of least privilege, security teams can prevent attackers from moving freely within the environment. If an attacker compromises one segment, they are unable to access other critical systems without additional credentials and verification. Network segmentation also allows for more targeted containment and remediation during an active attack.

Privileged Access Management (PAM) helps reduce the risk of credential theft and privilege escalation. APT actors often target administrative accounts and service accounts because they provide elevated access to sensitive systems and data. PAM solutions enforce strict controls on privileged account usage, requiring multi-factor authentication, session monitoring, and automated credential rotation. Just-in-time access provisioning ensures that privileged accounts are only active when necessary, reducing the window of opportunity for attackers.

Data Loss Prevention (DLP) and User and Entity Behavior Analytics (UEBA) solutions provide additional layers of protection against data exfiltration—a common objective of APTs. DLP systems monitor the movement of sensitive data and enforce encryption, access restrictions, and transfer controls to prevent unauthorized extraction. UEBA tools analyze user activity to identify unusual patterns that may indicate insider threats or compromised credentials, such as unauthorized file access or large-scale data transfers.

Security Information and Event Management (SIEM) platforms play a central role in APT defense by aggregating and correlating data from multiple security tools. SIEM systems provide real-time monitoring, threat analysis, and automated incident response. Advanced SIEM platforms use machine learning to detect subtle attack patterns and prioritize alerts based on threat severity. By integrating SIEM with SOAR (Security Orchestration, Automation, and Response) platforms, security teams can automate threat containment and remediation actions, reducing response times and minimizing damage.

Incident response planning and red team exercises are essential for preparing organizations to handle APT attacks. An effective incident response plan defines the roles, responsibilities, and escalation paths for detecting, containing, eradicating, and recovering from an attack. Red team exercises, where internal security teams simulate real-world APT scenarios, help identify gaps in detection and response capabilities. Blue team defenders can refine their tactics based on these exercises, improving overall readiness and response times.

Preparation and training are just as important as technological defenses. APT actors often exploit human error—weak passwords, poor patching practices, and misplaced trust. Employee training programs are essential to strengthening the human firewall. And defending against APTs. Because APTs often rely on social engineering for initial access, training employees to recognize phishing attempts, suspicious links, and unusual requests can reduce the likelihood of a successful breach. Organizations should foster a culture of skepticism, encouraging employees to question unexpected requests and verify communications through trusted channels before taking action.

Finally, supply chain security is a growing focus in APT defense. The SolarWinds attack demonstrated how a compromised vendor can serve as a vector for a large-scale breach. Organizations must conduct rigorous security assessments of third-party vendors, enforce secure coding practices, and monitor software supply chains for signs of tampering. Code signing, integrity checks, and secure software development frameworks (such as DevSecOps) help prevent malicious code from being introduced into production environments.

A comprehensive defense against APTs requires a blend of advanced technology, human expertise, and strategic foresight. Attackers are constantly evolving their tactics, and defenders must remain adaptive and proactive to stay ahead of the threat landscape. While no single solution can provide complete protection against APTs, a multi-layered strategy—combining Zero Trust principles, threat intelligence, advanced detection tools, and human resilience—creates a robust defense capable of withstanding even the most sophisticated attacks.

Advanced threats are not going away. If anything, they are becoming more sophisticated and more dangerous. The involvement of nation-states and well-funded criminal organizations means that APTs are no longer isolated incidents —they are part of a broader geopolitical and economic struggle. The challenge for defenders is not simply to stop an attack but to anticipate and neutralize it before it begins. Success requires a combination of advanced technology, strategic foresight, and organizational resilience. The battlefield has moved to the digital domain, and the adversaries are more dangerous than ever. The only way to win is to stay one step ahead.

CHAPTER 23: CYBER RESILIENCE AND BUSINESS CONTINUITY

"It's not whether you get knocked down, it's whether you get up."
— Vince Lombardi

Vince Lombardi's quote reflects a fundamental truth about resilience, both in life and in cybersecurity. In the context of cyber resilience, the inevitability of setbacks and breaches is not a sign of failure—it's a reality of the modern threat landscape. The strength of an organization's security posture is not determined by whether it can prevent every attack, but by how effectively it can withstand and recover from them. Just as success in sports comes from adapting to setbacks and responding with strength, cyber resilience is about limiting the impact of breaches and restoring normal operations quickly. The ability to recover and respond to cyber incidents defines an organization's true strength. Cyberattacks are no longer a question of "if" but "when." Therefore, the focus of modern cybersecurity strategies has shifted from achieving absolute protection to building systems capable of absorbing damage and bouncing back. Lombardi's insight serves as a reminder that success in cybersecurity is not about perfection—it's about resilience.

In the modern threat landscape, no organization is immune to cyberattacks. Even the most sophisticated defenses—firewalls, endpoint detection, and multi-factor authentication—can be bypassed by a well-executed phishing attempt, a zero-day exploit, or a supply chain attack. Advanced Persistent Threats (APTs) and state-sponsored actors, in particular, are capable of maintaining long-term access to networks, manipulating systems, and exfiltrating data without immediate detection. The reality of this environment makes one thing clear: complete prevention is no longer a realistic goal. The focus, therefore, must shift from purely preventing attacks to developing the capacity to withstand and recover from them. This is the essence of cyber resilience.

Cyber resilience refers to an organization's ability to continue delivering critical services and maintaining core business functions even in the face of a cyberattack. It combines proactive defense with responsive recovery, ensuring that even if defenses are breached, the impact is contained and business operations can resume quickly. Cyber resilience recognizes that breaches are inevitable—but catastrophic damage is not. A resilient organization anticipates threats, absorbs the impact, and rapidly recovers with minimal disruption.

Building cyber resilience requires careful preparation, rapid response, and effective recovery. Preparation begins with identifying and protecting critical assets, understanding business priorities, and defining acceptable levels of risk. Organizations must conduct thorough risk assessments to identify vulnerabilities, assess the potential impact of different attack scenarios, and develop mitigation strategies. Business impact analysis (BIA) helps organizations determine which systems and processes are essential for maintaining operations and which can afford to experience downtime. Preparedness also includes developing a business continuity plan (BCP) and an incident response plan (IRP). A BCP outlines how the organization will continue to operate during a disruption, detailing backup systems, alternative communication channels, and resource allocation. An IRP defines the specific steps for detecting, containing, and eradicating threats, as well as the roles and responsibilities of the incident response team. These plans should be tested regularly through tabletop exercises and red team/blue team simulations to ensure that they remain effective under pressure.

Once a breach occurs, the ability to respond effectively is central to cyber resilience. A well-designed incident response process follows the NIST framework: detect, contain, eradicate, recover, and learn. The first step is to identify anomalies, intrusions, and signs of compromise using tools like SIEM (Security Information and Event Management) and behavioral analytics. Once an attack is detected, the next step is to contain the damage by isolating affected systems and preventing the attacker from moving laterally within the network. The threat must then be eradicated by removing malicious code, cleaning infected systems, and identifying the root cause to prevent recurrence. Recovery involves restoring affected systems and resuming normal operations as quickly as possible. Finally, the organization must conduct a post-mortem analysis to identify weaknesses, improve response protocols, and strengthen future defenses.

Automation plays a key role in enhancing response capabilities. Security Orchestration, Automation, and Response (SOAR) platforms allow organizations to respond to threats in real-time by automatically isolating compromised endpoints, blocking malicious traffic, and initiating forensic analysis. Automated response reduces human error, accelerates containment, and minimizes damage. Communication is another critical element of response. Organizations must have pre-established communication protocols for informing stakeholders, customers, regulators, and law enforcement. Transparency and accuracy are key to maintaining trust and minimizing reputational damage. Mismanaging the flow of information during an incident can amplify the negative consequences and erode stakeholder confidence.

Recovery focuses on restoring systems and data to a trusted state while minimizing downtime. Cyber resilience requires organizations to have reliable data backups and failover systems in place. Backups should be stored in secure, geographically diverse locations, and regularly tested to ensure they are functional and up to date. Failover systems—such as redundant data centers, cloud-based infrastructure, and disaster recovery sites—allow critical services to continue operating even if the primary infrastructure is compromised. Recovery time objectives (RTO) and recovery point objectives (RPO) should be defined for all critical systems, ensuring that recovery efforts are aligned with business priorities. Cyber resilience also involves rebuilding trust in systems after an attack. Once systems are restored, they should undergo forensic analysis and security validation to ensure that backdoors, hidden malware, or compromised credentials are not lingering within the network. The organization must also evaluate its overall response and identify gaps in defense, incorporating lessons learned into future security planning.

Business continuity is a core element of cyber resilience. A business continuity plan (BCP) outlines how an organization will maintain essential services and business functions during and after a cyber incident. Unlike disaster recovery, which focuses on restoring technical infrastructure, business continuity ensures that the organization can continue to deliver products and services even under degraded conditions. An effective BCP includes identification of critical processes, alternate communication channels, cross-functional response teams, and coordination with third-party vendors and partners. Ensuring that employees and stakeholders can communicate even if primary systems are offline is essential for maintaining operational integrity during an attack. Establishing alternative supply chain agreements and vendor contracts also reduces the impact of disruptions caused by ransomware or data breaches.

One of the most high-profile examples of business continuity failure is the NotPetya attack in 2017. Maersk, the world's largest shipping company, faced one of the most devastating cyberattacks in history when it was hit by the NotPetya ransomware in June 2017. NotPetya, which originated in Ukraine, spread rapidly using the EternalBlue exploit, encrypting data and rendering entire systems inoperable. Maersk's entire global IT infrastructure collapsed, including 49,000 laptops, 1,200 applications, and over 4,000 servers. Operations ground to a halt, and ports managed by Maersk were left paralyzed. Yet remarkably, the company managed to recover relatively quickly. A single surviving domain controller in Ghana—offline due to a power outage—provided the foundation for the recovery effort. Engineers used this backup to rebuild Maersk's infrastructure from scratch. Maersk was forced to rebuild its entire IT infrastructure from scratch—a process that took several weeks and resulted in hundreds of millions of dollars in losses. Maersk's lack of adequate backups and failover systems significantly prolonged the recovery process. The company's resilience came from having a clear recovery strategy, a strong business continuity plan, and a coordinated global response. Within ten days, 90% of Maersk's operations were back online, and the company resumed full operations shortly thereafter.

In 2014, JP Morgan Chase experienced one of the largest data breaches in the financial sector, affecting over 76 million households and 7 million small businesses. The breach occurred when attackers gained access through a single compromised server that lacked multi-factor authentication. Although sensitive customer data was exposed, JP Morgan Chase's quick response prevented further escalation. The company rapidly isolated the compromised server, activated incident response protocols, and reinforced its network defenses. After the attack, JP Morgan Chase invested over $500 million annually to strengthen its cybersecurity infrastructure. It implemented Zero Trust Architecture, increased network segmentation, and enhanced access controls to limit future vulnerabilities. By treating the breach as a learning opportunity, JP Morgan Chase demonstrated resilience by improving its ability to detect and respond to threats more effectively in the future.

The Colonial Pipeline ransomware attack in May 2021 demonstrated how effective business continuity planning can limit the impact of a cyberattack. Colonial Pipeline, which supplies 45% of the fuel to the U.S. East Coast, was forced to shut down its operations after attackers deployed ransomware that encrypted critical operational data. The attack caused widespread fuel shortages and price spikes, leading to panic buying across the East Coast. However, Colonial Pipeline's incident response plan enabled the company to recover quickly. By relying on segmented backups and failover systems, Colonial Pipeline was able to restore critical systems and resume fuel distribution within days. The company's ability to recover quickly and minimize economic disruption highlighted the importance of having a structured recovery plan and secure backup infrastructure.

In 2013, Target suffered a high-profile data breach that exposed the payment card details of over 40 million customers. The attackers gained entry through compromised credentials from a third-party HVAC contractor, which allowed them to infiltrate Target's network and install malware on point-of-sale systems. The breach resulted in significant financial losses and reputational damage. However, Target responded by overhauling its cybersecurity framework. The company invested $100 million to enhance network segmentation, improve endpoint security, and deploy behavioral analytics to detect suspicious activity. Target also introduced chip-and-PIN technology at checkout terminals, reducing the risk of payment card fraud. Target's recovery strategy not only strengthened its defenses but also restored consumer trust, demonstrating how resilience is about adapting and improving after a failure.

Microsoft faced a serious challenge during the SolarWinds supply chain attack in 2020. Russian state-sponsored hackers inserted malicious code into SolarWinds' Orion software update, compromising the systems of thousands of companies and government agencies, including Microsoft. Despite the severity of the breach, Microsoft's threat intelligence platform and advanced monitoring capabilities allowed it to detect the attack early and respond swiftly. The company isolated affected systems, conducted a thorough forensic investigation, and deployed security updates to close the vulnerability. Microsoft's ability to limit the damage and coordinate with other affected companies and government agencies demonstrated the value of strong monitoring, early detection, and coordinated response.

Sony Pictures experienced a devastating cyberattack in 2014 when North Korean hackers targeted the company in retaliation for the release of the film *The Interview*. The attackers stole internal data, including executive emails and unreleased films, and deployed destructive malware that wiped data from Sony's systems. Despite the severity of the attack, Sony Pictures was able to recover by executing its business continuity plan. The company restored critical systems from backups and reinforced endpoint security to prevent future breaches. Sony's ability to maintain operations and release major films on schedule demonstrated the importance of a well-structured recovery plan and secure data backups.

Equifax suffered one of the largest data breaches in history in 2017, when attackers exploited an unpatched Apache Struts vulnerability, exposing the personal information of over 147 million Americans. The breach resulted in significant financial and reputational damage. Equifax responded by implementing a comprehensive resilience strategy, including the establishment of a dedicated cybersecurity task force, automated patch management systems, and stronger encryption protocols. The company also enhanced access controls and introduced multi-factor authentication to reduce future vulnerabilities. Equifax's ability to strengthen its defenses and improve threat detection demonstrated how organizations can turn a crisis into an opportunity for long-term improvement.

These examples highlight several key elements of cyber resilience and business continuity. First, rapid detection and response are critical to limiting the damage from a cyberattack. Microsoft and Colonial Pipeline minimized disruption because they were able to detect the breach early and respond swiftly. Second, effective business continuity plans enable organizations to maintain operations even during an attack. Maersk and Sony Pictures demonstrated that having reliable backups and failover systems allows for a faster recovery and reduces the impact of operational downtime. Third, learning from an incident and adapting to new threats strengthens long-term resilience. JP Morgan Chase, Target, and Equifax all improved their cybersecurity posture by analyzing the root causes of their breaches and implementing stronger controls. Finally, threat intelligence and early detection improve the ability to anticipate attacks and neutralize them before they escalate. Microsoft's response to the SolarWinds attack illustrated how strong threat intelligence and rapid containment can prevent broader damage.

Cyber resilience is not about preventing every attack—it's about preparing for them and responding effectively when they occur. The ability to detect, contain, and recover from cyberattacks defines an organization's strength and stability. The examples of Maersk, JP Morgan Chase, Colonial Pipeline, Target, Microsoft, Sony Pictures, and Equifax illustrate that resilience is built through preparation, strategic response, and continuous improvement. Organizations that treat cybersecurity as a dynamic and evolving challenge are better positioned to withstand future attacks and minimize disruption.

By contrast, the Colonial Pipeline attack in 2021 demonstrated the importance of a strong business continuity plan. Although the ransomware attack forced Colonial Pipeline to shut down its operations temporarily, the company was able to restore service relatively quickly by relying on segmented backups and secure failover systems. This allowed fuel distribution to resume within days, minimizing the long-term impact on supply chains.

Cyber resilience is not static—it requires continuous evaluation and improvement. Regular penetration testing, red team exercises, and post-incident analysis provide valuable insights into how well an organization's defenses hold up under real-world attack conditions. Metrics such as Mean Time to Detect (MTTD) and Mean Time to Respond (MTTR) provide quantitative indicators of an organization's ability to contain and resolve threats. Reducing MTTD and MTTR is a key measure of improving cyber resilience. Additionally, evaluating recovery time objectives (RTO) and recovery point objectives (RPO) helps organizations gauge how quickly systems can be restored and how much data loss is acceptable. Cyber resilience also requires a feedback loop. Lessons learned from previous incidents should inform future security strategies and business continuity plans. Threat intelligence feeds should be used to update incident response protocols and adjust network configurations to prevent repeat attacks. Effective organizations treat every attack as an opportunity to improve and strengthen defenses.

Cyber resilience recognizes that breaches are inevitable—but catastrophic damage is not. Effective cyber resilience strategies enable organizations to anticipate, contain, and recover from attacks while maintaining core business functions. Business continuity planning ensures that essential services continue even under adverse conditions, reducing the financial and operational impact of an attack. Ultimately, the strength of a cyber resilience program is measured not by whether an organization can avoid attacks, but by how quickly and effectively it can detect, respond to, and recover from them. In a world where cyberattacks are a constant threat, resilience is the key to long-term security and stability. Preparing for failure is the only way to ensure success.

CHAPTER 24 - CONCLUSION

Cybersecurity has become one of the defining challenges of the modern era. The rapid digital transformation of industries, the rise of sophisticated threat actors, and the increasing complexity of global supply chains have created an environment where cyber risk is not only inevitable—it is continuous. The evolution of cyber threats, from simple malware to state-sponsored espionage and targeted ransomware campaigns, has exposed vulnerabilities at every level of society, from financial institutions and healthcare providers to government agencies and critical infrastructure. In this rapidly changing landscape, cybersecurity is no longer just a technical concern—it is a strategic imperative.

This book has explored the full spectrum of cybersecurity, from foundational principles to advanced threat mitigation strategies. It began with an introduction to the CIA Triad —confidentiality, integrity, and availability—which forms the backbone of any security program. Understanding how to protect sensitive data, maintain data accuracy, and ensure operational availability is the starting point for any effective cybersecurity strategy. The concept of Defense in Depth —layering security controls across network, endpoint, and application levels—further reinforces the need to build resilience at every point in the digital ecosystem.

Building a cybersecurity program requires more than just deploying firewalls and endpoint protection—it demands a strategic and operational framework that integrates governance, risk management, and compliance into the core of business operations. A successful security program anticipates threats rather than simply reacting to them. It incorporates threat intelligence to understand attacker behavior and anticipate future attack vectors. It relies on continuous monitoring to detect anomalies in real-time and initiate automated responses before an attacker can establish a foothold. And it integrates adaptive security models that adjust defenses based on evolving threats and vulnerabilities.

At the heart of any successful cybersecurity strategy is the recognition that breaches are not a matter of "if" but "when." This is why the concept of cyber resilience has become central to modern security programs. Cyber resilience is not about preventing every attack—it's about ensuring that when an attack happens, the damage is contained, operations can continue, and recovery is swift. Resilience depends on strong incident response plans, reliable backups, network segmentation, and the ability to isolate and neutralize threats before they spread.

One of the key themes that emerged throughout this book is the importance of the human factor in cybersecurity. While technical defenses are essential, the most common entry point for cyberattacks remains human error. Phishing, social engineering, and credential theft are still among the most successful methods of infiltration. Building a culture of security awareness through training and accountability is just as important as deploying technical controls. Employees should not only understand the basics of secure behavior but also feel empowered to report suspicious activity without fear of punishment. A well-informed and vigilant workforce is one of the most powerful assets in a cybersecurity program.

Another central theme is the importance of governance and leadership. Cybersecurity is not an IT function—it is a business function that requires board-level oversight and executive alignment. Effective governance ensures that security policies are enforced, that resources are allocated appropriately, and that accountability exists at every level of the organization. Regulatory frameworks like GDPR and CCPA have added new layers of complexity to security governance, requiring organizations to protect sensitive data or face significant financial and reputational penalties. Strong governance ensures that security programs align with both business goals and regulatory requirements. Without clear leadership and accountability, even the most sophisticated security controls will fail to protect the organization from evolving threats.

Testing and validation emerged as another essential component of an effective cybersecurity program. A program that is not regularly tested is a program that will fail under pressure. Penetration testing, red team exercises, and tabletop incident response simulations help organizations identify weaknesses before attackers can exploit them. Metrics like Mean Time to Detect (MTTD) and Mean Time to Respond (MTTR) provide insights into the efficiency of security operations and help organizations improve over time. Successful programs are those that embrace continuous improvement, adapting to new threats and refining security controls based on performance data and threat intelligence. Organizations that fail to test their defenses risk being caught off guard when a real-world attack occurs.

This book also explored the broader strategic landscape of cybersecurity, including the rise of Advanced Persistent Threats (APTs) and the geopolitical dimensions of cyber warfare. Nation-state actors, cybercriminal syndicates, and hacktivist groups have introduced a new layer of complexity to the threat environment. Supply chain vulnerabilities, third-party risk, and the rise of deepfake technology further complicate the security equation. The future of cybersecurity will require not just stronger defenses but greater international cooperation and intelligence sharing to combat these evolving threats. The increasing interconnectedness of global infrastructure means that an attack on one system can have cascading effects on others. Governments and private organizations must work together to strengthen collective resilience against these types of systemic risks.

Cybersecurity is ultimately a continuous process. Security

programs must evolve with the threat landscape, incorporating new tools, techniques, and threat intelligence to remain effective. A static security program is a vulnerable security program. The future of cybersecurity will be defined by both technological and geopolitical trends. The increasing adoption of cloud computing, artificial intelligence, and machine learning will create new opportunities for automation and threat detection—but they will also create new vulnerabilities. The expansion of the Internet of Things (IoT) will introduce billions of new connected devices, each representing a potential attack surface. At the same time, the growing sophistication of nation-state actors and cybercriminal organizations will challenge even the most well-defended networks.

To meet these challenges, cybersecurity programs must remain dynamic and adaptable. Security teams will need to embrace automation and machine learning to keep pace with the speed and scale of modern threats. The principles of Zero Trust Architecture—assuming that no user or device is inherently trusted—will become even more essential in a perimeter-less network environment. Regulatory pressures will continue to shape the way organizations handle data privacy and security, requiring constant vigilance to avoid financial and reputational damage. The next phase of cybersecurity will require greater collaboration between the public and private sectors. Threat intelligence sharing, joint defense exercises, and coordinated incident response will become critical components of national and global security.

The role of the Chief Information Security Officer (CISO) will continue to expand beyond technical expertise to include strategic thinking, risk management, and crisis response. The rise of cyber insurance, evolving legal frameworks, and increasing investor scrutiny will add new dimensions to cybersecurity leadership. Cybersecurity professionals will need to develop a broader understanding of business strategy and risk management to effectively communicate the value of security investments to executive leadership and board members.

Cybersecurity is not a destination—it is an ongoing journey. It requires continuous adaptation, learning, and improvement. The goal is not perfection but resilience: the ability to withstand attacks, adapt to new threats, and emerge stronger. The strategies, frameworks, and principles outlined in this book provide a roadmap for building an effective and resilient cybersecurity program. Whether you are a security professional, a business leader, or a decision-maker, the tools and insights presented here will help you navigate the complex and evolving world of cybersecurity with confidence.

The future of cybersecurity will be shaped not just by technology, but by the choices we make today. A secure future is possible—but it will require vision, leadership, and a relentless commitment to resilience. The path forward is not easy, but with the right strategy, the right tools, and the right mindset, organizations can build a cybersecurity program that not only defends against attacks but also enables long-term growth and stability. The next chapter in the story of cybersecurity will be written by those who understand that resilience—not just defense—is the key to success.

ABOUT THE AUTHOR

Bill Johns began his journey into the world of computing over 45 years ago, starting as a hobbyist building and upgrading computer hardware at a time when understanding every component by hand was essential. His technical aptitude and natural curiosity soon expanded into networking, and before long, he had built a large Bulletin Board System (BBS) that became a hub for early online communities. At the same time, Bill was designing and building corporate networks, helping businesses adapt to the new landscape of interconnected systems long before cybersecurity became a formal discipline.

When the internet began to take shape, Bill transitioned his BBS into the online world, studying internet protocols firsthand through RFCs (Request for Comments) and collaborating with fellow pioneers on early forums like Undernet, Dalnet, and EfNet. His deep understanding of networks and security caught the attention of a major social networking platform, where, motivated by relentless attacks, he gained administrative access to the network's servers through sheer skill and ingenuity. Offered a choice—explain how he did it and help defend the network, or face consequences—Bill chose to build. That decision launched him into years of live-fire cyber defense, defending critical systems under constant attack, long before the modern frameworks for cybersecurity even existed.

This experience on the front lines opened the door to high-stakes consulting engagements, including the recovery of networks crippled by malware like Code Red and Nimda. Bill was called in when others had written systems off as lost causes—and succeeded where others had failed. From there, his work expanded into securing networks for U.S. Department of Defense (DoD) contractors, helping to protect critical national infrastructure from increasingly sophisticated threats.

As cybersecurity evolved, so did Bill's mission. Over the past two decades, he turned his expertise toward critical infrastructure protection, securing IT and OT/ICS environments across industries such as energy, nuclear power, manufacturing, water and wastewater, pharmaceuticals, and oil and gas. His work spanned both operational networks and regulatory domains. But beyond simply implementing cybersecurity controls within regulated environments, Bill spent years embedded within the regulatory ecosystem itself.

In a contractual role supporting a major critical infrastructure regulator, Bill was directly involved in shaping cybersecurity policy and oversight. He helped develop, refine, and negotiate regulatory language, supported regulatory inspections and enforcement actions, and taught regulatory interpretation and compliance strategies to both operators and inspectors. His work influenced how cybersecurity standards and related guidance were not only implemented in the field, but understood, adjudicated, and enforced. He spent years operating at the intersection of engineering, cybersecurity, regulatory law, and operational risk—where the stakes were public health and safety, environmental protection, and national security.

Following his time in the regulatory space, Bill worked with numerous corporate entities to extend their understanding of cybersecurity beyond the minimum expectations of compliance. He helped organizations bridge the gap between regulatory adherence and true operational resilience, guiding them to see their IT and OT environments not as separate silos, but as deeply interconnected ecosystems. His work focused on helping companies understand the full scope of cyber risk within converged environments—where engineering, operations, and digital threats intersect—and on building defensible architectures capable of surviving real-world attacks, not just passing audits.

Drawing on a career that spans the earliest days of interconnected computing to the modern challenges of defending converged critical infrastructure, Bill's books reflect more than just technical expertise. They capture the hard-won lessons of a lifetime spent not only building and defending critical systems, but also shaping the very frameworks that govern them—and helping others move beyond compliance toward true operational security.

GLOSSARY

A

Access Control – The process of limiting and regulating access to systems, networks, and data based on user identity and permissions.

Access Management – The process of managing and controlling how users and systems interact with resources, including user authentication and authorization.

Advanced Persistent Threat (APT) – A prolonged and targeted cyberattack in which an attacker gains access to a network and remains undetected for an extended period, often conducted by nation-states or organized cybercriminal groups.

Artificial Intelligence (AI) – The use of machine learning and complex algorithms to automate decision-making and threat detection in cybersecurity.

Attack Surface – The total set of entry points through which an attacker can attempt to gain access to a system or network.

Attack Vector – The method or pathway used by an attacker to gain unauthorized access to a system or network.

Authentication – The process of verifying the identity of a user, device, or application, often using methods like passwords, multi-factor authentication (MFA), or biometrics.

B

Backup – A copy of data that is stored separately from the primary system to enable recovery in case of a system failure, corruption, or data breach.

Behavioral Analytics – The use of machine learning and data analysis to identify abnormal patterns of behavior that may indicate a security threat.

Brute Force Attack – A trial-and-error method used by attackers to guess passwords or encryption keys.

Business Continuity Plan (BCP) – A plan that outlines how an organization will maintain critical operations during and after a disruption, including cyberattacks.

Business Impact Analysis (BIA) – The process of evaluating the potential effects of an interruption to critical business operations due to a cyber incident.

C

CIA Triad – The three core principles of cybersecurity: **Confidentiality** (ensuring data is accessible only to authorized users), **Integrity** (ensuring data is accurate and trustworthy), and **Availability** (ensuring systems and data are accessible when needed).

Cloud Security – The set of policies, controls, and technologies used to protect data, applications, and services in cloud environments.

Compliance – Adhering to regulations, industry standards, and internal security policies designed to protect data and systems.

Confidentiality – Ensuring that sensitive information is accessible only to authorized parties.

Containment – The process of limiting the spread of a cyberattack after it has been detected.

Credential Stuffing – An attack where stolen account credentials are used to gain unauthorized access to user accounts.

Cross-Site Scripting (XSS) – A type of attack in which malicious scripts are injected into otherwise trusted websites to steal data or manipulate users.

Cyber Resilience – The ability of an organization to anticipate, withstand, respond to, and recover from cyberattacks while maintaining essential business operations.

Cyber Threat Intelligence – The collection and analysis of information about potential or actual cyber threats to anticipate and prevent future attacks.

D

Data Loss Prevention (DLP) – Technologies and policies designed to prevent the unauthorized transmission or leakage of sensitive data.

Defense in Depth – A layered security strategy that combines multiple independent security controls to protect systems and data from attacks.

Denial of Service (DoS) Attack – A cyberattack designed to overwhelm a network, system, or service, rendering it unavailable to legitimate users.

Detection – The process of identifying potential threats or suspicious activity within a system or network.

Digital Signature – A cryptographic method used to verify the authenticity and integrity of digital messages or documents.

Distributed Denial of Service (DDoS) Attack – A more powerful version of a DoS attack in which multiple systems are used to flood a network or service, overwhelming its capacity.

Domain Name System (DNS) Hijacking – An attack in which an attacker manipulates DNS settings to redirect users to malicious websites.

E

Elevated Privileges – Administrative-level access that allows a user to modify system configurations or access sensitive data.

Email Spoofing – A technique used in phishing attacks where the sender's email address is forged to appear as if it comes from a trusted source.

Encryption – The process of converting data into a coded format to prevent unauthorized access.

Endpoint – Any device that connects to a network, such as a computer, smartphone, or tablet.

Endpoint Detection and Response (EDR) – A security solution that monitors endpoint activity to detect, investigate, and respond to threats.

F

Failover – The process of automatically switching to a backup system or redundant infrastructure when the primary system fails.

Federated Identity – A system that allows users to use a single identity to access multiple systems or applications across different organizations.

Fileless Malware – Malware that operates in a system's memory rather than from a file, making it harder to detect.

Firewall – A network security system that monitors and controls incoming and outgoing traffic based on predetermined security rules.

H

Hashing – A cryptographic process that converts data into a fixed-size value or code, which is used to verify data integrity.

Honeypot – A decoy system or network designed to attract and monitor attackers to study their behavior.

Hypervisor – A virtual machine manager that creates and manages virtual machines.

I

Identity and Access Management (IAM) – A framework for managing digital identities and controlling access to systems and data.

Incident Handling – The process of managing and resolving a security incident, including detection, containment, and recovery.

Infrastructure as Code (IaC) – The practice of managing and provisioning computing infrastructure using code rather than manual processes.

Insider Threat – A security risk posed by employees, contractors, or business partners who have authorized access to systems but misuse that access.

Integrity – Ensuring that data is accurate and has not been tampered with.

L

Lateral Movement – The technique used by attackers to move within a network after gaining initial access, often in search of high-value targets.

Least Privilege – A security principle that grants users and systems the minimum level of access necessary to perform their functions.

Living Off the Land (LotL) – A type of attack where attackers use legitimate administrative tools within a system to carry out malicious activity.

M

Malware – Malicious software designed to disrupt, damage, or gain unauthorized access to a system.

Man-in-the-Middle (MITM) Attack – An attack where an adversary secretly intercepts and manipulates communication between two parties.

Multi-Factor Authentication (MFA) – A security process that requires users to provide two or more forms of verification to access a system.

N

Network Segmentation – The practice of dividing a network into separate zones to limit lateral movement and contain breaches.

Nonce – A randomly generated value used in encryption to prevent replay attacks.

P

Patch Management – The process of applying software updates to fix vulnerabilities and improve security.

Phishing – A social engineering attack that tricks users into revealing sensitive information.

Privilege Escalation – The act of gaining higher levels of access within a system after gaining initial access.

R

Ransomware – A type of malware that encrypts a victim's data and demands payment for the decryption key.

Risk Appetite – The level of risk an organization is willing to accept in pursuit of its business objectives.

T

Tokenization – The process of replacing sensitive data with a unique identifier or token that cannot be reverse-engineered.

Trojan – Malware disguised as legitimate software that is used to gain access to systems or install additional malware.

Z

Zero-Day Exploit – A vulnerability that is exploited before a patch or fix is available.

Zero Trust Architecture (ZTA) – A security model that assumes no user, device, or system is inherently trusted.

www.ingramcontent.com/pod-product-compliance
Lightning Source LLC
LaVergne TN
LVHW051438050326
832903LV00030BD/3141